W9-CNU-282

THE WOMEN'S PROJECT 2

The Women's Project 2

THE BROTHERS
Kathleen Collins

LITTLE VICTORIES
Lavonne Mueller

TERRITORIAL RITES
Carol K. Mack

HEART OF A DOG
Terry Galloway

CANDY & SHELLEY GO TO THE DESERT
Paula Cizmar

Edited by Julia Miles

Performing Arts Journal Publications
New York

THE WOMEN'S PROJECT 2
© 1984 Copyright by Performing Arts Journal Publications

Introduction
© 1984 Copyright by Julia Miles
The Brothers
© 1982, 1984 Copyright by Kathleen Collins
Little Victories
© 1981, 1984 Copyright by Lavonne Mueller
Territorial Rites
© 1982, 1984 Copyright by Carol K. Mack
Heart of a Dog
© 1984 Copyright by Terry Galloway
Candy & Shelley Go to the Desert
© 1984 Copyright by Paula Cizmar

Library of Congress Cataloging in Publication Data
THE WOMEN'S PROJECT 2
Library of Congress Catalog Card No.: 84-61624
ISBN: 0-933826-73-7 (cloth)
ISBN: 0-933826-74-5 (paper)

Design: Gautam Dasgupta
Printed in the United States of America

Publication of this book has been made possible in part by a grant from the National Endowment for the Arts, Washington, D.C., a federal agency, and public funds received from the New York State Council on the Arts.

PAJ Playscripts/General Editors:
Bonnie Marranca and Gautam Dasgupta

Contents

To My Granddaughter Allie Grace

Acknowledgements

I'm deeply grateful to and wish to thank all the participants in The Women's Project: the playwrights, directors, actors, stage managers, designers, and technical staff who made the readings and productions possible, as well as The Women's Project Advisory Board, Board of Trustees of The American Place Theatre, and the Patrons, Sponsors and Friends of the Project who have supported the Project both financially and by their presence and response to the work. I am thankful as well for the interest and enthusiasm of the many playwrights and directors who submitted their plays or their expressions of interest, but whom we were not able to include in the Project.

I want to thank The Ford Foundation for its continuing support and especially Ruth Mayleas of the Division of Education and Culture. Other financial support was gratefully received from the following sources: National Endowment for the Arts, New York State Council on the Arts, New York State Council on the Arts Literature Program, The John Golden Fund, ICM, Paramount Pictures, The Beverly and Harvey Karp Foundation, American Theatre Wing, Mrs. James P. Warburg, Warner Communications, Con Edison, and The Rockefeller Foundation.

Thanks also to Wynn Handman, Director of The American Place Theatre, Scott Allison, Ron Spetrino and the staff of the theatre for all their help on the

Project, and special thanks to my assistant Elaine De Leon.

Lastly, I want to express my thanks to and appreciation of the staff—paid and volunteer—of The Women's Project without whose dedication the work could not continue: to Suzanne Bennett whose energy and intelligence has given the Project a great boost; to Elissa Myers and her assistant in casting Mark Teschner; to Carolyn Anderson for her enthusiasm and aid; to Arlene Markinson for founding the Friends of The Women's Project; to all the young, intelligent interns and production assistants with particular gratitude to Claire Gleitman, Cynthia Stokes and Paul Garten, this season, and I want to end with thanking two young women who have been part of the Project since its inception, Nancy Harrington, Production Supervisor, and Gayle Austin, Literary Manager, who have contributed much to the Project and to this anthology.

Julia Miles
Director
The Women's Project

Introduction

Much has happened for women in the theatre since the publication of the first Women's Project Anthology in 1980. More women have been writing plays and become more visible in many ways in the theatre, including two Pulitzer Prize winners: Beth Henley and Marsha Norman. The Women's Project has completed its sixth season of working with women playwrights and directors. Over this time we've produced 160 Workshop and Rehearsed Readings, Studio Productions of 22 plays and 4 mainstage productions. We have received support from The Ford Foundation as well as corporations and expanded our bases of support through many individual "friends" of the Project. Funding for the Project, along with most nonprofit theatres, remains a constant problem. Rehearsed Readings are a tool in helping playwrights and directors, but the necessary step is a production—and productions cost money.

The number of playwright and director members of the Project has increased to over 170 and we have far more women wanting to participate than we are able to accommodate. Many of our productions and readings have gone on to be produced at other theatres: among them are *Still Life,* written and directed by Emily Mann, which has won four Obie Awards including Best Production and has been produced throughout this country and abroad; *A Weekend Near Madison* by Kathleen Tolan at Actors Theatre of Louisville and

Off-Broadway; *Postcards* by Carol K. Mack at Ensemble Studio Theatre; *Winterplay* by Adele Edling Shank at Second Stage; and *Madonna of the Powder Room* by Paula Cizmar and *Native American* by Constance Congdon at The Portland Stage Company.

This past season (1983-1984) *A . . . My Name Is Alice,* a comedy and music revue, conceived and directed by Joan Micklin Silver and Julianne Boyd, was produced in the fall and was so well received that it transferred Off-Broadway in the Spring for a commercial run. This spring we produced our first Festival of Six One-Act Plays, funded by a Ford Foundation Directing Grant (of which *Candy & Shelley Go to the Desert* is included here), and a one-woman play about Louisa May Alcott, *To Heaven in a Swing* by Katharine Houghton. All seven plays were taped for The Lincoln Center for the Performing Arts Film Library.

Awards and honors for members of the Project have included one Guggenheim Fellowship, three Rockefeller Playwright Grants, five NEA Playwriting Fellowships, two NEA Directing Fellowships, and two NYSCA Literature Grants. Four plays have been selected for the TCG Plays-In-Progress series of publications and many others have been published in acting editions.

The networking aspect of the Project has expanded, including connections with The Women's Program of The American Theatre Association, the Women's Committee of The Dramatists Guild, many individual theatres and organizations, and the formation of The League of Professional Theatre Women/New York, an invitational organization which began meeting at The American Place Theatre in 1981.

Our purpose continues to be to seek out and nurture women playwrights of courage and originality, to help them find their voices in the theatre until such time as their numbers equal men and they will not be ''women playwrights''—only artists writing in the compressed, tense and very personal art form that is theatre. We also want to help them enter the necessary collaboration of producers, directors, actors, designers and technicians—so their plays can engage an audience in that ''willing suspension of disbelief'' for a brief time and communicate in a direct and pure way with living people—the audience.

After the play has been written, the playwright cannot just mail it out, she must leave her cocoon and begin the campaign to obtain a production. This necessitates aggressive behavior on her part that is alien to most women. It is not for the ''writer as recluse''—as Lavonne Mueller has said, ''Emily Dickinson could not be a playwright.'' When a production is in place, the playwright must use a new skill and become a team member of the production. In the past (but not any more I'm happy to say) most women were deprived of the team experience in school sports, and now find the joint effort with producers, directors, actors and designers difficult. Sometimes the playwright must fight for her artistic vision, while realizing that collaboration with these artists under the best conditions can enhance and clarify that vision. The last hurdle the playwright must face is the critical response to her play. Sometimes it seems as if critics do not know that we're all on the same side. Good reviews are necessary to achieve the final step for a playwright: finding her audience. She must use the reviews when they're good, and continue with her work when they're not. There is no "perfect" formula, but prolonged and prodigious practice is necessary for a playwright.

I continue to find it difficult to define a "feminine aesthetic." Does it exist? If so, what is it, or what should it be? I believe the artistic soul is androgynous and encompasses the experience of both sexes. The adjective I use in explaining the quality of talent is "mysterious." Women have their particular and unique mysteries and I want them to bring them to life on stage and show more of the secrets between women that men, for the most part, have not experienced—women as leading characters, women in action, women in conflict, and women using language. With women playwrights there is an increase in the number of roles for actresses (the plays in this book show that clearly) and I am happy for that. The plays selected show us these qualities. The playwrights are all gifted and all different.

In *The Brothers* by Kathleen Collins, five black women—four wives and one sister—review their lives, past and present, in the context of their relationships to four brothers. Each comes to recognize that the men, with their ambitions to succeed in spite of racial obstacles, have dominated the landscapes of their lives.

Little Victories by Lavonne Mueller juxtaposes Susan B. Anthony, travelling in the American West, with the military and personal exploits of Joan of Arc. The author chose to put them together in a play because they both survived in a landscape of men. They have their "Little Victories," but both died believing themselves failures. In the same year, 1920, Joan was canonized and woman finally won the right to vote.

Territorial Rites by Carol K. Mack is about two daughters "coming to terms" with their past in order to define their journey to maturity and a reasonable relationship with their dominant mother. It is also a contemporary fairy tale with an imperfect knight, a maiden who doesn't want to be rescued, a guardian-parent and the inevitable other sister, who has seen the larger world.

Heart of a Dog by Terry Galloway is a highly personal, poetic one-woman performance piece in which a woman, who is deaf, relives parts of her life in talking to her familiar dog. The influence of the past on the present and the tensions between the inner spirit and the outer world propel the woman on her journey.

In *Candy & Shelley Go to the Desert,* a comedy by Paula Cizmar, two women friends on a literal journey are thrown back upon themselves and each other when their car breaks down in the desert during a cross-country trip. The desert itself and a young male biker force the women to some hard realizations about their friendship.

Women playwrights today need to be encouraged by the fact that there is a history of women writers in the commercial theatre which is only beginning to be rediscovered. In 1980 Shirley Lauro, author of *Open Admissions,* said in the *New York Times,* "I always thought of playwrights as men, so when I started as a writer I began with fiction." Our Literary Manager, Gayle Austin, in researching American women playwrights of the past, has found many women from whom we all can take heart. Frances Hodgson Burnett's *Little Lord Fauntleroy* (1888) was the non-musical *Annie* of its time. There were many others. Martha Morton wrote many plays from 1888 to 1915, encouraged other women to write, and in 1907 founded an organization for women playwrights that eventually combined with the earlier men's club and later became the Dramatists Guild.

In the 1902-1903 season, women wrote 22% of the new, original plays. (I don't believe we've reached that number again yet—but we will). Their activities continued strongly through the 1920s, forming a precedent for Rachel Crothers, Lillian Hellman, and the others with whom we are more familiar. Between the Depression and the Post-War period production declined and the number of women playwrights fell drastically.

Fortunately the tide has turned. Mel Gussow in his Women Playwrights article in the *New York Times Magazine,* May 1, 1983, calls women playwrights "a proliferation that is the most encouraging and auspicious aspect of the current American theater." He is right and the Women's Project is proud to have contributed to this surge of women playwrights by creating a temporary home in which they can flourish. This, I believe, is the most one can do for an artist.

Julia Miles
Director
The Women's Project

May 1984

The Brothers

Kathleen Collins

to The Conwell Family

The Brothers was first presented at the American Place Theatre on March 31, 1982. The play was directed by Billie Allen, with set by Christina Weppner, costumes by K.L. Fredericks and lighting by Ann Wrightson. Music was composed by Michael Minard. The cast was as follows:

DANIELLE EDWARDS	Josephine Premice
MARIETTA EDWARDS	Trazana Beverley
MR. NORRELL	Duane Jones
LILLIE EDWARDS	Janet League
ROSIE GOULD	Leila Danette
LETITIA EDWARDS	Marie Thomas
CAROLINE EDWARDS	Seret Scott
THE DOCTOR	Duane Jones
VOICE OF NEWSCASTER	Duane Jones

The Brothers was also produced by the Kuntu Repertory Theatre in Pittsburgh from February 19 through March 12, 1982.

The present version of the play was revised by the author as of July 1982. In this revision the characters of Mr. Norrell and The Doctor were eliminated.

CHARACTERS

Marietta Edwards, the sister
Lillie Edwards, a wife
Rosie Gould, Lillie's mother
Danielle Edwards, a wife
Caroline Edwards, a wife
Letitia Edwards, a wife

All of the characters are Negro.

TIME
Act I—Sunday, February 1, 1948
Act II—A Sunday four months later
Act III—Friday, April 5, 1968

PLACE
The living room of Danielle Edwards' house; adjacent spaces that exist in the minds and memories of the characters.

ACT I

Living room of Danielle Edwards' house, Sunday, February 1, 1948.

In the center, a living room, furnished in middle-class taste. Prominent in the room a staircase that leads to an upstairs that is not visible. Characters disappear upstairs but can still be heard. Various noises—thumps, footsteps, even snatches of conversation drift down from up there. In fact, it might be fair to say that the real drama takes place in that Upper Room and what we witness below is its sheer reverberation.

Off from the living room should be other horizontal spaces fanning out in all directions. Spaces that can be almost anything—a kitchen, a garden, a memory, for these spaces exist more profoundly in the characters' minds than in actual fact.

When the play opens, Lillie Edwards is alone in the living room, pacing. A stunning woman around 30, she is fair enough to pass for white. Dressed in a simple silk, her manner polished and well-bred, she is an imposing figure with a shy, defensive sense of humour.

A radio is on. We hear a Newscaster speaking.

NEWSCASTER'S VOICE: . . . and President Truman expressed the hope that the assassination would not retard the peace of India and the world. Similar expressions of regret were voiced in London, where the King and the Queen and Prime Minister Attlee were among the many leaders to pay tribute to Mr. Gandhi and to deplore the violence that struck him down . . .

(A high-pitched female voice, that of Marietta Edwards, screeches across the Newscaster's Voice.)

MARIETTA: *(From upstairs.)* You don't mean to say he's thinking of never leaving his bed, he can't mean to do such a stubborn, morbid thing . . .

(*Like a shrill burst, Marietta Edwards comes bounding down the stairs. She is a well dressed woman in her mid 30's with an anxious, intense face. There is an old-maidish quality about her, an abruptness, an edgy dissatisfaction. She can be funny, is always sharply observant, but there is something profoundly off-center about her. She rushes over to Lillie.*)

MARIETTA: There's nothing wrong with him so the doctors say except a touch of asthma causing him to snort and groan, lose his breath every now and then . . .

LILLIE: Good, I can breathe again! I feel as if I'd been roped in at the waist!

MARIETTA: But he won't move! He's declared that he has no intention of ever leaving his bed!

LILLIE: Why, in God's name . . .

MARIETTA: (*Embarrassed.*) It's not easy to repeat . . .

LILLIE: Tell me . . . what reason he could possibly give . . .

MARIETTA: He says it's futile . . . that negro life is a void . . .

LILLIE: (*Almost laughing.*) Stop it, Marietta.

MARIETTA: His words exactly.

LILLIE: (*Without conviction.*) That's silly.

MARIETTA: Nelson, our baby . . .

LILLIE: And stubborn . . .

MARIETTA: What in God's name made him think of such a thing . . .

(*The women are lost momentarily in their private thoughts.*)

LILLIE: (*Out of the blue.*) Gandhi's dead.

MARIETTA: (*Confused.*) That refers to what?

LILLIE: (*Almost giggling.*) Chaos, both large and small.

(*Marietta gives Lillie a long, disapproving look. Then footsteps are heard overhead and she is instantly distracted.*)

MARIETTA: That must be Franklin, about to ask the Lord's intervention . . .

(*She rushes up the steps, colliding with Danielle Edwards who is on her way down. Marietta rushes past without a word.*)

DANIELLE: (*To Lillie.*) Aren't you going up, the ceremony's about to begin, the stars are gathering in the Upper Room.

LILLIE: I'm not dressed for the occasion . . .

(*Danielle continues down the steps, amused. She is around 27, stunning too but without Lillie's polished grace. Earthy, easy-going with a deep, raspy voice from too much smoking, she is a woman whose dry sense of humour sets her apart. Unwilling to take life at more than face value, she approaches everything with good-natured mockery.*)

DANIELLE: (*To Lillie.*) You want some coffee—though something sharper would cut the taste.
LILLIE: Coffee.

(*Danielle goes into the kitchen, returns with both coffee and a drink. She hands the coffee to Lillie who sits there shivering.*)

DANIELLE: Cold? I could turn up the heat . . .
LILLIE: Don't bother, I'm sure it's me. (*She sips her coffee.*) Marietta says he's not sick, not really . . .
DANIELLE: That's right, though he snorts and grunts like an old steam engine. The man's 31, his body's just as tight and trim as the last time he flew down that track, now you tell me where it comes from, all this maudlin despair . . . (*Restless, she lights a cigarette.*) Franklin can pray all he wants, Christ Himself could not get Nelson to rise from that bed. (*Just then, Marietta appears on the steps.*)
MARIETTA: (*Breathless.*) He's calling for you, Danielle.
DANIELLE: (*Annoyed.*) He's not dying, Marietta, these are not his final words, he either wants to pee, or he's finally decided on breakfast. No doubt Franklin's prayers have released his appetite . . .

(*Reluctantly, she starts up the steps. Seconds later, Marietta comes down. Lillie sits shivering, her hands wrapped around her coffee cup.*)

MARIETTA: (*Without feeling.*) You look cold.
LILLIE: It's 5° below outside, so the radio says. The idea must influence me. (*She shivers. Marietta looks annoyed.*)
MARIETTA: You should have heard Franklin's prayer, a splendid plea for God's speedy intervention . . . (*Eyeing Lillie accusingly.*) . . . you didn't come up.
LILLIE: I said my own prayer, Marietta, a private chorus to Franklin's strident notes . . .
MARIETTA: (*Baffled.*) That's such a literary turn of phrase, I'm never sure I follow you . . . what did Lillie say, I ask myself, what did Lillie really say. (*Annoyed, upset, Nelson's announcement preys on her mind.*) He *can't* mean it . . .
LILLIE: (*Deliberately obtuse.*) Mean what?
MARIETTA: This morbid decision not to leave his bed.
LILLIE: I've never heard of a more ridiculous thing. (*Suddenly giggling.*) . . . though it is restful. (*Marietta gives her a disapproving glance.*)
MARIETTA: Has Lawrence arrived?
LILLIE: (*Still feeling silly.*) Not before my eyes.
MARIETTA: He'll pump some sense into him, it's Lawrence's cruel and heavy

hand we need.

LILLIE: (*Suddenly impatient.*) Is he coming down soon?

MARIETTA: (*Deliberately obtuse.*) Who?

LILLIE: (*Defiantly.*) My Frankie Boy.

MARIETTA: (*It's her turn to giggle.*) There she goes again with those *descriptive* phrases.

LILLIE: He'll stay up there too long, let Nelson bend his ear with all that mournful talk. (*Getting more annoyed.*) Nelson's just spoiled, that's all, all of you let him have his way too often and too long.

MARIETTA: (*Proudly.*) He's our baby . . . (*She goes over to the mantelpiece, looks admiringly at several of his trophies.*) . . . flew through the air two Olympics in a row, glittered with medals, broke one world's record after another . . . Nelson, our baby . . .

LILLIE: I'm going up. (*She runs into Danielle who's on her way down.*)

DANIELLE: (*With dry humour.*) I wouldn't go up right now, they're heaving a heart-to-heart about Nelson's despair.

LILLIE: Franklin can't talk any sense into him, it'll wind up in a fight . . . wait and see . . .

(*They look at each other sympathetically. Danielle goes into the kitchen. Irritated, Lillie turns on Marietta.*)

LILLIE: . . . there's something in all of you that defies a happy ending.

MARIETTA: (*With placid meanness.*) This is no story, Lillie, we're not polished souls, smooth and prim. (*She makes an affected gesture, then is off on a new track.*) . . . where's Lawrence, where's my fast, determined brother who tolerates no confusion! Lawrence will get him out of that bed, if he were here now, Nelson would be standing once again on his own two feet . . .

(*Suddenly upset, she begins to weep. Danielle comes in, drink in one hand, cigarette in the other. She stops when she notices Marietta.*)

DANIELLE: What's the matter . . . what sudden Edwards flutter did I miss? (*Marietta looks disapprovingly at the drink. Danielle raises her glass defiantly.*) What about a little music, or is that an unholy thought?

MARIETTA: It's Sunday.

LILLIE: (*Mischievously.*) And Gandhi's dead . . .

MARIETTA: (*With sudden fury.*) What has *that* got to do with a thing!

DANIELLE: (*Giggling.*) Please, Marietta, save your fury for the Upper Room . . . (*She looks upstairs imagining the scene.*) I bet the old boy's down on his knees by now, weeping and gnashing, confessing his despair . . . (*She falls to her knees, begins a prayer-like intonation, mimicking Nelson's whining voice.*)
Yea that the Negro athlete
Could forever wear his crown

Never stumble
Never falter
Never end his race victorious
In that somber Negro void . . .

MARIETTA: (*Rising.*) That's blasphemous!

LILLIE: (*Amused.*) They call it poetic license, Marietta, truth in the form of free-fallen verse . . . (*She and Danielle exchange amused glances. Marietta moves indignantly towards the steps.*)

MARIETTA: It's no easy thing for a man to fall from grace.

DANIELLE: (*Rising.*) He didn't fall, Marietta, he took off his track shoes, grew mortal and flat-footed like the rest of us . . .

MARIETTA: (*To both of them.*) I don't know which I find more distasteful, your queasy way of putting things, or Lillie's overblown prose . . .

(*Just then there is a loud scuffling noise from upstairs, the sound of male voices raised in anger.*)

MARIETTA: (*Instantly hysterical.*) My boys, my boys, what's going on with my boys? (*She flies up the stairs. Danielle almost follows, then stops.*)

DANIELLE: I will *not* go up.

LILLIE: (*Backing away.*) They're fighting . . .

DANIELLE: (*Dryly.*) . . . or we could pretend they're choirboys struggling to reach high C . . .

LILLIE: It always finishes in a fight . . .

MARIETTA: (*From upstairs.*) Stop this silly, childish skirmishing, what provoked you boys to rage . . .

LILLIE: (*Angry.*) All this high-pitched fury, time and time again! (*There is the sound of further scuffling.*)

MARIETTA: (*From upstairs.*) Stop it, I say! Give your poor sister a chance to intervene!

LILLIE: (*Inside her own fury.*) Screeching and screaming like black crows in heat!

MARIETTA: (*From upstairs.*) Look what you've done! Driven Franklin to distraction, caused him to strike out against your nasty old spells, you deserve a whipping . . . (*Furiously clapping her hands.*) . . . one two three, I'd have you up in a minute . . . it's not fitting for an Edwards to languish in despair! (*She begins to cry.*)

LILLIE: (*Outraged.*) And it always ends with the damn weeping! (*Danielle comes over to calm her down.*)

DANIELLE: Why don't you go up, try and persuade Franklin to take time-out from the ring. (*Lillie hesitates.*) Go on . . .

LILLIE: I'll do my best . . .

(*She disappears upstairs. Danielle goes into the kitchen, returns with a fresh drink, then raises the volume on the radio. We come in on the end of another newscast.*)

NEWSCASTER'S VOICE: . . . elsewhere, Orville Wright who with his brother, the late Wilbur Wright, invented the airplane, died last night at Miami Valley Hospital at the age of 76 . . .

(Late 40's cool jazz [early Monk or Miles] blares out as Danielle switches the station then begins puttering around the room.)

DANIELLE: *(To herself.)* . . . before despair there was the glitter and the glamour! London, Germany, the New York track scene when it was all the way with Nelson! He was cruising! Legs flying . . . light years ahead of whoever took second! Caught his trophies from princes and queens! *(She begins to preen.)* . . . I powdered my nose, rouged my cheeks, slipped in and out of silks, we were flying! Jet-settin' it negro-style across the Continent . . . breakfast at the Carleton at two in the afternoon, lavish old parties we dropped in on at dawn. We had a flair for the hot-steppin' life . . . *(She looks upstairs.)* . . . didn't we . . . *(Suddenly outraged.)* Now you tell me why you're up there crying in your pillow when there are midnight bars across the continent to make life a slow, *easy* kind of thing! *(She grows sullen.)* . . . places we could stroll, drift along on a little whiskey and gin . . . *(She drifts into a song.)* . . . I took a trip on a train and I thought about you . . . two or three stars caught under the sky . . . a winding road . . . *(She gets even more moody.)* . . . I'm hanging loose on the vine, while he's up there playing the Buddha! Turning himself into the Negro Job . . . *(Amused by her own humour.)* And God said: "Let there be Despair!" And Nelson *dropped* from the sky . . . oh boy oh boy . . . *(She giggles to herself, when Marietta's voice interrupts.)*
MARIETTA: *(From upstairs.)* Danielle! *(Startled, Danielle turns around. Marietta is standing on the steps.)* He wants his Ralston . . .
DANIELLE: *(Quick on the trigger.)* Piping hot, with raisins and brown sugar . . .
MARIETTA: *(Taken aback.)* He did put it that way, yes . . .
DANIELLE: Tell him I couldn't get any Ralston, only Wheatena, but I can fix it the same, he won't even know the difference . . .
MARIETTA: I'll tell him that, yes . . .

(She disappears upstairs. Danielle goes into the kitchen. We hear her clattering about, among the pots and pans, making an awful racket.)

DANIELLE: *(From the kitchen.)* . . . is this the Big Time, is this what Nelson meant by the Big Time . . .

(Marietta appears on the steps, leans over the railing, and yells into the kitchen.)

MARIETTA: He insists that it's not the same . . .

(Danielle comes to the doorway, looks up at her.)

MARIETTA: (*Proudly.*) He has fond memories of Momma fixing only Ralston in the morning.

DANIELLE: (*Biting her tongue.*) Tell him it will be crunchy, and creamy sweet just like Ralston . . .

(*Marietta hesitates, gives off suspicious airs.*)

DANIELLE: (*Moving in for the kill.*) With all her teeth out, and her hair falling into the bowl, your *Mother* could have eaten it . . .

(*Shocked, Marietta retreats up the steps. Satisfied, Danielle goes back into the kitchen.*)

DANIELLE: (*Mumbling.*) Let's see now . . . I got my tray, a dainty napkin for his Highness, the raisins and brown sugar, a little fresh cream . . . (*She emerges carrying her tray, crosses the room and starts upstairs.*) . . . now I ask you, is this the life for a woman of my quality . . . have I fallen, have I fallen . . . (*She disappears upstairs. We hear her talking to Nelson.*) . . . you keep telling yourself it's Ralston, it's got raisins and brown sugar, it's crunchy and creamy sweet, just like Ralston . . . eat the cereal, Nelson . . . (*Getting louder.*) Taste it, for God's sake . . . (*And louder.*) Taste it! You . . . baby! (*Lillie emerges, slips down the stairs.*) . . . did anyone ever tell you you're a baby baby baby!!!

(*Lillie crosses the room. Sudden pain makes her double up, almost lose her balance. She sits down in the nearest chair.*)

LILLIE: (*To herself.*) I can't stand it, not one more minute of it . . .

(*She closes her eyes. Lights dim. Fade-up on Rosie Gould, standing in her doorway wrapped in a shawl. She is a woman in her 60's with silver hair, skin as fair as Lillie's. She has a charming manner, gracious, yet not without a sharp, rather aloof edge. Lillie comes rushing up the steps in a fur coat and hat, shivering intensely. There is a feeling of wind, bitter cold in the air.*)

LILLIE: (*Breathless.*) I brought the children, Momma. Nelson's sick, we might have to be there all day, do you mind?

ROSIE: Where's Franklin?

LILLIE: In the car . . . is it alright, Momma, it's not any fun for them at Nelson's . . .

ROSIE: It's cold, child, go bring them in, I know they're in a mood for hot chocolate and cake . . .

LILLIE: (*Relieved.*) Thank you, Momma . . . when I told them they might be coming to you, Rowena squealed, "We're going to Rosie's, our Rosie's, our Rosie's," she shouted . . . (*Laughing oddly.*) . . . where it's sweet-smelling and clear and the odor of death is nowhere about.

ROSIE: (*Stiffening.*) Those are no child's words.

LILLIE: (*Ashamed.*) I'm sorry, Momma . . . I'm not well, I feel like I'm coming apart. The house is too small, there's no room to breathe. I have to stay by the phone and record who's died. Franklin depends on me to keep track of all the details, when the funeral will be, what flowers will go on the grave, what size casket they need. I could almost embalm them, Momma, I've grown so familiar with the rituals of death.

ROSIE: (*Distancing herself.*) Stop, child, stop whining as if life were no more than a morbid dream! (*A car horn honks briskly.*)

LILLIE: That's my Frankie Boy . . . I'll feel better, Momma . . . soon Franklin will have his degree and this catering to death will be over. (*The horn honks again.*) He's bound to succeed, a man that impatient is bound to succeed. All the Edwards ride a proud, hungry edge. (*She rushes down the steps.*)

ROSIE: (*Under her breath.*) So do race horses and fools.

(*We hear the car door open and Lillie speaking to the children.*)

LILLIE: (*Out of sight.*) See Rosie, our sweet Rosie . . . (*Marietta's voice cuts across.*)

MARIETTA: (*Out of the dark.*) Lillie . . .

(*Lights go out on Rosie, come up on Marietta tiptoeing down the steps.*)

Lillie . . . (*No answer. She looks around, the room remains mostly in shadow.*) I'll bet you anything she's gone for a walk, that's just like her to tiptoe away, come rushing back all a-flutter about her Frankie Boy. (*She mimicks Lillie's genteel tone.*) ". . . oh Frankie Boy, don't get yourself so worked up, oh Frankie Boy . . ." (*Annoyed.*) . . . while Franklin looks at her with moony eyes. He's too stern for such foolishness . . . it's not often he laughs, except with me . . . there are things between us that make us fall out in a fit . . . secret things that go back to childhood, to heavy rooms, Pop's stern forbidding ways . . .

(*Lights change as she drifts into the past and relives a conversation with Franklin. Her voice changes to whispered fright.*)

Pop's in a fury, Franklin. Lawrence failed the Post Office exam . . . you should hear him. Lawrence came within inches of getting the thrashing of his life. (*She mimicks her father's violent, stentorian tone.*) ". . . I expected one of my boys to put in a good show down there . . . you keep out of this, Margaret, I know what each and every one of these boys better turn out to be. I may be too skin deep, locked forever behind this stone wall but I will not tolerate from my boys any *scrawny colored lives!''* (*Nervous and excited.*) Oh Franklin, he pitched a fit! You know how he gets . . . his glasses fall off and he has to squint . . . he can't see two feet in front of him but he keeps *roaring* away! (*They laugh.*) I guess Lawrence couldn't find a way to cheat . . . he would have and you know it. I don't care what you say, he's a schemer, he can think of more devious things . . . that's because you refuse to see bad in anything, you're too . . . (*She searches for the right word.*) . . . *upstanding* . . . the righteous one in the clan. Lawrence will knock people over to get where he wants to go . . . not you, you'll work hard, be truthful, persevere . . . of course you'll make it, you'll be First Colored at something just the way Pop dreams. (*They laugh.*) . . . you met who . . . when did this happen . . . oh Franklin, tell me everything . . . who is she . . . a Gould! Why they're queer, eccentric, the haughtiest Negroes around! Live off by themselves on their own private acres, never mingle nor mix with any other souls . . . how did you meet her . . . oh I know she's beautiful, they're a handsome tribe, take great pride in their land and their color, breed themselves as white as any negro stock can be. (*That provokes a chuckle.*) Do the boys know? Lawrence will be jealous, I can tell you that much . . . not Jeremy, he's always good-natured. (*She mimicks Jeremy's stuttering.*) . . . th . . . th . . . that's j . . . j . . . jus . . . st gr . . . gr . . . and, Fr . . . Fr . . . Franklin . . . I . . . 'm s . . . so ha . . . ha . . . ppy f . . . f . . . for y . . . ou . . . Dear dear Jeremy . . . and of course Nelson will think it's wonderful, he thinks the world of you . . . me? Why ask such a thing. I'm sure I'll like her, I can't see why not, unless she's flighty or silly . . . or doesn't like me . . . well I might be too plain for her taste . . . there's nothing fancy about me . . . I'm not subtle or delicate as I suspect her to be. (*Suddenly feeling self-conscious.*) She's not been raised around four boys all her life . . . pushing and pulling and tugging at me . . . till sometimes I feel like an abrupt male thing. (*Growing even more self-conscious.*) . . . who am I anyway . . . am I just you boys' shadow that no one will ever see? (*Lillie's voice interrupts.*)

LILLIE: (*Out of the dark.*) Marietta . . .

(*Lights go out quickly. Come up on Lillie still sitting in the chair where she's fallen asleep.*)

Marietta . . . I thought I heard her speak . . . where is everyone? (*She goes towards the steps when Marietta appears startling her.*) I thought I heard you . . .

MARIETTA: I was in the kitchen fixing myself some tea.

LILLIE: I fell asleep.

MARIETTA: I thought you'd gone for a walk.

LILLIE: (*Shivering.*) Too cold.

MARIETTA: (*Oddly.*) I said to myself, Lillie's walking around . . .

LILLIE: (*Amused.*) You talk about me like I'm not here. Is there more tea?

MARIETTA: I made a fresh pot. (*Lillie starts towards the kitchen, Marietta blocks her path.*) Don't move, don't move. (*She goes quickly into the kitchen, returns almost as quickly with tea and things on a tray.*) Bring that coffee table over here. (*Lillie does as she's told, Marietta puts down the tray.*) Sit down. (*Again, Lillie obeys. Marietta begins ceremoniously to serve tea.*) Those are sweets. Danielle baked them, so I'm sure they're no good. (*She mimicks Lawrence's acid tongue.*) ". . . it should be clear to all of us by now that Danielle has no flair for the domestic sciences . . ." (*Giggling.*) . . . that's how Lawrence put it.

LILLIE: (*Gently.*) . . . though her humour is often better than a good meal. (*Silence reigns. After a while.*) Tell me what it is *I* do wrong in your eyes.

MARIETTA: (*Annoyed.*) Now how am I supposed to answer that, by taking you apart?

LILLIE: You think I'm too flat, too low-keyed for someone with Franklin's temperament.

MARIETTA: (*Growing testy.*) And what does that mean . . . flat, low-keyed, as if you were a piece of music, you have this irritating way of speaking in tongues, alluding to things, as if nothing had a proper name.

LILLIE: (*Bluntly.*) You think I'm weak.

MARIETTA: (*Backing off.*) Slow . . . for the Edwards speed.

LILLIE: Haughty.

MARIETTA: Too refined.

LILLIE: (*Bizarrely.*) A clinging vine.

MARIETTA: (*Getting nasty.*) All sweetness and light.

LILLIE: (*Bluntly.*) You don't like me.

MARIETTA: (*Spitefully.*) What has *that* got to do with a thing! (*Silence.*)

DANIELLE: (*From upstairs.*) . . . that's exactly right, that's the least he can do.

(*She comes stomping down the steps. Marietta, uneasy, gets up and starts towards the steps.*)

Where are my cigarettes? (*Marietta brushes past her and goes upstairs.*)

LILLIE: How is it up there?

DANIELLE: There's an effort underway to get him to use the bathroom. (*She grabs a cigarette.*) Depression is one thing, urinary warfare is quite another.

LILLIE: (*Angry.*) What's the point?

DANIELLE: Of never getting out of bed? (*They look at each other. The absurdity of the thing hits them and they break out laughing.*) He thinks he has a right to his despair.

LILLIE: Because he's colored. (*They can't stop laughing.*)

DANIELLE: (*Giggling.*) You should hear him up there pontificating . . . (*She begins to mimick Nelson's dry, whining drawl.*) ". . . now Franklin, you and I both know that the Negro athlete, once he falls from grace has nowhere to run . . . the track and field were his last line of defense, once that falls, he returns to the void, negro life is a void, Franklin, you and I both know that." (*She giggles.*) Then Franklin starts in on him. (*Assuming Franklin's crisper, sterner tone.*) "... It does none of us any good to hear you talk like that, Nelson ... what would we do if the whole race went back to bed." (*They can't stop laughing.*)

LILLIE: (*Giggling.*) Can't you see it ... armies of Negroes taking to their beds ...

DANIELLE: (*Giggling.*) Declaring Nelson King of the Void ... (*The laughter subsides.*) ... which makes me what ... Queen of the Bed Pans ... (*She can't help wincing.*) ... that's kind of hard to get dressed up for. (*Suddenly frightened.*) I could lose my bearings, Lillie. I'm only built for speed.

(*Just then there is a loud scream from upstairs.*)

MARIETTA: (*Upstairs.*) Don't do that! Stop it, Nelson. Franklin, stop him, he could suffocate. Take it from him ... he's mad, completely mad, abuses all our kindness, oh God, I can't stand to see him treat himself this way! (*She comes rushing down the steps.*) He just tried to bury himself under his pillow! (*The doorbell rings.*) ... it's Lawrence, thank God! Our charger's on the scene! (*She starts towards the door. Lights go out.*)

END OF ACT 1

ACT II

Scene 1
Danielle Edwards' living room, Rosie Gould's garden.
A Sunday four months later.

Lights fade up on Danielle's living room. We hear her upstairs talking to Nelson.

DANIELLE: (*From upstairs.*) I'm applying all my culinary skills to this meal, the least you could do is make it to the table. I'm asking you to walk a few hundred feet, crawl, if you have to, I don't give a damn how you get there . . . speak up, god damnit, or else write me one of your notes . . . what's no use? What are you always crying about . . . (*She comes to the steps, shouts back at him.*) . . . you think you're the Prophet, Nelson the Negro Prophet leading his people through the Valley of Tears! (*She stomps down the steps.*) Just get up and go to work! We could have a few drinks, a few kids, *then* you can die. Honest to God, Nelson, I'm gonna get old, how much longer you want to play this Job scenario . . . the whole damn race is Job, what makes you so special . . . (*She sits down at the bottom of the steps.*) This could get bleak . . . me, a bottle of gin and a looney-tune colored man. (*That makes her laugh in spite of herself.*) Colored or not, I'm not built for despair . . . must be a high yaller impulse to keep things light. I'm descended from too long a line of sallow women who taught me to look stylish and shut my mouth . . . wear my skin like it was a precious jewel . . . wait for choice negro offerings to line up at my door. I was supposed to have myself a doctor, or a lawyer, why I chose Nelson is more than I can explain. (*She laughs at herself.*) It must have been those quick-moving limbs, that sly baby-face grin, the old boy looked like he was good for many years in the fast lane. Together I thought we'd ride above the storms, turn negro life into a stardust melody . . . no bleak strolls into despair, no questions asked at all. (*She yells loud enough for him to hear.*) It was not my intention to think life through! Wind up with answers that lead nowhere but down! (*The phone rings throwing her off-balance.*

She takes her time answering.) Hello . . . yes, Franklin . . . is Lillie any better? . . . I'm sorry, Franklin, tell her I'll try to come see her next week but it's hard for me to get away . . . no he hasn't moved . . . I told him you were all coming to dinner but I think that made things worse . . . I can't say, it's rare nowadays that he uses the spoken word . . . he prefers to write notes . . . (*Just then there is a loud thump overhead.*) . . . and when that fails, he pounds on the floor like a damn inmate . . . hold on a second. (*She goes over to the steps, furious.*) What's the matter with you, I'm talking to Franklin. (*Now the doorbell rings, followed by another loud thump or two from upstairs. Danielle is beside herself.*) And I'm supposed to *manage* this act. (*She goes to the door. Marietta comes in, just as Nelson thump-thumps again. Marietta looks puzzled.*) He started that yesterday, will you go upstairs and shut him up, Franklin's on the phone. (*Marietta rushes upstairs. Danielle goes back to the phone.*) I'm sorry, Franklin, maybe it would be better if you all didn't come, the idea seems to have set him off, he swears there's some kind of conspiracy to get him to go to work. (*The thumping starts again.*)

MARIETTA: (*From upstairs. Urgent.*) Danielle.

DANIELLE: (*Quickly.*) I gotta go, if you can't reach Lawrence, then please come, I can't handle the charger by myself . . . alright. (*She hangs up, starts immediately up the steps.*) . . . I'm coming, though I wish to hell they'd put me in a strait-jacket, and cart me off. (*She disappears upstairs, talking to Nelson.*) His Highness rang.

(*The doorbell rings. No one seems to hear it. It rings again. Finally, the door opens, and Caroline Edwards steps in. She is a woman in her mid 30's, exquisitely dressed in an expensive fur coat that fits her to perfection. A sense of style, clothes-wise, and an instinct to flaunt it, should strike one immediately. There is, in general, a defiant quality about her, a gruff way of speaking and behaving that lacks refinement. She crosses the stairway, talking to herself.*)

CAROLINE: Where's everybody . . . probably gathered already in the Upper Room. (*She starts to go up, changes her mind.*) . . . I'll wait for Lawrence . . . though the minute he hits that door he'll fly right by me. (*Amused by that, she mimicks his brusque manner to perfection.*) ". . . gotta check on Nelson, gotta check on Nelson, fix me a drink, fix me a drink . . ." Then he'll *charge* up the steps, and the fireworks will begin. Maybe I should warn them that he's on his way . . . give them a chance to cool Nelson down. (*She acts out the idea with amusement.*) Greetings everybody, Lawrence sent me on ahead. He's hot on the trail of some fast-moving real estate deal, suggested I play advance man for his act. (*That truly amuses her.*) . . . that'll set things off, Marietta will have to pee, the thought of Lawrence always sends her racing to the bathroom. Danielle will sneak three quickies before he gets through the door. Nelson will bury himself under his pillows, while Franklin tries in vain to raise him from the dead. Poor Lillie will miss all the fun and explosions, I guess too many sparks have flown in her eye. (*Again she starts to go up, but changes her mind.*) I need the charger. (*Restless, she goes to a mirror to check her appearance. She is taking off her coat, when Marietta appears on the steps, sees her, rushes down quickly.*)

MARIETTA: When did you come in, where's Lawrence?

CAROLINE: He'll be late. How's Nelson?

MARIETTA: I think he's gone to the moon, or some other planet where depressed souls go. He's propped up in bed, and if you ask him anything, he writes you a note. I said to him, wouldn't you like to come downstairs for dinner . . . he thought about it awhile, then wrote: (*Reciting the note.*) "He who lives in silence defies negro pain." Now what has that got to do with coming down to dinner? He won't let Danielle out of his sight, has a fit whenever she tries to leave the room . . . which reminds me, she sent me down here to check the roast.

(*She goes quickly into the kitchen. Caroline goes to the window, looking for Lawrence. When Marietta comes back in, she picks up Caroline's fur coat.*)

Is that new?

CAROLINE: Sort of.

MARIETTA: (*Coolly.*) There are tangible benefits to Lawrence's brutal deals. (*She drops the coat, plops down in a chair.*) I'm tired, I spent the morning with Lillie who looks appropriately languid as only Lillie can look.

CAROLINE: But she's sick, really sick, according to Lawrence, they say there's something wrong with her spine.

MARIETTA: Well, she's staying with Rosie who I'm sure will pamper her back to health.

(*She closes her eyes. Caroline remains by the window. Neither of them speaks for the longest time. Intruding on their silence is Danielle's laughter.*)

DANIELLE: (*From upstairs.*) That's very good, but I can't think of any words that rhyme with negro . . . how about gigolo? (*She laughs even harder, as if in response to something Nelson says.*) . . . that's better yet, you have the makings of a real bard. (*Danielle's laughter subsides.*)

MARIETTA: (*Touched.*) Nelson, our baby.

(*Caroline looks at her oddly but her eyes are closed. The silence continues until Caroline, feeling restless, lights a cigarette. The sharp striking of the match startles Marietta who jumps awake.*)

I thought I heard Lawrence, it's just like him to surprise me with his presence.

CAROLINE: (*Amused.*) The charger never rings nor announces his arrival.

MARIETTA: (*Agreeing.*) All of a sudden, he's here . . . it's the same with you. You carry around his atmosphere.

CAROLINE: (*Distant.*) I've heard you say that we look alike.

MARIETTA: (*Agreeing.*) That Lawrence would find his match has always surprised me, he was such a separate child, we had to remind ourselves that he was our brother. But the moment you entered the house, I thought to myself—Lawrence went off and found his twin. (*Amused.*) Two sleekly polished souls have we, two sleekly polished souls.

CAROLINE: I don't know whether to be flattered or not. (*Marietta laughingly repeats the same refrain.*)

MARIETTA: Two sleekly polished souls . . .

(*Over this refrain, "cool" music drifts in, disembodied like a memory. Caroline moves forward responding to it.*)

CAROLINE: (*Remembering.*) I'm standing on a cool balcony on a hot summer night. Alone. In a new floral gown. It's hot. The dance floor's crowded. I refuse to go down and sweat with the crowd. I look too good. I will not get all souped-up for some silly young thing . . . all of a sudden, Lawrence walks in. I watch him glide acoss the floor with his shiny black hair. He looks up, sees me . . . (*Mimicking Lawrence's gruff, raspy voice.*) "What you doin', what you doin' up there?" (*As herself.*) I don't want to sweat, it's nice and cool up here. (*As Lawrence.*) "I'll keep it the same down here." And he holds out his hand, his eyes leaping at me. (*She shivers.*) Down I go . . . wrapped in those cool arms before I know what hit me . . . that was the beginning.

(*She moves as if dancing. Cross-fade to Marietta who, too, has drifted back into the past and is once again talking with Franklin.*)

MARIETTA: Who? Lawrence and that sleek little Fieldsboro thing? That story's as clear as a bell, those two will most certainly marry, they have the same greedy high-pitched dreams . . . who else was there . . . old Bus? With a girl? (*Slightly embarrassed.*) . . . oh I guess I was hoping he'd ask me . . . never mind. Did you meet Rosie . . . I could have told you that, they don't like anyone who's brown. Tell me what Lillie was wearing . . . that sounds exactly like her with her "Frankie Boy" this and her "Frankie Boy" that, really, Franklin, that's a truly embarrassing name, only Lillie would think of such a thing out of her wide-ranging memory for the coy, romantic touch she calls you her Frankie Boy. (*She shakes her head disapprovingly.*) . . . I do like her, she's kind, even funny in a sweet, poetic way . . . and she certainly loves you . . . I don't know, that's her idea of romance, a singular adoration fixed forever on one chosen soul . . . I don't know if love everlasting fits the hard Edwards mold for dreams. (*Suddenly uptight.*) I'm not jealous and I won't be teased like already I'm some spinster fool . . . who . . . oh . . . Bus . . . don't call him that, Franklin, he's nice and he has a good job with the railroad, too . . . you mock anyone who comes near my door . . . (*Mimicking him.*) "He's not good enough for you, Marietta, not that scrawny negro fool." (*They laugh.*) . . . . you're as bad as Pop . . . will he be among the first of the first of the coloreds, he'd say . . . (*They begin to giggle.*) . . . poor Bus, I bet you scared him away . . . well, he is a little slow . . . and he's got big feet . . . (*They are really giggling by now.*) And as Pop would say, he's a bit too colored for me. (*Laughter explodes out of her.*) . . . oh Franklin, there's nobody but nobody I ever laugh with like you. (*She leans over conspiratorially.*) Tell me again about old Slade Wilson, it's not true, Franklin, that he almost got himself embalmed. (*She giggles, listening, when a loud cry from Danielle cuts across.*)

DANIELLE: (*From upstairs. Hysterical.*) Marietta!

(*Lights go out quickly on Marietta, come up on Danielle standing on the steps as Marietta rushes in to see what's wrong.*)

I can't wake him . . . he's not breathing, or am I seeing things . . . call someone quick, my God, I better not leave him. (*Starts back up the steps, as Marietta rushes to dial the phone.*) . . . he's faking, that is just like him to fool me, he's good at holding his breath for as long as he wants. (*She disappears upstairs.*)

MARIETTA: (*On the phone.*) Dr. Wilkins, please . . . and quickly . . . it's my brother, Nelson Edwards, he's not breathing at all . . .

DANIELLE: (*From upstairs. Hysterical.*) Marietta!

(*Just then the doorbell rings with quick, insistent strokes. Marietta drops the phone.*)

MARIETTA: . . . oh thank God, it's the charger . . . he'll wake him up alright, pump some sense into that playful spirit, always scaring us with his games. (*As she rushes to answer the door, Lillie's voice cuts across.*)

LILLIE: (*Out of the dark.*) Momma!

(*Lights black out on Marietta, a dim light fades up on Lillie's face. Her eyes are closed, she moves restlessly, as if talking in her sleep.*)

What happened then . . . oh Frankie boy, he's not dead, no one ever dies . . . they sleep, they dream, nothing is as it seems . . .

ROSIE: (*Out of the dark.*) Lillie . . .

(*Lights come up. We're in Rosie's garden. Lillie is stretched out on a chaise lounge, an afghan thrown across her. She wakes up in confusion, while Rosie stands there holding a tray.*)

LILLIE: I fell asleep. Marietta always wears me out. I was dreaming about Nelson, he was trying to strangle himself with his pillow. I thought it was funny but Franklin thought he was dead. I was sure he wasn't, I kept saying, you can't strangle yourself with a pillow, no one can strangle themselves with a pillow but he wouldn't listen and started to cry . . . (*She looks at Rosie who gives her back an aloof gaze.*) I suppose you'd call that a morbid dream.

ROSIE: It has no bright overtones, no . . . (*She sets down her tray.*) I brought you some tea, a slice of lemon pound cake and some strawberries, the first from my garden.

LILLIE: They look lovely, Momma, plump and cheerful like you'd like me to be. (*She smiles at her mother.*) I've seen everything come into bloom, watched your forsythia spread along that fence, followed your magnolia and dogwood as they burst open, now your roses have come and almost gone. Do they watch me, I wonder, laugh and shake their heads at this dying old vine . . . (*She grows nervous.*) . . . where are the children?

ROSIE: Rowena's in the kitchen learning to make floating island, I just put the baby down for a nap.

LILLIE: They tiptoe around me like they knew I needed silence to keep me alive. (*Rosie stiffens.*) I don't get better, do I, Momma, and it's me not the illness that's wasting away.

ROSIE: Don't talk like that, child. (*She serves her some tea.*)

LILLIE: I'll brighten up, I'll be just like those peonies, haughty and proud as you raised me to be. (*Suddenly anxious.*) Did Franklin call?

ROSIE: Not since this morning.

LILLIE: (*Upset.*) You should have wakened me, Momma, it upsets him to feel cut off from me. He has a funeral today, his classes this evening, then he'll try to run by Nelson's before he goes to work. He won't call if he thinks it's too late.

ROSIE: I should go in, I promised to teach Rowena how to separate eggs. (*Lillie tries to get up.*)

LILLIE: (*In pain.*) Help me up, Momma. (*Rosie goes to help her. Together they manage to get her on her feet which pleases Lillie greatly.*) Now, what can I do . . . if I were home, I could answer the phone for my Frankie Boy, tell him who died, it's always a proud moment when I rush down the stairs. Frankie Boy, someone's dead, we can pay our bills, go out to dinner, have a night on the town, we're rich, Frankie Boy, look at the pleasures death will loan us for an hour! (*She holds tight to Rosie.*) Let's walk a bit, Momma, it's the least I can do. (*They begin to walk. She falters, grabs hold of Rosie, crying out in pain.*) I can't even do that, my back's too broken to carry me to the gate . . . it's funny to watch this body splinter itself to bits. (*Rosie leads her back.*)

ROSIE: (*Matter-of-factly.*) It's the sun that's too hot, we'll wait till it's cool and there's a breeze to carry us.

LILLIE: That's just like you, Momma, keep things clear and simple, like tea

and flowers were the only real things. (*She mocks her Mother in nursery rhyme prose.*)
My Rosie lives outside of race
She never lets it reach her gate
She grows her flowers
Bakes her sweets
Race is a stranger she never meets.

ROSIE: (*Furious.*) Stop it! I won't be made fun of! I said to you what any Mother would have said. It was the best advice I could offer, don't mock me because it's true. (*She tries to soften her anger.*) I shouldn't leave the children this long . . . try to sleep and dream for once of all the *bright* things that surround you. (*She leaves. Lillie, on the verge of crying, tries to get up but can't.*)

LILLIE: (*Sad and upset.*) Oh Momma, you don't know my Frankie Boy when he's at his best . . .

(*She begins to cry, drifts fretfully into sleep. The scenes that follow are her dreams: 40's music, the cool early jazz of Miles Davis, drifts across. Lights fade up on what must feel like a dance hall. Lillie drifts in as if dancing with someone. She is vibrant and bright in a silk gown and responds to her partner as if engaged in conversation.*)

. . . I came with my cousin, Winston Gould. (*Responding.*) . . . I agree, it's a dark, morbid name but it fits him, he's (*Drifting into rhyme.*)
Always stiff
Always sad
Never does anything
Good or bad
(*Responding.*) I always do that, I learn who people are by putting them in verse. (*Responding.*) I don't know you well enough. Tell me at least three things about you. Mortuary science, you mean corpses, embalming, that kind of thing . . . that's morbid, going to school to learn about death! . . . then what are you really studying . . . I see you better as that, you'll make a wonderful teacher, eager, upstanding, stern to a fault . . . (*She stops dancing.*) . . . I don't know. You don't smile—that's a sign of sternness and there's a crease in your forehead . . . right there . . . it's frowning at me even though you're trying to smile. You're too serious! (*She giggles, suddenly excited.*) Momma!

(*Lights come up on Rosie, sitting in a rocking chair crocheting. Lillie rushes in, breathless and excited.*)

It was a lovely dance! I danced every dance with Franklin Edwards from Riverview, a handsome man who will be magnificent one day . . . not now, he's only a mortician, a watchman at night to make ends meet. But he's in

school, an education major like myself, he'll be a teacher one day, then a principal, he's determined to succeed, it's written all over his face. (*Hesitant.*) . . . he's brown, Momma, not very, but a little browner than any of us. (*She waits for an answer. Rosie doesn't say a thing. Lillie bursts out laughing.*) I call him my Frankie Boy. (*She drifts into rhyme.*)
Last night at a dance
I fell into a trance
A silly old spell
Perhaps no one could tell
Except the stranger
I met and married at a glance
It's he, of course
Who put me in a trance.
(*She kneels beside her mother.*) Tell me why you don't like my Frankie Boy.
ROSIE: (*Distant.*) You already know the answer . . . every bit of the answer.
LILLIE: You think I'm weak.
ROSIE: To ask for trouble, brooding negro trouble is a weakness, yes.
LILLIE: But there must be room for love, Momma.
ROSIE: A slippery platform, child, don't plant your feet on such a slippery platform.

(*Lights go out. In the dark: somber organ music. We come up slowly on Lillie sitting by an open window writing.*)

LILLIE: From my window I can see
Death arrive, it follows me
In and out my door it goes,
Caskets, flowers, tales of woe
No one smiles
No one rejoices
Somber faces, somber choices . . .

(*Footsteps are heard. She gets up, puts her writing aside.*)

Is that you, Frankie Boy? (*Responding.*)
No . . . no calls,
No deaths
No one sees fit
To take their rest
(*Amused.*) I've been sitting at the window all morning making up verses. Come hold me, I don't mind anything when you hold me. (*She moves towards him when a sudden pain grips her.*) . . . I don't know, ever since Rowena it comes and goes as if something came apart at her birth. Don't frown, it's only plumbing, a loose valve, you're back, now it will dissolve. (*She reaches*

out to touch him but he doesn't respond.) Don't brood, it's only the warehouse. It's our prison, it keeps us apart in the still of the night, makes mornings come in slow and somber . . . (*Refusing depression.*) . . . but it won't last forever! Soon you'll have those degrees . . . oh Frankie Boy, don't brood, every second of life's not dangerous and sad . . . hold me, please, hold me.

(*Rosie's voice cuts across the scene. Lights go out quickly.*)

ROSIE: (*Out of the dark.*) Lillie . . .

(*Come up on Rosie, like a shadow. She hovers a moment over Lillie eclipsing her from our sight.*)

Wake up, child . . .

(*Lillie wakes up in confusion like she was a small child again.*)

LILLIE: (*Defensively.*) Don't blame me for my dreams, Momma, I tried hard to make them bright and harmless.
ROSIE: Franklin just called, he'll be here shortly after his classes, he has the night off from the midnight shift. I'll bring you your dinner. (*Excited, Lillie starts to get up.*)
LILLIE: I can get up, Momma, I'd like to eat with the children, my Frankie Boy's coming, I think I'll even change.

(*She pulls herself up violently. The effort sends her sprawling, knocking over the table and chair beside her lounge.*)

I'm a joke, Momma. (*Rosie tries to lift her but can't.*)
ROSIE: I'll need help to lift you, child, just lay still for a moment. (*She rushes away. Lillie lays there growing increasingly delirious.*)
LILLIE: Frankie Boy, here lies your Lillie, a crumpled heap . . . (*She cries out in pain.*) Oh God, what a mess dying is. I don't want him to find me all disordered like this. (*She tries to move but the pain defeats her.*) Rosie will fix me, she'll make me look lovely, I can see myself stretched out under her gaze . . . surrounded by flowers . . . lillies of the valley, white roses, delphiniums, I'll be decked out like a queen . . . Queen of the Bed Pans. (*She giggles. By now she is completely delirious.*) . . . oh Danielle . . . don't let their pride defeat you, it's sickness, they're all too angry to breathe . . . (*With sudden defiance.*) I will *not* live off of anger, dead bodies, defeated dreams! Watch my Frankie Boy brood on all the unfair negro things . . . no, the drab passages are too much for me! (*Collapsing with shame.*) What a mess I've made of things. (*Weeping.*) Frankie Boy, my Frankie Boy . . . (*Something begins to change inside her body.*) My strength's coming back, my

body feels so light and free just as if it were leaving me. (*She screams out in panic.*) Momma! I don't want to die just yet, tell my children they don't have to remember me. (*A violent movement rocks her body.*) . . . flowers *burst* into bloom, Momma, all of a sudden they thrust themselves free!

(*She dies. Lights fade slowly. After awhile, they come up on Rosie sitting in her rocking chair in a darkened corner.*)

ROSIE: A dead daughter, that's a fine thing to talk about, I never speak of a dead daughter. There are letters, of course, photographs taken up to the age of 30, a little child who screams from the top of the stairs . . . where's my Mommie. (*Retreating into haughtiness.*) How many times do I have to tell you, child, your Mother has gone to Heaven, where all dead Mothers go . . . to Heaven where it is fragrant, sweet-smelling, and white lilacs are in bloom the year round.

(*She claps her hands feverishly. Lights go out.*)

Scene 2
Danielle Edwards' living room, a few days later.

A dim light surrounds Danielle, who is standing on the steps, dressed in black.

DANIELLE: He's asleep, worn out like a baby . . . looks just as peaceful, too, all the brooding gone from his face, you'd never imagine he was the least bit unhappy.

(*As she starts down the steps, lights fade up, and we see Marietta, also dressed in black, standing at the bottom of the steps.*)

MARIETTA: The car will be here shortly.

(*Caroline comes in from the kitchen. She is not dressed in black, wears instead a handsome beige outfit, with her hair pulled back severely.*)

CAROLINE: I boiled water for coffee or tea, which would you prefer?
DANIELLE: (*Coming down.*) Neither.
MARIETTA: You're not going to drink before Lillie's wake! (*Danielle glares at her. Marietta goes all mournful.*) Dear Lillie, dead Lillie, why did she go so fast . . . (*She moves away, upset.*) Already, Franklin is not the same, has shut himself up, closed the door on me . . .
DANIELLE: He's in shock, Marietta, all of us are. (*She looks upstairs.*) . . . he

liked Lillie so, she used to scold him with her rhymes, try to tease him out of
bed . . . (*Gently mimicking Lillie.*)
Nelson Nelson
Isn't it a shame
For you to stay in bed like this
As if you were lame!
Pretending to be sick
With the negro blues
When all you really want
Is to take a snooze . . .
(*Fondly amused.*) There are verses like that, sent to him from Rosie's, when
she was too sick to move . . . he'd write back, send her his own brand of
wit, and poetic humour. (*Taking on Nelson's dry, whining drawl.*)
Dear Lillie
Isn't it silly
That we're both in bed
Playing dead
While the world goes on around us . . .
(*She grows sad, uneasy, can't help looking upstairs.*)

MARIETTA: (*Like a refrain.*) Dear Lillie, dead Lillie, why did she go so fast
. . . ? (*She shifts into indignation.*) I can hear Rosie's people now, they'll
swear Lillie didn't die a natural death, that it had to do with Franklin being
too dark, too poor, and not yet finished with school . . . in their hearts
they'll blame Franklin . . . and Franklin will blame himself, that's the
worst of the story. (*This upsets her. Danielle goes to comfort her, when the phone
rings. Caroline answers it.*)

CAROLINE: Hello . . . No, they're waiting for the car . . . I'm staying with
Nelson until she gets back . . . he can't . . . stop foaming, I'll be here about
two hours, then I'll meet you at the wake . . .

MARIETTA: Is that Lawrence? (*Caroline nods.*) May I speak to him? (*Caroline
coolly yields the phone.*) Lawrence . . . tell me first about Jeremy and when
he's due to arrive . . . someone has to meet him . . . don't talk that way
. . . stop it, Lawrence, that's too unkind, it's as if he were an orphan, or
step-child in the clan . . . (*Adamant.*) It's not fair that he come so far without
a welcome, if you won't do it, I'll ask Mr. Norrell to send a car . . . alright
. . . really? That's just like them, no pomp and circumstance, if it were up
to Rosie there'd be no funeral at all . . . who . . . the cousins? Aren't they a
sight . . . all washed out and anemic looking with those faded blue eyes . . .
(*She mimicks their light Southern twang.*) ". . . Rosie's child had no business
takin' up with no undertaker . . . why she spent her last days playin'
secretary to the dead . . . " (*Growing more upset.*) They will blame it all on
Franklin. (*She goes to pieces. Caroline takes the phone.*)

CAROLINE: I'll come as soon as they get back . . . how much . . . I don't
know, you could get burned in a deal like that . . .

MARIETTA: (*Eavesdropping.*) He can't be wheeling and dealing behind Lillie's grave!

CAROLINE: (*Uneasy.*) I better go . . . I wouldn't move too fast on that. (*She hangs up.*)

MARIETTA: (*Pouncing.*) All of us grieving, while he hustles some nasty deal!

CAROLINE: There's no need to take it personally, Marietta.

MARIETTA: (*Indignant.*) His own brother left unattended!

CAROLINE: (*With growing irritation.*) He said he'd pick him up.

MARIETTA: (*Consumed with indignation.*) Poor Jeremy will look for a welcome, and where will Lawrence be . . . around the corner shaking some greasy palm. (*Now she turns on Caroline.*) And *you* in sleek disdain, won't even dress for mourning!

CAROLINE: (*Defiant.*) What I put on my back has no place in this exchange. (*She moves aggressively close. Marietta retreats slightly.*)

MARIETTA: Dear Lillie, dead Lillie, why did she go so fast . . . (*Caroline turns to Danielle.*)

CAROLINE: Will he wake up for lunch?

DANIELLE: I couldn't say, he's got no predictable habits. I gave him his medicine. I hope that'll make him sleep until I get back. But he's very good at faking. (*She looks upstairs.*) . . . it's possible he's not asleep at all. (*The door bell rings.*)

MARIETTA: (*Abruptly.*) That will be the car. (*She opens the door, disappears quickly down the steps.*)

DANIELLE: (*To Caroline.*) I guess I better follow suit . . .

(*She bows with mock graciousness, then exits. Caroline goes to the window.*)

CAROLINE: (*Watching Marietta.*) Look at her, she can't even get in the car without giving instructions to the driver . . . that woman . . . (*We hear the car drive away. Still irritated, Caroline moves away from the window.*) . . . the charger will straighten her out, one of his fast verbal punches, and she'll keel over quick . . . (*She jabs the air playfully, like a boxer.*) . . . I'd like a good match with her myself. None of this hit-and-run stuff either . . . always playing the lady when it gets too hot. (*Almost unconsciously she slips on her fur coat, seeks out the nearest mirror for reassurance.*) . . . the sleeves are too short, he's right about that, though he only says it to get my goat. (*There is a sudden thumping overhead.*) No, he didn't . . . go and wake up the second she's gone.

(*She goes to the steps and waits. The thumping is repeated. She yells up.*)

Danielle's gone, Nelson, she went to Lillie's wake. (*A loud, angry thump in response, followed by intermittent sobs.*) Oh God, he's crying . . . he must be having one of his fits . . . I wish the charger were here . . . (*She disapperars upstairs.*) What's the matter . . . are you upset about Lillie . . . we all feel pretty bad . . . you want some lunch, Danielle left you some soup and there's chicken for a sandwich . . . what . . . a piece of paper . . . and a pen . . . alright. . . (*We hear her moving around.*) . . . there you go . . . (*Reading his note.*) . . . she ran away . . . who . . . Lillie? No, she died, Nelson, Lillie died, she didn't run away . . . (*Reading more.*) . . . she ran away into death . . . oh, that's a bit morbid, Nelson, she just got sick, that's all and died . . . let me fix you some lunch . . . no? What about a cup of tea . . . nothing? You're sure? Well, thump . . . I mean call if you need anything, alright?

(*She emerges hugging her coat. Once downstairs, she lets out a sigh.*)

The man's a basket case . . . he makes Lawrence seem almost sane.

(*Uneasy and restless, she walks over to the mantelpiece and looks at photographs of the brothers.*)

. . . though none of them are too with it. (*She looks at each one of them in turn. Lights dim on Caroline, while the photographs begin to loom large in the light.*) . . .there's Franklin, the Righteous One presiding as usual over all family disputes . . . look at Nelson, pampered and spoiled in the days of his athletic glory . . . and Jeremy . . . what's there to say about Jeremy except that he had the good sense to put distance between himself and the clan, moved to Chicago where he slaughters sheep and stutters to his heart's content . . . and Lawrence, my Lawrence, the mad stallion of the clan . . . riding herd over all of them with his lies and maneuvers . . . for a colored man Lawrence takes up a *tremendous* amount of space . . .

(*She chuckles. We hear the sudden, brutal slamming of a door. Caroline moves forward clutching her coat. We hear footsteps, the sound of someone entering the room. Caroline slips eerily into Lawrence's voice.*)

"What you doin', what you doin' " . . . (*As herself.*) I'm watching you, that's all, you don't enter a room like normal people, you charge in, the door *flies* open and there you are. (*As Lawrence.*) "Nothin' special about me . . ." (*We hear footsteps pacing, the sound of furniture being moved.*) ". . . genuine Chippendale chair. I like that chair . . . man's comin' next week with two genuine Persian rugs, I'm gonna put one in the dining room, put one right here . . . what you think, what you think . . ." (*As herself.*) You have a fine eye for things, it's an Edwards trait, you should've all been born white, you spend your lives trying to jump out of your skin . . . (*That amuses her but makes Lawrence turn mean.*) "Listen to the maid . . . got five cents worth of education and she's tryin' out *ideas* . . ." (*As herself.*) Stop saying that! That's how you got through all those schools! (*As Lawrence.*) "That's right, I thank Caroline the maid." (*Screaming at him.*) Cut it out! I scrubbed floors alright, while you *cheated* your way through school! I thought we were pretty evenly matched . . . tit for tat, tit for tat! (*As Lawrence.*) "Get dressed for the theatre . . . and look sleek, look sleek, I don't want to be seen with you unless you look sleek." (*As herself, hesitant.*) Well, I won't be looking sleek for too much longer. (*As Lawrence, pacing.*) "What's that supposed to mean . . . huh, what's that supposed to mean?" (*As herself, almost girlish.*) . . . that even in your quick, hurried fashion, something must've took . . . (*As Lawrence.*) "What you tryin' to say . . . ?" (*As herself.*) I'm having a baby! The charger *raced* through me and look what he left behind! (*As Lawrence.*) ". . . that's pretty funny, pretty funny . . ." (*As herself.*) If it's a boy, I know he'll fly through my womb in the Edwards style! (*As Lawrence.*) ". . . could be a girl, some fussy thing with your instincts to serve." (*She winces, deeply wounded.*) Don't keep turning things nasty, I want this child to breathe something new between us.

(*There is a sudden rapid thumping from upstairs. Disoriented, Caroline spins around.*)

What . . .

(*Lights come up as she moves towards the steps. The thumping is relentless, harsh, angry. It puts Caroline in a fury.*)

What's the mattter with you . . . what's the matter with *all* of you! You think we're a bunch of bleeding stagehands! (*She stomps up the steps and disappears. Lights go out.*)

END OF ACT II

ACT III

Danielle Edwards' living room, Friday, April 5, 1968.

Lights fade up on Letitia Edwards, alone in the living room. She stands rather stiffly by the window. She is a woman in her late '50s with hair that is neatly composed, a prim, overly polite manner that disguises many bitter edges. When she speaks, there is a sing-song quality about her voice that conveys a kind of false elegance.

After awhile, Marietta appears on the steps. Always nervous, Marietta has grown more hysterical with the years, approaching life now with constant suspicion, as if treachery and bad tidings lay in wait at every turn. Her voice, never melodic, is now even more astringent, and masculine in intensity. She leans over the balcony addressing Letitia.

MARIETTA: No word from Lawrence?

LETITIA: No, Marietta. (*Marietta slips down the steps, looking back several times.*)

MARIETTA: I shouldn't leave her alone . . .

LETITIA: Does she have anything to make her sleep?

MARIETTA: (*Scornfully.*) There are Nelson's left-over drugs, if she wants something like that.

LETITIA: I was thinking of something milder.

MARIETTA: (*Switching gears.*) Has Franklin called?

LETITIA: Not yet, Marietta.

MARIETTA: He promised to call from Mr. Norrell's.

LETITIA: He can only just have arrived, Marietta.

MARIETTA: (*Switching again.*) It's to be a midnight service with the casket closed. No eulogy. He's asked that no words be spoken on his behalf. It's not right that no one should speak! He was an athlete of great stature who went down in defeat!

LETITIA: (*Matter-of-factly.*) He died of asthma, Marietta, he simply couldn't breathe.

MARIETTA: (*Ignoring that.*) And the tombstone's to read: He who labors in a colored vineyard labors in vain! Where did he come up with such a morbid saying . . . oh God, I can't stand it . . . Nelson, our baby . . . (*She grows more upset.*)

LETITIA: Don't get yourself all worked up, Marietta.

MARIETTA: (*Looking around.*) Every Sunday for twenty years we have gathered in this house . . . gone up those steps to greet Nelson in his tomb . . . that's what it was, you know, that bed was really his tomb! All of us coaxed and prayed over him, did everything we could to bring him back to life! If I had a nickel for every prayer Franklin offered in his behalf...and Lawrence with that nasty temper of his tried to whip him out of bed more times than I care to remember . . . (*With more gentleness.*) I'd just sit with him . . . Sometimes I'd get him to walk with me as far as the window . . . look at Old Man Hawkins, I'd say, sitting under the trees enjoying the sunshine! Take a walk with me, Nelson, look at life from outside where it's sunny and bright! (*She takes on Nelson's moroseness.*) "Nobody can see me, Marietta . . . it's too dark inside my skin." (*Snapping herself out of it.*) Oh, Nelson . . . why take it to heart! Life goes on anyway! (*Pulled under again.*) "Well it can go on without me . . ." and he'd start back to his bed. (*Outraged.*) He was young! He once flew around that track like a bird on wings! There was *haughty* negro blood in his veins! (*She is beside herself.*)

LETITIA: Try not to upset yourself, Marietta. Can I fix you some coffee or tea, which would you prefer? (*Marietta shivers violently.*) Are you alright, Marietta?

MARIETTA: (*Uneasy.*) For a second I thought I heard Lillie speak . . . Gandhi's dead, she said . . . clear as a bell . . . (*She shivers again.*)

LETITIA: Let me make you some tea, Marietta.

(*Letitia goes into the kitchen. Intuitively, as if drawn to it, Marietta turns on the radio. We hear a Newscaster speaking.*)

NEWSCASTER'S VOICE: . . . of the AFL-CIO urged Vice-President Humphrey to enter the race . . . the National Guard has been called out in Memphis where just last night the Reverend Martin Luther King was fatally shot by a gunman as he stood on the balcony of his motel. President Johnson postponed his scheduled trip to Hawaii to confer with his military strategists about Vietnam. Instead, he telephoned Mrs. King in Atlanta and made a brief television appeal for calm and nonviolence to prevail . . .

(*She shuts it off abruptly. When she turns around, she is startled to find Letitia standing there with her tea. She jumps back.*)

LETITIA: I didn't mean to startle you . . .

MARIETTA: King's dead.

LETITIA: I heard.

MARIETTA: I bet Lillie's laughing at me . . . (*Letitia looks at her strangely. Lost in her thoughts, Marietta wanders over to the window.*) There'll probably be Negroes rioting . . .

LETITIA: It could happen, though the irony is that he deplored such things.

MARIETTA: Who?

LETITIA: Martin Luther King.

MARIETTA: If Lillie were here I'd apologize for that.

LETITIA: (*Confused.*) I'm not following you, Marietta.

MARIETTA: King's dead, I'd say, that's the same as Gandhi any day . . . (*She begins to cry uncontrollably.*)

LETITIA: Don't get yourself all worked up, Marietta.

MARIETTA: (*Weeping.*) Maybe Nelson was right to have slept through it all. (*She stands staring out the window. Letitia picks up her knitting and sits down.*)

LETITIA: They'll want Franklin to speak about him in the Assembly . . . (*Marietta doesn't seem to hear.*) . . . he'll say something gracious, though he'll be mad as can be. I can hear him now . . . (*Speaking like Franklin.*) "Just because I'm the only . . . (*She has a hard time saying the word.*) . . . Black, they'll expect me to speak . . . like I was the spokesman for negro grief." (*She sighs.*) He hates the race stuff politics locks him into.

(*Marietta doesn't respond. She seems to have drifted inside her own grief. After awhile, she moves almost hypnotically towards the steps.*)

MARIETTA: (*Thinking of Nelson.*) He choked on his own saliva.

LETITIA: It could not have been a pleasant death, Marietta.

MARIETTA: When Danielle came in, she found him buried under his pillow.

LETITIA: As I recall, Marietta, that was one of his favorite tricks.

MARIETTA: He must have been crying. Recently, he cried almost all the time.

LETITIA: (*With some bite.*) He made no effort to hide his despair. (*Marietta grows increasingly sad, almost morbid.*)

MARIETTA: Jeremy's sick . . . he won't even be able to make the funeral . . .

LETITIA: I'm sure he feels badly about that, Marietta . . . he's loyal to the family in his own way.

MARIETTA: He's so far away, we never see him . . . with Nelson gone that leaves just us three.

LETITIA: (*Ironic.*) Well, together you keep up a pretty lively chorus, Marietta.

MARIETTA: (*Increasingly morbid.*) Franklin could go in a flash . . . and Lawrence . . . both of them move at breathtaking speed.

LETITIA: It's an Edwards trait . . . you go at a pretty fast clip yourself, Marietta.

MARIETTA: (*Snapping.*) Don't "Marietta" me this and "Marietta" me that. (*Letitia visibly draws in her breath as if accustomed to Marietta's rude outbursts.*)

LETITIA: I was obliging you with polite conversation, Marietta.

MARIETTA: (*Malicious.*) That's all you *can* do with your dry understanding. (*She grows violently impatient, starts to pace.*) Franklin should have called by now. I should make a list of who's to be notified . . . what food we'll need prepared . . .

(*She disappears into the kitchen in a few rapid strides. Letitia sits aggressively knitting, her needles making a loud, clicking sound.*)

LETITIA: (*To herself.*) . . . I suppose she expects that to roll off my back as if I were so thick-skinned nothing got through. (*She grunts.*) Hmph . . . to all of them I'm the Rock, the Buddha, the Immovable Object between Franklin and dead Lillie. (*Pained.*) . . . they have never recovered from my intrusion on the scene. When I was first introduced as the replacement for dead Lillie, mouths fell, heads turned as if Franklin had dragged me up from the bottom of the sea. All of them flared and snorted like race horses at the gate. Lawrence had the awful dramatic gall to call me a negro nun. (*Wounded.*) . . . the scenes I have witnessed in this room . . . (*Returning to the present.*) . . . I should try and reach the girls. Lillian will be quite upset, he was her favorite uncle though I never understood why. Rowena will go to pieces but for no good reason, she found Nelson's behavior embarrassing in the extreme but in the end she'll give in to hysteria . . . she has the Edwards need for dramatic release. (*Her needles click hard.*) . . . I suppose that's what they hold against me, that I have no performance value . . . (*Grunting.*) . . . and as they are all fine performers, they expect us in-laws to measure up. (*Reviewing the scene.*) . . . Danielle holds her own with a kind of dry repartee . . . the quick draw, I call it, Danielle is the mistress of the quick draw . . . Lawrence certainly found his match in Caroline, they are forever at each other violent tit for tat . . . Nobody speaks of Aurora but then nobody speaks of Jeremy who dare not speak for himself because he stutters too badly. Aurora and Jeremy are the poor relations in the clan . . . I suppose Marietta never found anyone brave enough to match wits with her brothers, she is herself a *hard* act to follow . . . (*Marietta, at that very moment, comes bustling in.*)

MARIETTA: (*Brusquely.*) I thought I heard voices.

LETITIA: . . . just my knitting needles, Marietta, they make a loud sound.

(*The phone rings. Instantly, Marietta grabs for it.*)

MARIETTA: Hello . . . oh Franklin . . . have you spoken to Lawrence . . . no, we haven't heard a word, I can't imagine where he can be . . . have you seen his body . . . poor baby . . . I know it's too hard to believe . . . oh Franklin, don't you start to grieve, I won't be able to stand it. (*She grows more upset. Letitia, worried, gets up.*) . . . no, Franklin, we did everything we could . . . he just wouldn't budge. I just never expected he'd go like this

. . . just shrivel up and die . . . (*Both she and Franklin are crying by now.*) I'd like to sit with him, Franklin . . . just you and me for awhile . . . alright . . . (*She starts to hang up, Letitia signals her to hold the line.*) . . . Franklin . . . (*No answer. Coldly.*) He's upset about Nelson . . .

LETITIA: That's no reason why we couldn't speak. (*They stare at each other. Danielle's voice startles them.*)

DANIELLE: They'll be asking for a suit. . .

(*They look up. She stands at the top of the stairs. A great deal older, she wears the years well as if that mocking sense of humour had held her in good stead. There is, however, a nervousness in the way she moves, a slight trembling around the face and neck, the result of too much booze. As she comes down the steps, it should be clear that she's already a bit drunk.*)

How's everybody holding up . . . where's Franklin and Lawrence?

MARIETTA: Franklin's over at Mr. Norrell's, no one's heard from the charger since we told him the news.

DANIELLE: He'll be along . . . blow in like a drill sergeant and ruffle everybody's feathers . . . it's an Edwards trait to make their women jump . . . (*She chuckles inwardly.*) . . . here we sit in the eye of the storm . . . blown around like they were the wind. (*She looks around, badly in need of another drink.*) Now, what was I about to do . . . ?

MARIETTA: You said we have to choose a suit.

DANIELLE: (*Mechanically.*) . . . a final statement for Nelson to wear.

MARIETTA: (*Brusquely.*) And you should have something to eat, some coffee, too . . .

DANIELLE: (*Mechanically.*) . . . whatever it takes to dry the old girl out . . .

MARIETTA: (*Brusquely.*) There are things to be done, cards to be sent out, people to call . . .

DANIELLE: (*Mechanically.*) . . . all the details of death the dead leave behind . . .

MARIETTA: (*Snapping.*) Stop this weary repetition and get a grip on yourself! (*Danielle stares at her.*) Would you like me to go up and look for a suit?

DANIELLE: (*Quietly.*) You do that, Marietta, you go up there and rummage around among the ruins.

(*They look at each other. Marietta moves quickly past her and up the steps.*)

That oughta keep her pants on for awhile . . . (*She becomes aware of Letitia sitting in a corner knitting.*) You gotta watch out for the steam roller or she'll mow you down. (*She chuckles loudly. Letitia gives her a wan smile. Shrugging it off, Danielle disappears into the kitchen.*) . . . all my sterling good humour is lost on that one . . . (*Mocking Letitia.*) . . . you need a sense of humour, Letitia, you cannot gather ye among the clan without a sense of humour! (*We hear her opening and closing cupboards.*) Damnit, there must be one somewhere that I hid from myself.

(*Smarting from Danielle's remark, Letitia starts to retreat to her chair but catches herself in the mirror and can't help a moment's awkward preening.*)

LETITIA: (*Flustered.*) . . . in his crueler moments Franklin has been known to remark that I'm one of those women whose dresses are always getting caught between their buttocks. (*Embarrassed, she tugs at herself.*) . . . I see myself still in the early days of our marriage struggling in and out of silks and gabardines only to provoke again and again the sharp rebuke that my dress had slipped somewhere between my buttocks. (*She turns away, no longer willing to look at herself.*) . . . there is reason to still ask why he married me. He needed a mother for his children and he needed one quick before Rosie went to court to keep them. I think I came along in the nick of time. Franklin moved with his usual swiftness and snatched me up. I was 38 . . . there were no long lines blocking his way. (*Any minute, one gets the feeling, she might run and hide.*) . . . I was most certainly untouched . . . no man had ever laid a finger on me . . . when it came Franklin's turn, I lay exceedingly still . . . he was very handsome with his light eyes, his fine crinkly hair, I think I was flattered, that his speed and daring overwhelmed me. (*Trying to recover her balance.*) . . . why else would a woman almost forty marry a man with two daughters! Rowena had just turned six, Lillian was less than two . . . a shy child who fastened herself to me, became my shadow. (*A sense of maternal pride touches her, then shifts.*) Not so Rowena, she was too full of memory, it was dead Lillie this and dead Lillie that and where oh where could dead Lillie be now! There was no end to her whining and stomping about. Franklin would come home, the child would start to flail and scream he'd swear I'd been beating her, come after me, fists raised, eyes burning . . . (*With sudden indignation.*) . . . he has the *worst*, the very worst temper I've ever witnessed in my life! I'm told his father was the same . . . a terrifying kind of anger that comes at you in violent doses! All of them have it. Marietta goes shrill the moment she enters a room. Lawrence would kill if he could just go unpunished. Nelson turned his inwards and beat himself to death . . . poor Jeremy hides his behind a stutter and a twitch. Mad souls every one of them! I landed smack dab in the lion's den!

(*From the kitchen there is a sudden loud crash of broken dishes falling to the floor. We hear Danielle muttering and cursing.*)

DANIELLE: (*From the kitchen.*) Don't tell me I'm left high and dry without a nickel's worth of gin! (*Letitia shudders, retreats to her chair.*)
LETITIA: . . . I did not leave . . . I think that is my great accomplishment, that I did not leave.

(*Danielle wanders in looking for a drink. She seems not to be at all aware of Letitia. She looks everywhere, finally gets down on her knees and begins peeking under the couch. She pulls something out.*)

DANIELLE: (*Triumphant.*) I knew there was one somewhere. (*She holds up a bottle.*) . . . if I didn't know myself better, I'd swear I must have hid it myself . . . but why would I do such a dumb thing when I'm the only one who drinks . . . couldn't have been Nelson, he hasn't been down those steps in twenty years, except today . . . when they wheeled him away . . . (*She stares at the steps as if seeing Nelson carried down them, goes to pour herself a drink.*) I bet you a fat man Marietta hid that bottle, the way she sneaks around whenever my back is turned. (*As she starts to drink, she notices Letitia.*) . . . it's hard to remember you're around.

LETITIA: (*Carefully.*) Without a sense of humour I'm hard to see.

DANIELLE: (*Chuckling.*) Touché, touché . . . (*There is a moment of sympathy.*) Where's the steam roller?

LETITIA: Upstairs, looking for a suit.

DANIELLE: Right . . . I should tell her to pick out one of his ditty bop numbers from the jazz days . . . the old boy might like to go out in style.

LETITIA: Would you like me to fix you something to eat?

DANIELLE: (*With mock daintiness.*) No tea or toast, thank you.

LETITIA: (*Embarrassed.*) I was just trying to . . . (*Danielle stops her with a wave of her bottle which she holds out proudly.*)

DANIELLE: This must have been a present from one of Nelson's track buddies. They always came back to check on the old boy. He's read them his usual Sermon on the Void and when they'd had enough of that, they'd come down and chew the fat with me, polish off a taste or two, reminisce, until the room was full of smoke and booze just like the old days . . . do you mind a little music?

LETITIA: No.

(*She goes and puts on Carmen McCrae or Anita O'Day singing ''Isn't This a Lovely Day'' and begins to dance in a clumsy way.*)

DANIELLE: . . . they'd get me up on my feet . . . (*As if talking to Nelson's cronies.*) The old girl can still hop about . . . I'm fading fast in the ring but I still got my hand in . . . (*Sadness overwhelms her.*) But the sallow beauty's cracking under the strain . . . I've been living too long in the Land of Oz and all the glitter's gone. (*She almost breaks down.*)

LETITIA: (*Trying to save her.*) You're still light on your feet. (*For some reason that makes Danielle chuckle.*)

DANIELLE: I was built for speed . . .

(*Marietta's voice cuts across. She's standing at the top of the steps holding a suit.*)

MARIETTA: Does this look fitting . . . ? He'll look handsome in gray, don't you think? I must remember to tell Mr. Norrell to part his hair in the middle and smoothe it back away from his face, that's how he wore it in the old days with a mustache . . . his light eyes . . .

DANIELLE: (*Angry but fighting tears.*) . . . the baby-faced prince working his act . . .

MARIETTA: What kind of tie, something a little splashy or should we keep it simple?

DANIELLE: Suit yourself, Marietta . . . do what you can to resurrect his charm.

(*She turns away, pained. Marietta feels it, too.*)

MARIETTA: He's the first of my boys to go . . . one by one they'll leave me, I'll be the last to go.

(*She retreats into a conversation with Franklin. The light changes so that she is spotlighted while the women below become shadows.*)

. . . She's not dead, Franklin, she can't be. I saw her this afternoon . . . she looked a little tired but nowhere near dead . . . we just put Pop in the ground, it seems like just the other day . . . dead . . . not Lillie . . . she was too snappy and fresh for death. I'm so sorry, Franklin. How could such a thing be . . . (*Suddenly seeing.*) There's something morbid about us, isn't there, Franklin? . . . something in how fast we breathe . . . all steamed-up and running the hard course that Pop set. We'll never be happy, will we . . . (*Frightened by what she sees.*) Look at Nelson . . . he's going to take it to an extreme . . . this terrible brooding in us over what being colored really means.

(*She seems to drift away. Lights come up on Danielle taking a huge swig from the bottle.*)

DANIELLE: . . . they'll be crowding in here soon, I should straighten things up a bit . . . these rooms are all my living, I should put them on good display . . . (*She makes an effort to straighten things when the doorbell rings with a sharp insistence. Danielle stops dead in her tracks.*) There he is . . . the North Wind himself.

LETITIA: (*Unnerved herself.*) Lawrence . . .

DANIELLE: . . . he'll come in here and blow us to bits . . .

(*The bell rings again, more insistently. Danielle doesn't move. It's Letitia who gets up finally to open the door Caroline stands on the threshold.*)

CAROLINE: (*Defiantly.*) Where is he?

(*She steps into the room wearing as always an expensive fur coat. With the years her face has grown severe and she wears too much make-up. Her voice, never pleasant, is now a good deal harsher and there is something a bit disheveled about her appearance as if the coat was thrown over the first outfit she grabbed.*)

LETITIA: Was he on his way here?
CAROLINE: He's been gone all night, he's gone a lot of nights. I expected Nelson's death would bring him home for a change . . .
LETITIA: We haven't seen him.
DANIELLE: (*Mischievously.*) Maybe he went up in smoke . . . he does everything so fast he could blow himself up.

(*A childish giggle escapes. Fast on its heels is a faint chuckle from Letitia that she cannot quite repress. Caroline looks from one to the other.*)

CAROLINE: I don't get the joke.
LETITIA: Could I get you some coffee, I bet Lawrence will be along any second now.

(*Caroline waves aside the idea of coffee, begins to pace with increasing agitation.*)

CAROLINE: Where is he? It'll be the same old story . . . a sudden real estate deal, legal tie-ups that lasted through the night. (*She shakes her head disbelieving.*) There's only one thing that keeps him out through the night.
DANIELLE: (*Opening that line wide.*) . . . the charger lets it *rip* . . . pummels his way up San Juan Hill . . . (*She breaks out in raucous laughter.*) . . . SEX with the Brothers! (*Subsiding to a giggle.*) . . . not exactly your all-time bawdy romp in the hay . . .

(*At this point Danielle and Caroline should be separated by isolated pools of light as if revealing their intimate feelings only to themselves.*)

CAROLINE: (*To herself.*) . . . I tell myself that if he's out there looking, it can only be for a shot in the dark, he wouldn't linger long enough to call anybody's name. (*Feeling lost.*) . . . it's Laura's death that sends him out there . . . the house is too silent, it was her childish cries that made it feel like a home.
DANIELLE: (*To herself.*) . . . Even with him laying up there flat on his back, it was rare that the old boy *rose* to the occasion. (*She mimicks his whining drawl.*) ". . . Colored people can't have true intimate relations . . . we are too exposed in this world for any further undressing . . ." (*Numb.*) . . . ain't *that* the cat's meow.

(*Silence. Then the sharp jangle of the phone. Caroline grabs for it aggressively.*)

CAROLINE: Hello . . . where are you . . . where are you and where have you been . . . don't give me that, honest to God, I don't want to hear it again . . . no, they're all here . . . I don't know . . . (*To Letitia.*) Where's Franklin?

LETITIA: He's at Mr. Norrell's.

CAROLINE: (*To Lawrence.*) . . . at Mr. Norrell's . . . are you coming here . . . what do you want me to do . . . I'm not dressed to go to the Funeral Home. (*She becomes more aware of her disshevelled look.*) . . . could you pick me up . . . I'd like it if you picked me up . . . that's not the point . . . I'd just like it, that's all . . . (*Getting crazy.*) . . . Would you pick me up, *please.* You want me to bow and scrape . . . (*Going out of control.*) . . . I've already done that, remember, that's how it began with me down on my knees . . . Lawrence . . . (*There is no answer. She screams as if it were wrenched from the center of her.*) Lawrence!!!!

(*The room grows quiet, the women having withdrawn into their own silence. Only Danielle continues to move about in an uneasy, drunken way. After a while, she even begins to sing, softly, snatches of melodies.*)

DANIELLE: (*Singing.*) . . . I took a trip on a train and I thought about you . . . two or three stars caught under the sky . . . a winding road . . . (*She starts talking to Nelson as if she were standing by his bed.*) They're gonna serve the Edwards Requiem on you soon, old boy . . . milk that final act for all it's worth. (*As if fluffing his pillows.*) How are your pillows . . . you should let me change the sheets, those are getting bed-ridden . . . get up Nelson and let me make the bed . . . Go take a bath and shave . . . you can't be . . . how can you be tired when you never move! (*The absurdity of it hits her.*) Get up . . . long enough for me to change the sheets . . . you can sit in that chair if you won't bathe . . . (*She begins changing the sheets.*) . . . what do you mean . . . because I was too lazy, I guess to lift myself up . . . go somewhere, anywhere . . . even across the street . . . (*She smoothes the sheets.*) . . . instead I sat around with you . . . let time go backwards on me . . . let your grieving get into my bones, like a damp chill . . . (*She shivers.*) Are you cold . . . come on, you can lay back down . . . then I drifted inside your shadow the way women can do . . . (*She fluffs his pillows again.*) . . . drift and drift like they got no place to go . . . (*A terrible weariness seeps in.*) . . . next thing I know I've been sitting here for years . . . soaked clean through on the thin excuses you exchanged for a life . . . (*Numb with anger.*) . . . I'm fixing your pillows, changing your sheets, carrying Ralston up and down the steps like the joke was still funny . . . you're waking me up in the middle of the night, full of questions about the Negro's place in time, his reasons for being in the scheme of things . . . (*She relives a conversation.*) . . . I don't know why, Nelson, why they think we're dumb or different or inhuman . . . I can't answer those questions for you . . . it's late, Nelson, try to go back to sleep, don't torment yourself like this . . . and don't start to cry, oh God, Nelson, please, don't weep . . . (*Panic seeps in.*) Stop it, Nelson . . . you'll have a convulsion if you go on like this . . . shut off the tears before the damn flood gates burst! You're spilling all over the place, your sheets and pillows are drenched with tears . . . (*Going out of control.*) Stop it, stop acting like a baby! I'll have to leave the planet if you don't cut out this act! (*Then with real violence, she acts it out.*) Stop it, I say, or I'll drown you my own self, hold this pillow over you till you're blue in the face . . .

(*Which she does, pressing it down harder and harder until death stops his tears and her own can start. Danielle begins to sob uncontrollably. In the heat of the wreckage, Marietta's voice drifts across carrying its own private excitement that is oblivious to the scene below.*)

MARIETTA: Look what I found . . . (*She comes to the top of the steps.*) . . . one of Lillie's poems . . . hidden under Nelson's pillow . . . (*She giggles.*) . . . I bet it's some silly thing . . . (*She starts to read it quite frivolously.*)
Gandhi's dead
so I said
She only turned and stared
Nelson's in bed
so she said
I only laughed and glared
Gandhi's dead
I said again
What's that to me, she replied
Nelson's in bed
Again she said
All colored men do is die.

(*Hold. For a long time. Then let the lights come down.*)

END

Little Victories

Lavonne Mueller

Whatever you can do, or dream you can, begin it;
Boldness has genius, power and magic in it.
Goethe

**To the new women:
Chris, Stacey, Lisa, Marya and Allie**

Little Victories was first presented by The Women's Project on January 26, 1983. It was directed by Bryna Wortman, with set by William M. Barclay, lighting by Phil Monat, costumes by Mimi Maxmen, music by Clay Fullum, sound design by Regina M. Mullen, and the following cast:

SUSAN B. ANTHONY	Caroline Kava
JOAN OF ARC	Linda Hunt
MARSHAL/CAPTAIN BATTAU	Terrence Markovich
HOTEL OWNER/TAILOR/BAR DOG	Bill Cwikowski
CAPTAIN LAVOUR/BEN CALEB	Jimmy Smits
DOUBLE UGLY/ARCHER/LIMPY BOB	John Griesemer
VOICE OF JUDGE AND CARDINAL	Terrence Markovich

PLAYWRIGHT'S NOTES

The Play: Several years ago, at a midwestern writers' conference, I encouraged participants to write about war. I felt it was important for women to examine an issue dominated by men. After all, I said to the group, one of the greatest generals the world has known was a woman. I was astounded that nobody knew who that general was. This was the "germ" for Joan of Arc in *Little Victories.*

The "germ" for Susan B. Anthony came about in a more subtle way. I randomly picked up a biography of Anthony and was startled to find that she traveled out West at a time when few women were there and the life was one of enormous hardships.

I chose to put Susan B. Anthony and Joan of Arc in a play because they both survived in a landscape of men. They not only survived but triumphed, yet they died believing themselves failures. It was possible to shake the world and not know it.

Susan died in 1906; women received the right to vote in 1920. Joan died in 1431; she was canonized a saint in 1920.

The Staging: The staging of the play should be simple and fluid so that whatever minimal elements are used in the setting—benches, crates, burlap curtains—can serve to create the worlds of both women. The "stove area" and "billiard room area" of the hotel in Act I, Joan's "battlefield," the Bar Dog's "bar" and Susan and Ben's "campfire" in Act II should be suggested rather than represented in any literal way.

The men's roles should be doubled or tripled as indicated in the list of characters.

L.M.

CHARACTERS:

Susan B. Anthony
Joan of Arc
Marshal/Captain Battau
Hotel Owner/Tailor/Bar Dog
Captain Lavour/Ben
Saddle Tramp/Archer/Miner
Taped Voices, including Susan's Mother, Judge, Cardinal

TIME: Last half of the 1880s and 1429.

PLACE: Various locations in the American West and in medieval France.

ACT I ˙

Susan enters carrying a lasso. Joan enters and remains at the side of the stage. Susan begins to swing the lasso as her mother's voice is heard.

MOTHER'S VOICE: (*Over speaker.*) Susan . . . Sus . . . an? (*Pause.*) Where is that girl? (*Susan continues to rope.*) Stop that this minute. I just ironed that dress. (*Pause.*) Mind me, young lady. You're not in the wild West . . . You're in Rochester. (*Susan continues to rope.*) I thought I told you to stop that.

SUSAN: A lot of people never mind their mothers.

(*Susan throws the lasso towards Joan, who crosses and steps on the loop. They remain in a freeze as lights come up on the Hotel Owner.*)

MARSHAL: (*Entering the hotel area; to Hotel Owner.*) You see a woman? Dark hair? Totin' these pamphlets? (*Pause. No answer from Hotel Owner.*) History is [has] traced wars to women like that. They incite folks to take up arms and rescue them. (*Pause. No answer from Hotel Owner.*) I followed her through the heat on ten days now. Sun raised blood blisters on my face. (*Pause.*) You seen her?

(*Hotel Owner spits. Marshal and Hotel Owner remain in a freeze. Small sound of sheep bells is heard.*)

JOAN: (*To Susan.*) I'm hunting my sheep. They follow the wind.
SUSAN: (*Singsong.*) Leave them alone and they'll come home . . .
JOAN: Lost sheep never come gome. You go after them!
SUSAN: I'll help you get them back. . . . Then we can go to the firehouse in

town and watch the horses come out at six. (*Pause.*) We'll play firemen and save widow-ladies and their babies from burning houses.

JOAN: (*Stops looking around for her sheep.*) Look at this. . . . Just like my place . . . only trees . . . a barn fallen in on itself . . . dumb cows bored with the pain of milk . . . dirty pigs. (*Pause.*) A big healthy calf was born today, and Mother likes it better than me.

SUSAN: Mother calls me "savage" . . . her little "savage." (*Pause.*) I swing from so many trees, I've stretched my arms and I look awful in dresses.

JOAN: (*Abruptly.*) I have an eye that doesn't close. It doesn't even blink. (*Pause.*) I know about eyes. One always wants out. (*Susan and Joan remain in a freeze.*)

MARSHAL: (*To Hotel Owner.*) You the owner of this place?

HOTEL OWNER: Yep.

MARSHAL: Where's your deed?

HOTEL OWNER: (*Takes out his gun.*) Here's my deed . . . 'n nobody's questioned it, either.

MARSHAL: (*Shows his badge.*) I'm the U.S. Marshal.

HOTEL OWNER: I know you ain't no cowpuncher by the way ya siddle up ta me. (*Pause.*) What'd she do?

MARSHAL: Broke the law. Voted.

HOTEL OWNER: We wouldn't let that happen out here.

MARSHAL: Ya seen her? (*A long silence.*) I kin haul ya in fer questions.

HOTEL OWNER: Jist a minute. Hold on now. I gotta transfer my quid of tobacco ta the other jaw . . . 'n free my talkin' side.

MARSHAL: Well?

HOTEL OWNER: Nope. (*Spits.*)

(*The Marshal looks at him disgustedly, then strikes an official pose.*)

MARSHAL: (*Shouting.*) I'm here ta tell folks . . . no wagons start out beyond Dog Town 'less they got theirselves a hundred men. 'Cause of the Indians.

HOTEL OWNER: Yer talkin' loud 'nough fer Indians to hear.

MARSHAL: (*Still talking loudly.*) Sioux sure love ta capture them a woman.

HOTEL OWNER: (*Loud.*) So I hear.

MARSHAL: A woman might find it better off ta be caught by a marshal. (*He starts to exit.*) Injuns in the area—mind yer hair. (*He exits.*)

(*Susan is standing watching Joan pluck a flower. After a pause, she walks to Joan.*)

JOAN: Loves me . . . Loves me not . . .

SUSAN: (*Takes the flower from Joan.*) I pull purple skirts off morning glories. I love a flower's spine. A fortune teller came by our farm last week. He set me on the kitchen table and felt my head. Then he says: "You'll live a long time . . . and . . . and sleep in a lot of different beds!" My mother started right in crying . . . and Daddy, he told me I couldn't go any farther than the pasture posts without telling him.

JOAN: Mama says women who follow soldiers are whores. Girls like us are whores . . . in some places.

SUSAN: Who told you that?

JOAN: Uncle Tony's a sailor and he went to this island and child whores there got a special name. It means "small opening."

SUSAN: That's awful.

JOAN: Men don't think so. Do you think about getting married?

SUSAN: I watch the horses mate . . . and . . . it looks scary and thrilling . . .

JOAN: Maybe it's that way with people. Do you think about marriage?

SUSAN: I don't want to sit around for anybody. I want to go away . . . and . . . find the big empty room that's the whole world. Sometimes I see a tired housewife, bending over a washtub . . . and . . . well . . . it makes me want to be a man . . . just to help her.

JOAN: Nuns never marry—and their veils cure headaches. I saw a beautiful parade today. With gold-painted statues and six priests with red robes.

SUSAN: The only parades I ever see are old men . . . walking slowly in faded blues and faded grays.

JOAN: Those soldiers fought for their home.

SUSAN: Parades make me sad. (*Pause. Joan sees Susan is holding an orange in her hand.*)

JOAN: How can you eat that thing? I hate oranges.

SUSAN: You do?

JOAN: They're putrid.

SUSAN: Summer's flesh is in an orange.

JOAN: Not to me. (*She makes a face. Susan looks at the orange carefully, turning it around. Then she puts it down on the ground in front of her and stares at it.*) Go on . . . You're the one eating it.

SUSAN: If I could taste this the way you do . . . I guess I wouldn't like it either. (*Pause. Rolling the orange slowly in her hand.*) We're all so alone . . . aren't we? (*Pause.*)

JOAN: Can . . . you keep a secret?

SUSAN: Anything you tell me, I'll keep dark.

JOAN: I hear things. (*Joan takes Susan's hand and leads her to the side of the stage.*) Hear it? Soldiers' feet. Marching to war. Marching for France. Tramp . . . tramp . . . Little pounding feet saying: "You come . . . you come . . ." (*She stops abruptly and looks at Susan. She holds out an arm.*) See this arm? It's older than the other one. (*Pause.*) My mama tried to birth me for three days. This arm was all that poked out at first . . . till . . . till finally the rest of me came. Some day . . . some day I'll follow those soldiers . . . and march with this (*holds out arm*) . . . to carry a big green hawk that attacks Englishmen when I tell it to. (*Pause. She jiggles the arm at Susan.*) Touch it!

(*Pause. Joan shakes the arm more strongly at Susan. After another pause, Susan touches Joan's arm.*) Promise . . . by my oldest arm, you'll go with me. And be bold with me.

SUSAN: (*Hesitantly.*) Go . . . where?

JOAN: Where we have to? (*Susan is silent. Joan shakes her arm at Susan again.*) Promise!

SUSAN: I'm afraid.

JOAN: The thing you're scared of is the thing you have to do. (*Susan is still silent.*) Hurry. I don't have lots of time. (*Pause.*) Be a soldier with me. (*Susan stares silently at Joan.*) You got somebody better? (*Susan is still silent. Taunting Susan.*) You got anybody at all . . . fireman? (*Susan is still silent.*) Together. Partners. Stitched inside each other like a secret pocket in a spy's coat.

SUSAN: (*After a pause.*) I . . . promise.

JOAN: I was given this arm by heaven . . . (*Goes into her voices.*) Hear them . . . marching . . . left, right . . . left . . . right . . . right . . . left . . . right . . .

(*Joan and Susan march dreamily as the lights slowly fade on them. Lights come up on the hotel area.*)

HOTEL OWNER: You kin come out now. (*Pause.*) I know yer there. (*He sniffs and holds up a finger to the wind.*) Woman don't smell like a man. (*Susan enters the hotel area.*) They're after you like a fall buck.

SUSAN: I'm not an animal. I'm not some wild hog giving out babies.

HOTEL OWNER: What are you givin'?

SUSAN: These pamphlets . . . I want women to read them.

HOTEL OWNER: Why?

SUSAN: So they'll vote. (*Pause.*) And this bale of paper. I mean to fill it with names. Names of women from New York to California. Thousands of names to make the legislature change the laws.

HOTEL OWNER: I never did like pressure. I got me pressured into marriage once.

SUSAN: Right now . . . I have to get to California. In a hurry. For a rally— a woman's rally that will bridge this country from East to West.

HOTEL OWNER: You traveled in the West before?

SUSAN: First time.

HOTEL OWNER: Travelin' in the West don't be easy on a woman . . . especially with a marshal after her.

SUSAN: If I could have a room . . .

HOTEL OWNER: It's cheaper ta get some fella take you to his room ta-night.

SUSAN: (*Firmly.*) My own room, please.

HOTEL OWNER: (*Takes a deuce of diamonds card out of his pocket and hands it to her.*) Yer bed. (*He takes her bags, all the time staring at her clothing.*) I tote bags fer women even if they ain't. (*Pause.*) Britches! You wear a stovepipe hat, too?

SUSAN: Just for weddings. (*Hotel Owner leads Susan to another area of the stage, the "billiard room" of the hotel. Susan looks around her.*) Dear Lord, I never knew there'd be no walls.

HOTEL OWNER: (*He puts a deuce of hearts in Susan's hand next to the deuce of diamonds she is holding.*) Deuce of hearts and deuce of diamonds make a pair.

SUSAN: My bed? A billiard table? (*Pause.*)

HOTEL OWNER: Miner bunks inna dry goods box in the hall. Paid me six bucks. (*Pause.*) Two dollars by the stove. (*Pause.*) Women don't come ta Horse Creek. (*He picks up a string which has a cup, toothbrush, comb and soap on it.*) House facilities. (*He holds out the string to Susan.*) House facilities. Don't cost extra. Go on take it. Everybody uses it. (*Susan hands back the string.*) Breakfast whenever ya get up. You'll find mountain bread on the stove after six. I do the cookin' here. (*Pause.*) Window ta the privy blew out, but we got us a Chinese boy ta stand there till it's fixed. (*Pause.*) Inny rats over two feet is caught by the management. (*Susan looks around in disgust.*)

SUSAN: I've slept on parlor chairs . . . on corn husk mattresses smelly from tobacco juice . . . on dirty train benches . . . but never . . . (*They both stare at Susan's "bed." Pause. Susan turning to face the Hotel Owner.*) Mosquitoes . . . yes. And black deer flies. But . . . rats!

HOTEL OWNER: Go back East, like you belong ta do. You just hit the deep West!

SUSAN: Are you going to report me to the marshal?

HOTEL OWNER: Folks ta the West don't give out *no* information. Ta nobody. That's the only law around here. (*Pause.*) I don't like me no foreigners. (*Pause.*) If they're not women, Injuns, Mexicans . . . then they're strangers 'n that's jist as bad. (*Hotel Owner leaves Susan and goes and sits in the stove area of the hotel. He watches Susan as she looks around once more dejectedly, lights a candle, then begins to undress for bed. Hotel Owner snickering.*) Lady, spit out that thar candle, or ivver man in this here hotel is gonna see you naked through them curtains.

(*Susan reaches unthinkingly for a billiard stick and holds it up in front of her breasts. The Hotel Owner laughs. Susan then blows out the candle. Both hotel areas go dark.*)

VOICE: (*Over speaker.*) The State of New York calls Susan B. Anthony. (*Pause.*) Susan B. Anthony! Please take the stand. (*The pounding of a court gavel is heard.*)

JUDGE'S VOICE: (*Over speaker.*) What is your name?

SUSAN: (*Speaking from the darkened billiard-room area.*) Susan B. Anthony, Your Honor.

JUDGE'S VOICE: Where do you reside?

SUSAN: (*Scrambling in the dark for her jacket.*) Rochester, New York.

JUDGE'S VOICE: Speak louder, please.

SUSAN: (*Lighting the candle.*) Rochester, New York.

JUDGE'S VOICE: Again.

SUSAN: (*Angrily.*) A man just got shot. Right next door to me.

JUDGE'S VOICE: What can you say regarding your actions?

SUSAN: I have a stiff neck. (*Rubbing her rear.*) Other parts of me are stiff, too.

JUDGE'S VOICE: (*More firmly.*) What can you say regarding your actions?

SUSAN: I rode the Redbird stagecoach all week. Next to the driver. On the outside. My skin's cracked and dry like old stone burned in the sun.

JUDGE'S VOICE: What can you say regarding your actions?

SUSAN: I used to have good skin.

JUDGE'S VOICE: What can you . . .

SUSAN: I voted the Republican ticket. Straight. 7 a.m.

JUDGE'S VOICE: Whether you believe you have a right to vote or not is a question of law.

SUSAN: (*Defiantly.*) I did it, sir! I walked right into that poll booth, and I did it.

(*Shocked voices and pounding of gavel is heard. The light dims on Susan's area. Medieval music is heard. A Tailor comes onstage followed by Joan. The Tailor carries a basket of silk and plumes and a female dressmaker's dummy. He puts the basket down and sets the dummy in position. Then he opens the basket, fluffs up the silks, and turns to Joan.*)

TAILOR: Joan . . . Joan of Lorraine. Ahh, your neck will have the best boiled leather . . . (*He strokes Joan's neck. Joan smiles.*) Then . . . I'll caress these lovely appendages in fine steel. (*He touches her breasts, counting.*) One . . . two . . . and thick rings of chainmail under those deep, dark armpits. Beside these lovely moons . . . (*Joan is enjoying the stroking of the Tailor.*)

JOAN: (*Dreamily, as she strokes herself along with the Tailor.*) Yes . . . yes . . . more steel . . . more leather . . . more . . .

(*Lavour comes onstage and sees Joan and the Tailor.*)

LAVOUR: (*To Tailor.*) What in the hell are you doing? (*The Tailor drops his hands.*)

JOAN: (*To Lavour.*) Did you swear, soldier?

LAVOUR: Get that lecher out of this camp.

(*The Tailor skulks off, bowing unctuously to Joan as he scurries offstage.*)

JOAN: Soldier, say "Martin" every time you want to swear.

LAVOUR: (*Pause.*) I'm your adjutant, not "soldier." (*He stands at attention.*) Captain Lavour.

JOAN: Enchantee. (*Pause. She looks at him startled.*) I didn't know my adjutant would be so . . . young. You smell funny.

LAVOUR: I don't smell of manure. I don't come from a farm.

JOAN: (*Happily, sniffing his arm.*) Lemon soap. (*Pause. She goes on to touch his upper arm muscles.*) I bet you joust.

LAVOUR: I broke three lances fairly . . . in Reims.

JOAN: I've always wanted a knight to wear my scarf on his lance. (*She stares at him.*)

LAVOUR: (*Coldly.*) I'm not that kind of knight.

(*Joan smiles, realizing she can command him. She sorts through the basket of silks and plumes, and holds up a green scarf.*)

JOAN: Maybe green. Sheep grass is not as green. (*She ties the green scarf around Lavour's arm.*) Where is he?

LAVOUR: Who?

JOAN: The captain that hates me. I saw him slouching near the wagon yard this morning. (*Lavour remains silent. Joan turns away and begins lifting items from the basket.*) From the Dauphin. His personal plumes, scarves . . . sashes . . . (*She puts on more silks. She looks around royally.*) And he's promised me cannon-balls . . . as many as I want.

LAVOUR: Cannonballs! Those things destroy trees and bushes. They make gashes in the ground. They don't kill men.

(*A pause as Joan's face flushes in anger.*)

JOAN: (*She goes into a tantrum.*) I give the orders here. You soldiers are all alike. You don't think I know anything. Well I do. I know weapons when I see them. Don't bully me. I'll tell the Dauphin. Do you hear me? I'll tell the King. (*Stamping her feet.*)

LAVOUR: He's not the King yet. (*He looks at this childish commander with contempt. Then he briskly exits.*)

(*Joan stares after him, half-surprised and then slowly childishly victorious. After a pause, she goes to the basket to sort happily through all her plumes and silks.*)

CARDINAL'S VOICE: (*Over speaker.*) This inquisition will now begin. (*Pause.*) Please state your name before the cardinals present here in the name of the Holy Mother Church. Where were you born? (*Joan doesn't answer. She is too busy with her treasures.*) Where were you born?

JOAN: (*Happily.*) Gifts. From the Dauphin.

CARDINAL'S VOICE: Your birthplace?

JOAN: (*After a pause.*) Domremy.

CARDINAL'S VOICE: What can you say regarding your actions?

JOAN: I lead armies to unite France. Because of you, Holy Fathers. (*Pause. She holds up a scarf.*)

CARDINAL'S VOICE: Whether you have a right to lead armies or not is a question of this council.

JOAN: I love you all . . . I love the Holy Mother Church. And you love me.

(*She exits carrying the silks and plumes with her. Lights come up on the Hotel Owner sitting in the stove area of the hotel. He strums a guitar as the Saddle Tramp enters.*)

HOTEL OWNER: (*Singing.*)
   HORSE CREEK AIN'T CROSSIBLE,
   NOT EVEN HORSIBLE
   HORSE CREEK AIN'T PASSABLE
   NOT EVEN JACKASSABLE
   HORSE CREEK AIN'T . . .

(*Susan comes into the stove area. The Men stare at her.*)

SUSAN: I'm from the Billiard Suite.
SADDLE TRAMP: So yer the one that marshal's lookin' for. You a bigamist?
SUSAN: I'm a voter. (*Saddle Tramp reacts dramatically.*) I didn't say I spread smallpox. I said I voted. (*To Hotel Owner.*) I need a sheet. For my . . . bed.
HOTEL OWNER: We had a rush of business fer dinner (*he picks up a sheet and gives it to Susan*) . . . 'n used it fer a tablecloth. (*Susan takes the sheet gingerly.*) Youse 'at come from the East . . . we pamper you a spell. Sheet 'n tablecloth the first couple of days. (*Pause.*) We don't allow style as a regular thang.
SADDLE TRAMP: Welcome ta Hotel de Dirt.
SUSAN: Is there any water for washing in?
HOTEL OWNER: A kettle full ta the back stove.
SUSAN: That won't be enough.
HOTEL OWNER: You mean you're fixin' ta wash *all over?* (*Both men laugh at this.*) Damn that dog of mine. I've been scratchin' from Charlie's fleas all day. (*Pause.*) Wanna bet?
SADDLE TRAMP: Nice big fleas?
HOTEL OWNER: (*Pause.*) Put up a dollar.
SUSAN: (*Looks at men firmly.*) I've seen that game. In False Bottom. (*Pause.*) You drop fleas in a pan and see which one of these grayback scrambles out first.
HOTEL OWNER: That's right. (*Pause.*) Dollar a head.
SUSAN: I'm on.
HOTEL OWNER: Bet's a bet. (*Knowing wink to Saddle Tramp.*) Don't put up money ya can't lose. (*Pause.*) I'll warn ya . . . this ain't no New York "Parcheesi," "Hearts," or "Old Maid."
SADDLE TRAMP: (*Spits in a small fry pan.*) Pan's hot.

(*After a pause, the Hotel Owner scratches his sleeve furiously. The two men both take fleas from the Hotel Owner's arm. Then they hold the fleas poised over the frying pan. They*) *wait for Susan, looking at her intently to see what she will do. After a determined silence, Susan courageously scratches the Hotel Owner's sleeve.*)

SUSAN: (*Taking a flea from the Hotel Owner's sleeve, she dramatically holds it poised over the pan.*) On three! One . . . two . . . three!

(*They all drop their fleas into the pan at once. Soon they are cheering, Susan too.*)

HOTEL OWNER: (*After a pause, to Susan.*) Yers is out first. (*The men make a gesture to pay her.*)
SUSAN: I'll accept payment in bath water. (*The Saddle Tramp turns the pan over and clears it.*)
HOTEL OWNER: (*Cranky.*) Gotta be brought in from the creek. (*Pause.*) I need 'n feed Charlie, my dog . . . Charlie, my horse . . . 'n Charlie, the ox . . .
SUSAN: All your animals are named "Charlie"?
HOTEL OWNER: It don't confuse me inny that way. (*Pause.*)
SUSAN: I've got to wake up early tomorrow. My stage leaves at dawn . . . and I just can't miss it. (*She starts to leave.*)
HOTEL OWNER: If yer gettin' ready ta go ta California, then you'll be headed for Crystal Hills?
SUSAN: Yes that's right . . . in about a week . . . according to my map. There'll be a letter there from my friend.
HOTEL OWNER: Crystal Hills, huh?
SUSAN: Yes.
HOTEL OWNER: Nobody is told you about Crystal . . .

(*Saddle Tramp shakes his head gloomily.*)

SUSAN: Should they have? (*Pause.*) What's wrong with Crystal Hills? Is the marshal there?
HOTEL OWNER: Nope.
SUSAN: Indians?
SADDLE TRAMP: Nope.
HOTEL OWNER: Is it real important that you go that way?
SUSAN: Yes. I told you I have a letter waiting for me at Crystal Hills.
SADDLE TRAMP: You kin take the detour over Beaver Fork.
SUSAN: I'd lose seven or eight days that way.
HOTEL OWNER: Sometimes a detour is worth it. Lotta people was determined ta get there . . . once.
SADDLE TRAMP: I knew me a wagon train of cavalry that . . . well . . . they ain't livin' ta tell the story.
SUSAN: Will you please tell me what this is all about!
HOTEL OWNER: Hate ta see somebody alone took off for that place.
SADDLE TRAMP: God knows people in groups ain't fared no better.

SUSAN: What is this all about?

HOTEL OWNER: Crystal Hills is . . . is so clear ya can't see 'em . . . 'n people is run smack into 'em head-on 'n died.

SADDLE TRAMP: You'll see stacks of wagons which is broken their wheels by runnin' into 'em . . . bones of people 'n horses 'n birds with broken necks . . .

(*Susan stares at the men for a second; then the men can't hold out any longer and begin to laugh.*)

HOTEL OWNER: (*As he is laughing.*) Them hills is so . . . clear . . . they is invisible . . .

(*Hotel Owner and Saddle Tramp exit. Joan enters the hotel area.*)

SUSAN: (*Peeved; after a pause.*) The West!

JOAN: It's not just the West.

SUSAN: You'd think I'd wise up to their jokes.

JOAN: I know.

SUSAN: (*Looking after the men.*) I'm always standing by watching somebody else do something.

JOAN: (*Pause.*) You won at fleas.

SUSAN: I walk up to a minister's house. To give him these pamphlets. And you know what he says? (*After a pause.*) Are you the new hired girl? Did it ever occur to him that a woman standing at his doorstep just might be something else besides a . . . hired girl?

JOAN: Did he sign your petition?

SUSAN: (*After a pause; smiling.*) . . . After I scrubbed down his porch . . . (*She chuckles.*) OK . . . so he wasn't so bad. What about that jackass hotel owner . . . and the saddle tramp?

JOAN: (*Pause.*) My own first sergeant asks me if I do only "sitting work." (*Pause.*) He sees me drinking in muddy tanks, right alongside the horses. He sees me stripping bark off the trees for my bed. (*Pause.*)

SUSAN: I wouldn't mind it so much . . . if . . . we could be on the trail together.

JOAN: But we are.

SUSAN: All the time. I'm lonely. I never thought I'd be lonely. (*Pause.*) It seems like here in the West, you come upon a stranger . . . share his or her food and home and you're no closer to that person than a bird and a squirrel who happen upon the same tree branch.

JOAN: I saw a robin today and it made me think of home. (*Pause.*) My archers and lancers sit huddled together around the fire. They're homesick, too.

SUSAN: But they're homesick together. (*Pause.*) Maybe Mother's right . . . maybe a woman can't take it . . . the traveling . . . the weather . . . I have bad dreams.

JOAN: Dreams! They're only cats and dogs of the sky.

SUSAN: I dream . . . I never change anything. I see my face . . . old, weather-wrung. It's a homeless face. (*Pause.*) I'm afraid . . . afraid to stop . . . afraid to go on. (*Pause.*) A marshal's on my trail. (*Pause.*) If he gets me, I'll be hobbled like a horse. Taken back East on the same overland coach I came on. People gawking at every stage station. Finally thrown in a dark cell in Rochester. Tried with the speed of a miner's court. (*Pause.*) What if . . . I give up everything and lose? What if . . . I have no place to go . . . when I'm old.

(*After a pause, Joan picks up one of the hotel's communal hairbrushes, still on its string, and begins to brush Susan's hair.*)

JOAN: (*As she brushes.*) Maybe homeless is beautiful . . . maybe. Now . . . rest . . . rest . . . I'll brush your hair . . . then you brush mine. Women have always done that for each other.

(*The light slowly fades. Joan quietly exits. Susan remains in semi-darkness. Voices are heard over speaker, then the sound of a court gavel.*)

JUDGE'S VOICE: (*Over speaker.*) Did Elizabeth Cady Stanton get you to wear men's clothing?

SUSAN: (*Angrily.*) I wear bloomers and logger socks because I ride a horse and I'm freezing cold.

JUDGE'S VOICE: Did she?

SUSAN: It rains out here like . . . like a creek's fallen from the sky. A skirt drags in the mud. I refuse to get pulled down by the mud.

JUDGE'S VOICE: Even women jeer at you.

SUSAN: Not all of them. At a boarding house in Big Bear, the lady owner told me to pick my room and order dinner, adding there'd be no bill. In French Lick, a miner's wife . . .

JUDGE'S VOICE: You're Elizabeth Cady Stanton's lackey.

SUSAN: She writes my speeches.

JUDGE'S VOICE: At home.

SUSAN: She makes the bullets. I fire them.

JUDGE'S VOICE: But she stays home.

SUSAN: She has children. (*Pause.*) Seven of them. I don't believe there's a safe day in the month for her.

JUDGE'S VOICE: Children . . . now that's the normal function of women, Miss Anthony, isn't it?

SUSAN: What's normal for a woman is something she must determine for herself.

JUDGE'S VOICE: You, Miss Anthony, are unmarried, childless, dressed in men's attire, and traveling in a prairie of men. Am I correct?

SUSAN: Yes!

JUDGE'S VOICE: Mrs. Stanton is married, a mother, attired as a lady of her social class, and living in her family home. (*Pause.*) How nice for her that you . . . you are in the West . . . delivering her speeches.

SUSAN: I met Mrs. Stanton when she first came to Rochester. For a lecture. It was the most thrilling speech I've ever heard. (*Pause.*) She's a lawyer's daughter, Your Honor. When she was five, she ripped out all the pages in her father's law books that discriminated against women. She's been "ripping" ever since. (*Pause.*) After that first speech, I followed her from city to city. I heard every speech she made. And . . . then . . . (*Pause.*) One day in Seneca . . . one August day . . . when heat lightning split the sky . . . we sat on her lawn talking . . . and she said . . . "Susan, you can help women. You!" (*Pause. Angrily.*) She picked me! Me! Out of hundreds of others. Don't you dare call me her lackey. I'm chosen!

(*Susan remains standing for a moment. Lights dim on Susan and come up on the Archer, strumming his guitar in another area of the stage.*)

ARCHER: (*Sings.*)
JOAN
JOAN
WITHOUT NO KNIVES
   AT HOME
   HOME;
      SHE CAN'T WINK
      SHE CAN'T SIGH
      A VIRGIN KEEPS HER CHERRY PIE
      KEEPS HER CHERRY PIE.

(*After a pause, Lavour enters with Joan.*)

LAVOUR: Too many of your officers are refusing to follow you. More every day. (*Joan turns from Lavour and begins to strut.*) Desertion is increasing. Four corporals ran off with a full cart of supplies last night.

JOAN: (*Strutting.*) These spurs are five inches.

LAVOUR: The morning wind knocked down all the ammunition tents and blew off wagon covers.

JOAN: (*She struts again.*) Any traitor who comes near me will get it right between the legs.

LAVOUR: (*In contempt.*) My father always said: The farther you get from Paris, the darker the bread.

JOAN: That means I'm a stupid farm girl, right? (*Pause.*) A few weeks ago, I was kicking cows home from pasture . . . but now. Silks! Plumes!

LAVOUR: Battle will stink a long time in your nostrils.

JOAN: Is that a criticism of war. . . ?

LAVOUR: A criticism of fact. (*Pause.*) What is it you want . . . General?

JOAN: Want. I have no wants.

LAVOUR: Those who do not want something do not make war. They only endure it.

JOAN: Let me tell you something . . . Captain. I don't come from a fancy family in Paris . . . the way you do. I don't worry about low supplies of good wine . . . about losing my title. (*Pause.*) You know what war means to me? (*Pause.*) A mule! (*Pause.*) We had a plow mule called Belle. She was born the same day I was. (*Pause.*) Stray English soldiers would come by our farm asking for pack animals to carry their cannons and arrows. We couldn't let them have Belle. She was all we had for the fields. We'd starve. (*Pause.*) So Daddy took Belle to the shed and . . . cut up her legs . . . till they were bleeding and she was limping . . . so the enemy wouldn't take her. (*Pause.*) Belle's legs would heal . . . we'd work her . . till enemy stragglers came by . . . then we'd cut up Belle's legs again. (*Pause.*) We shared birthdays, Captain. (*Pause.*) And one day, after maybe the sixth time, I went to the shed where Belle was . . . all bleeding . . . and lame . . . and started pounding the walls. I screamed and pounded till my fists were bloody as Belle's legs. (*Pause.*) I learned something about myself that day. I learned that . . . when I'm mad, I'm stronger than I ever knew I could be. When I'm mad, I don't feel pain. I endure. (*Pause.*) It's France that wants, Captain. (*Pause.*) Now . . . I have a battle to win. I'm tired . . . and I don't have much time.

LAVOUR: (*Demanding.*) Why are you so sure you're the right person to win France back?

JOAN: (*Points.*) See how the wind moves those twigs against the fallen leaves? (*Pause.*) I believe in mirages, Captain. Mirages have their real side. That same little whirling war is being waged . . . and I (*she stamps her foot in the whirling leaves*) . . . I have won it.

(*Joan runs offstage. After a pause, Battau enters.*)

BATTAU: Some of our lancers stole tavern signs from town. They're drunk. Restless. (*Pause.*) I'm restless, too. (*Pause.*) You know what she's done now? (*Pause.*) Ordered half the line dismounted. She wants a flank movement on the other side of the river. (*Pause.*) No officer is going to walk into Orleans.

LAVOUR: If you're ordered to walk . . . you'll walk.

BATTAU: A farm girl tells us to walk. (*Pause. Laughs.*) I drew a map of this camp. I have it pretty well narrowed down.

LAVOUR: What do you have narrowed down?

BATTAU: Where her tent is. I'll put the scare of death in her. (*Sound of wood-chopping is heard.*)

LAVOUR: I don't like treason. (*Pause.*) My grandfather . . . father . . . we've served France. Honorably. I don't intend to be the first in the family to commit treason.

BATTAU: We figure she's to the east of the wagon yard.

LAVOUR: Get rid of the map, Battau. (*Pause.*) The Dauphin's made her official head of this battalion. Until he comes to his senses, we'll follow her.

BATTAU: (*Holding out the map.*) We got one big circle on the likely spot. (*Pause.*) She's a witch, you know that.

LAVOUR: You believe in goblins, too?

BATTAU: She's not normal. They say she sees things . . . hears things . . . she spooked the Dauphin! (*Pause.*) A witch, Lavour.

LAVOUR: A man . . . who graduated with me from the University of Paris . . . is now telling me he believes in witches.

BATTAU: You'll see. Check around. Babies in Rouen are being born deform-ed. People in Paris are losing teeth. (*He stares at Lavour for a second.*) All I want to do is kill a witch . . . that's all.

LAVOUR: She won't last ten minutes in battle. Let the English take her off our hands. They'd love to capture her. Think of the ransom they'll get. (*Sound of wood-chopping is louder. A pause as Battau looks toward the sound.*)

BATTAU: (*Still looking off.*) What the hell's that?

LAVOUR: Somebody chopping wood. (*They both stare off for several seconds.*) Do you think I want to ruin my career . . . maybe die because of a stupid farm girl? (*Pause.*) Trust me. (*Pause.*) If she isn't struck down when we breach the walls . . . she'll turn and run home to Mother the minute the English cannons start popping.

BATTAU: (*Pause.*) Lavour, why are you doing this to me? Let me stop her.

LAVOUR: She has to be stopped officially. You know that. It's only a matter of time . . .

BATTAU: (*Looking off again.*) What the hell! What . . .

LAVOUR: That tree's about to fall.

BATTAU: Jesus . . . it's going to fall on my tent!

LAVOUR: Timber! (*Loud noise.*) It went on your tent, all right.

(*Battau runs off. Joan comes onstage carrying a hatchet.*)

JOAN: I can cut a tree straight enough to drive a nail.

LAVOUR: I see. (*He can't help but be amused. He exits.*)

CARDINAL'S VOICE: (*Over speaker.*) Please tell this court if voices command you to wear men's clothing?

JOAN: I don't wear men's clothing by the counsel of any voices. I climb the underside of scaling ladders . . . using just my hands. The rest of me dangles in midair.

CARDINAL'S VOICE: What vision do you see?

JOAN: A long single line.

CARDINAL'S VOICE: A line of . . . men?

JOAN: Yes . . . Our men.

CARDINAL'S VOICE: Men with natural heads?

(*Lavour enters.*)

JOAN: French heads. Please . . . come back . . . please . . . let me tell you more . . . about the glories I do in your name . . . (*She sees Lavour.*) Captain (*Pauses, embarrassed.*) . . . I need your advice . . . Well, more like your help.

LAVOUR: (*Coldly.*) What is it, General?

JOAN: (*Slowly.*) How do you. . . ? (*Lavour is watching her curiously.*) How . . . (*gathering courage*) . . . how . . . do you . . . ride a horse?

LAVOUR: (*Stares at her in disbelief.*) You don't know how to ride a horse?

JOAN: I've only been in this army two weeks . . . Do they really bite?

LAVOUR: Worry about the ones that kick at you when they run away. (*Pause.*) Horse bites are downright friendly. (*Looks at her disgustedly.*) Don't let the horse know that you are afraid.

JOAN: I won't be afraid.

LAVOUR: (*Calling.*) Archer! Archer! (*Archer comes running onstage.*) Over here. Bend over.

ARCHER: Which direction do you want my ass? (*He giggles.*)

LAVOUR: Get down on all fours. (*To Joan.*) Your horse. (*To Archer.*) She'll ride you.

ARCHER: (*Happily and lewdly.*) Ahhhh!

LAVOUR: I'm only doing this for France. (*To Joan.*) Every horse worth anything has a natural distrust of human beings. Especially soldiers. It wants nothing bigger than a leaf on its back. (*Lavour helps Joan straddle the Archer's back. He takes a cord from around the Archer's waist and puts it through the Archer's mouth as reins for Joan to hold, then kicks the Archer so he will buck.*) Bucking is its way of making friends. So you both can get used to each other. Don't pull hard. That wrecks his mouth. Head up! Up! You don't have to watch the horse.

(*Joan is riding, feeling all the passion between her legs. In a frenzy she uses spurs. As she rides, she suddenly assumes command. She shouts authoritatively. Lavour watches amazed.*)

JOAN: Open the ranks! Let the English through! Group in single lines! No knight will be a shield for another! A single line! (*Pause.*) Close up those intervals! (*Pause.*) Knights in the front! Squires behind! Scale the wall!

ARCHER: Ahhhh! (*He bucks Joan off and rolls over on the ground in pain.*) She used them spurs on me! (*Pause.*) I'm bleeding. (*Pause.*) Find yourself another ass . . . fer soldiers' pay . . . twelve lousy deniers a day. (*He rolls away from*

Joan.)

JOAN: (*Sits on the ground panting.*) I like that . . . Oh, I like to ride a horse.

LAVOUR: Where did you learn to give commands like that?

JOAN: From peasant ignorance, Captain.

(*Lavour, Joan and Archer exit. Lights come up on the Saddle Tramp sitting in the stove area of the hotel.*)

SADDLE TRAMP: (*Sings.*)

   I NEVER CHANGE MY UNDERWEAR,
   I DON'T THROW 'EM AWAY
   'TIL THEY GET SO GRIMY
   I FINALLY HAVE TO SAY:
      GOODBYE OLD SWEAT-STIFF LEGGINGS
      IN ALL YOUR PRIDE OF GRIME,
      I'VE WORN YOU FOR SIX YEARS NOW
      AND THAT'S A PROPER TIME.
   I NEVER WASH . . .

(*Susan enters.*)

SADDLE TRAMP: You traveling all alone?

SUSAN: Yes. What line goes through Indian territory?

SADDLE TRAMP: Miles-Deadwood stage.

SUSAN: Not the kind of coach a lady would ride?

SADDLE TRAMP: Nope.

SUSAN: (*She smiles, puts a pan on her head and points to it.*) How's this? Will it fool the Indians?

SADDLE TRAMP: (*After pause.*) They is savages—not morons.

SUSAN: (*She shrugs and takes the pan off her head.*) Any food in Hotel de Dirt? Slice of bread? I missed supper.

SADDLE TRAMP: Built me some "trail stew." Ain't New York puff paste and cream fillin's. (*He takes out a jar and empties it into a pot.*)

SUSAN: (*Pause. She holds out her hand.*) I'm Susan.

SADDLE TRAMP: Double Ugly. My "front name." (*Points to his face.*) I was cut in two places in a fight in Crow Canyon. I give a first-class funeral ta my real name long time ago. (*He continues stirring the stew.*) So yer all by yerself?

SUSAN: Yes.

SADDLE TRAMP: I know what that is . . . being a cowpuncher . . . alone on the range . . . ridin' the fence line. Home's not where I throw my hat—but where I spread my blanket. (*He pours her a cup of coffee.*) Here, yodel this. (*Stares at her silently for a few seconds.*) Yer what we wranglers call a loner steer . . . prowlin' up and down the outside of a dusty cattle line. (*Pause as he tastes the stew. He motions to the pot.*) Go ahead, Susan. (*Pause.*) It'll make ya steal yer own clothes, bite off yer own nose . . . watcha waiting for? (*Susan stares at the pot. Reluctantly she tastes the stew. She slowly smiles.*)

SUSAN: Good. (*Eats another large spoonful.*)

SADDLE TRAMP: (*Gives her a big dish of the stew; sings.*)

THE COFFEE'S GOT CONSUMPTION
THE SPUDS ARE HIT WITH FLU
THE FLAPJACKS SUFFER DROPSY
THE BEEF IS SCALPED BY SIOUX

(*Susan laughs.*)

SADDLE TRAMP: I like yer laugh. It don't sound like a man's . . . 'n you don't try 'n soften it like some women do. I guess we give you a lot of razzin' while back. (*He watches her eat.*) You eat that much all the time?

SUSAN: I read somewhere that plenty of good food wards off the cholera. (*She continues eating heartily.*)

SADDLE TRAMP: (*After pausing to watch her eat.*) So how ya like the West?

SUSAN: I love cowboys.

SADDLE TRAMP: (*Pleased.*) Yah?

SUSAN: When I was little, I roped sheets off my mother's clotheslines.

SADDLE TRAMP: Big ones?

SUSAN: Big as boxcars. I still love sheet-behavior of horses when the wind blows.

SADDLE TRAMP: Well, Susan, I'll tell ya . . . I have broke horses 'n they have broke me. (*Pause.*) But a horse, once he's yers, you ain't never gonna find a more loyal friend. (*He reaches in her soup and takes out a bone.*) I'll jist take this fer Plenty.

SUSAN: Your horse chews bones?

SADDLE TRAMP: Rolls 'em in her mouth like a dog. (*Pause.*) She's old now . . . 'n grayin' up around the ears. I kin loosen her cinch 'n drop the reins on the ground 'n she stays right next ta me. (*Pause.*) I catch her innywhere with a biscuit. (*Pause.*) She comes ta a river now . . . she won't even try to swim . . . jist turns on her side 'n floats across. But she's the most horse I ever had.

SUSAN: Tell me . . . Double Ugly . . . what do you do when your horse gets sick . . . useless?

SADDLE TRAMP: (*After a long, reflective pause.*) I feed her. (*Pause.*) Some people don't feel fer critters, but I do. That's why I work with 'em. (*Pause.*)

SUSAN: Does it bother you . . . to think of cattle ending up on a plate?

SADDLE TRAMP: Nope. It's the way a critter's treated before he's eaten that bothers me.

SUSAN: (*Pausing; looking at him carefully.*) I stayed with some homesteaders in Calico Pass. The wife was sick . . . and do you know, Ugly, that they carried her right on her sick-cot to the washtub to do their clothes . . . 'cause washing is women's work. (*Pause.*)

SADDLE TRAMP: Don't it occur to you to blame nature fer what is done women?

SUSAN: Certainly not.

SADDLE TRAMP: A woman's body . . . how it's . . . formed . . . (*Gestures around his chest.*) . . . that's what is made your place in life. Nature don't make mistakes. These times scare me, Susan. Ya know they got them a machine fer hatching eggs by artificial warmth. A machine . . . ta take a mother's place. (*Pause.*) Now you talk about women votin'. Where's it all gonna end? (*Susan chews silently for a moment, then stops abruptly.*) That there's jist gravel in the beans.

SUSAN: (*She adjusts her mouth to accommodate the gravel; stops again.*) What's this tasty meat?

SADDLE TRAMP: Wolf.

(*There is a pause. Susan gives out a loud wolf howl. The Saddle Tramp laughs.*)

SUSAN: Wish the wolves around here were big enough to eat marshals. (*Pause as the Saddle Tramp watches her eat.*)

SADDLE TRAMP: I think I'd like to hear you speak, Susan. Yep, I'd like that all right. But I hit the trail early tomorrow . . . driving steer ta Fresno.

SUSAN: California?

SADDLE TRAMP: Yep.

SUSAN: Maybe . . . I could get you to sign my petition before you go. (*She hands him a paper. He just looks at the paper. After a second, she hands him a pen.*)

SADDLE TRAMP: (*He refuses the pen, crooking his hands.*) It takes me time ta git the crooks outta my hands from them bein' clamped 'round the saddle horn all day . . . 'n . . . well, I got ta think on somethang serous 's this.

SUSAN: Think, then. All you want. And hear me speak in California. 'Cause I'll be all over that state . . .

SADDLE TRAMP: You know somethin' . . . You don't match. (*He tenderly touches the side of her face.*) One side of your face is darker 'n the other.

SUSAN: That's my window-side . . . I get to the station early . . . for a window seat.

SADDLE TRAMP: (*He touches Susan's face again.*) I learn from horses to see how a person's eyes and ears work ta catch thangs . . . 'n Susan . . . all of yours is workin' fine . . . real fine like a good critter's . . .

SUSAN: Double Ugly, you aren't going to try and kiss me?

SADDLE TRAMP: Why . . . no.

SUSAN: (*Sighs in relief and turns away from Saddle Tramp. After a pause, she twirls around to face him.*) And why not! Aren't I pretty enough?

SADDLE TRAMP: A sweet hardy mountain flower.

SUSAN: Then why?

SADDLE TRAMP: Loner steer don't feel what the rest of the herd does.

SUSAN: I beg to differ with you, Ugly. These arms feel . . . These lips feel . . .

(*The Saddle Tramp slowly backs away from her and exits. Court gavel is heard.*)

JUDGE'S VOICE: (*Over speaker.*) Susan B. Anthony . . . do you travel out West? (*Susan looks around nervously, straightening her hair.*) Answer please.

SUSAN: The West is a curious place. Pigeon Creek . . . where there are no pigeons . . . White Woman . . . with no women at all.

JUDGE'S VOICE: Do you travel with men?

SUSAN: There's always a kind brakeman who's willing to slow down the switch engine for a few minutes so I can jump aboard a flatcar or gondola and hook a free ride to the next town. Sometimes I run for the caboose . . . huffing alongside, my cape flapping. I throw my bags at the platform and lunge at the handrails. (*Pause.*) Too often the train glides away with my belongings. But my luggage is always left at the next depot up the line.

JUDGE'S VOICE: (*More sternly.*) Do you only encounter men when you travel?

SUSAN: What does that have to do with this trial?

JUDGE'S VOICE: Your character, Miss Anthony, is on trial.

SUSAN: Some days I only eat a crab apple and an ear of parched corn. (*Angrily.*) I'll have no danger of getting gout . . . the alderman's death. Is that character enough!

JUDGE'S VOICE: Answer the question please. Do you see only men?

SUSAN: On a cold day, a trapper shoots a wolf, scalps the animal right then, and draws the warm skin on his head.

JUDGE'S VOICE: This court would like to know where the trapper sleeps at night.

SUSAN: (*Angrily.*) You can ask that . . . when . . . when even little school-children out here carry guns to school.

JUDGE'S VOICE: Is it true you're so close to men you hear their snores at night?

SUSAN: Not all men snore, Your Honor.

JUDGE'S VOICE: When men cry in the night . . . from their nightmares . . . do you comfort them? (*Pause.*) Do you let down your long thick hair . . . lean over them with your comforting veil of hair . . . ?

SUSAN: I will not answer to this, sir. I refuse to answer these slanderous, irrelevant questions.

(*After a pause, Susan sits down angrily. Joan has entered and is standing in the battlefield area of the stage. Susan slowly turns to look at her. Lavour enters and goes to Joan.*)

LAVOUR: I saw you by the river.

JOAN: Testing the banks.

LAVOUR: Send a squire for that.

JOAN: A good soldier always makes his own reconnaissance.

LAVOUR: How do you know that?

JOAN: I watch you, Captain. Has my riding improved?

LAVOUR: You've a talent for it.

JOAN: (*Smiles at Lavour.*) I have a good teacher. (*Pause.*) I ordered lancers to light hundreds of fires . . . so the English will think our camp is larger than it is.

LAVOUR: The food's improved.

JOAN: The men were complaining . . . I went to that ancient commissary sergeant and ordered beef . . . for the old soldiers in this unit. (*Pause. She mocks the sergeant's ancient tone.*) "Ah . . . old soldiers," he says. "How many old soldiers you have?" (*Pause.*) I said: "Plenty! And give them everything they deserve." (*Lavour chuckles. After a pause, Joan walks away to sit on the ground.*) I haven't slept in three days.

LAVOUR: Few generals do . . . before battle. (*Pause.*) Rumor is . . . the English are afraid of you. You're uncalculating . . . and naive. You've nearly panicked them.

JOAN: (*Calling.*) Seven! (*Shakes dice.*) I smell sulphur.

LAVOUR: There's always sulphur in a camp. For trench-itch. (*Pause.*) A powerful mystery has formed around you. (*Pause.*) It's a weapon.

JOAN: (*Disappointed.*) Eight! (*Pause. She shakes dice again.*) Are there plenty of trumpets? Drums? I want all the music of a tournament. (*She calls her dice.*) Ten!

LAVOUR: You'll have music. I learned about war from tournaments. (*Pause.*) You . . . you just might pull it off.

JOAN: (*Pleased; calling dice.*) Ah, seven!

LAVOUR: You've got a chance. More than a chance. You could take Orleans by simple boldness. (*Pause.*) Where did you get those dice?

JOAN: From the Dauphin. Pure ivory. (*Pause.*) It's the game of God. Chance belongs to Providence. (*Pause.*) Play with me.

LAVOUR: I have to watch the "watch." (*He starts to exit.*)

JOAN: Captain. (*Lavour stops.*) I was alone for years in the hills . . . with only sheep and cows. I finally have my own army now . . . ten thousand men . . . and still nobody talks to me. (*Pause.*) Don't leave. That's an order. (*After a pause.*) Captain, are you afraid? (*Pause.*) Is . . . is a knight ever afraid before battle?

LAVOUR: Knights are afraid.

JOAN: I thought so. (*Pause. Takes a breath.*) Because I am. (*Pause.*) What do you think about . . . Captain? (*Lavour turns and stares at the ground.*) What does a soldier from Paris think about . . . before battle?

LAVOUR: My father took me hunting when I was young. (*Pause.*) Once . . . we were ambushed by English knights . . . my father, me, a young peasant boy who acted as my father's page. (*Pause.*) We were ready to eat our catch of rabbit . . . when suddenly . . . English arrows flew at us. Father and I escaped into some heavy willows; our heads pushed close to the roots so we couldn't be seen. But the peasant boy didn't make it. He was killed.

(*Pause.*) I was frightened . . . afraid to move . . . but I could hear a soldier say: "I'll have a French chair while I eat." . . . I could see through the brush . . . he pulled the dead boy by the heels, dragged the little carcass toward the fire . . . and sat on him. (*Pause.*) The English soldier ate our food and sat on a runt of a child . . . a scrawny poor boy . . . no older than you. (*After a pause.*) Now . . . I see a child . . . and I'm fierce for France.

JOAN: Captain . . . you see mirages too. (*Pause.*) Follow me . . . follow me with all your heart. I can win. Will you help me?

LAVOUR: (*Softly.*) Yes. (*Pause. Strongly.*) Yes! (*He walks over to a standard at the side of the stage and brings it back to Joan.*)

(*Susan slowly walks to the center of the stage. She picks up Joan's hatchet and looks at it for a moment.*)

SUSAN: (*To Saddle Tramp.*) Please . . . cut my hair before I go.

(*The Saddle Tramp walks to her and takes the hatchet. Susan kneels and throws her long hair over a crate or bench. The Saddle Tramp stares at her hair. Pause.*)

JOAN: Captain, I am peasant France. (*She holds up her standard triumphantly.*)
LAVOUR: Yes!

(*The Saddle Tramp brings the hatchet down on Susan's hair. Blackout just as the hatchet touches her hair.*)

END OF ACT I

ACT II

The Bar Dog is onstage. A "Wanted" notice for Susan B. Anthony is posted hear him.

SUSAN: (*Enters through the audience, singing.*)
    COME ON NOW
    COME ON NOW
      SEE WHAT'S NEW,
    I'VE SPLIT THE SKIRT
    SPLIT IT RIGHT IN TWO
      AND THERE AIN'T NO HORSE THAT
      CAN'T BE RODE,
      AND THERE AIN'T NO MAN
      THAT CAN'T BE THROWED.
    (*To Bar Dog.*) You open to speakers? (*Bar Dog just looks at her.*) I've been on the road for six months and I've seen nothing but tent-saloons since Medicine Bow. (*Pause.*) I'd sure like to speak in here. (*Pause. Bar Dog looks at Susan blankly.*) I came over the Soda Springs Road. The Miles-Deadwood stage sunk up to its springs in slime.

BAR DOG: Where's your baggage?

SUSAN: We had to lighten up. I lost all my clothes, books, old letters. (*Pause.*)

BAR DOG: (*Looks at the "Wanted" poster.*) Well . . . if it ain't Susan B. Anthony, the chantoozie.

SUSAN: The speaker.

BAR DOG: Yer . . . wanted. (*Whistles to back room.*) Hey . . . the woman outlaw's here . . .

SUSAN: Speaker! (*She looks around nervously, then sees the poster and rips it down.*) That should make me a real good draw.

BAR DOG: A marshal came through here yesterday putting the "Wanted" sign up.

SUSAN: I know the marshal's close. I can smell his Kill-Dad tobacco. I've been smelling his tobacco since Echo Canyon. (*Pause.*) He draw the beard on me too?

BAR DOG: I did that.

SUSAN: You draw a good beard, Mister . . . Mister . . .

BAR DOG: Kibby. Kibby Newt.

SUSAN: Susan B. Anthony. How about it . . . Kibby? Can I speak here tonight?

BAR DOG: I don't like no howling woman ta my establishment. Man's gotta have a quiet place ta drink after drivin' cattle or minin' ore all day.

SUSAN: I promise not to "howl."

BAR DOG: I tell ya . . . it jist ain't the wilderness no more like it used ta be. I got me a claim shack this year 'n 'fore I knew it somebody was buildin' a sod hut ten feet from my privy. Yep, land's all took. Even the beavers is thinnin' out.

SUSAN: One hour. That's all. Let me speak for one hour.

BAR DOG: Thangs is quiet. Ain't been nobody shot in three days. (*Pause. He fingers a newspaper.*)

SUSAN: (*Takes the newspaper and looks at it. After a pause.*) The Caribou Sentinel. Yippeeeee! It says here the state of Kansas cast nine thousand votes for woman's suffrage. That's the first time it's been put to popular vote. (*Pause.*) Kibby, let me tell the folks in this town about women's right to vote.

BAR DOG: My wife says she ain't gonna vote . . . even if this here state says she can. I do the votin' in the family . . . just like I earn the wages.

SUSAN: Does your wife pray?

BAR DOG: Sure.

SUSAN: You tell your wife . . . what's your wife's name?

BAR DOG: Jane.

SUSAN: You tell her Susan B. Anthony said: "Jane, you do your own praying . . . you do your own voting." Tell Jane something else. A woman's brain is a hundred grams lighter than a man's. Dante's brain was a hundred grams lighter than Byron's. Does that mean Dante shouldn't vote?

BAR DOG: Can't say I know 'im.

SUSAN: Dante wrote *The Divine Comedy*. Maybe the greatest poem ever written.

BAR DOG: What's he ever done fer the West? (*Pause.*) I'm a bar dog. Can't say as I read me Dante. I kin look inna neck of a bottle of whiskey 'n tell the age jist like a cowpoke tells the age of a horse by lookin' in its mouth. I ain't never been ta the East. Afraid ta go. I'd get there 'n start wearin' celluloid collars 'n cuffs 'n never be worth a cuss no more.

SUSAN: Be the first man in your town, Kibby, to stand up for Freedom of Speech. Let me . . .

BAR DOG: I had me a man come in from New York jist last week. He says: "I think I'll have a cocktail." I said: "Ya don't think in here—ya drink—'n it comes straight . . . in a tin cup."

SUSAN: I'm asking for an hour . . . give me half an hour!

BAR DOG: So ya eat ice cream ta the East? I ain't never et none, but a North Platte fella had some once 'n told me it gives 'bout as much feed as loping a rough horse 'ginst a west wind with a funnel in yer mouth.

SUSAN: Thirty minutes . . .

BAR DOG: Is it true they keep water coolers filled with champagne ta fancy New York hotels?

SUSAN: I don't know about fancy hotels. I stoked a train from Navaho Twins for a free ride. Sometimes I stack wood for lunch.

BAR DOG: I use buffalo chips. (*Pause.*) Help yerself ta free biscuit. I shoot at 'em every morning ta see if they're soft 'nough ta eat.

SUSAN: Kibby Newt . . . do you believe in these United States?

BAR DOG: My daddy fought for fourteen dollars a month and the Union.

SUSAN: Then you believe in the Constitution of this country.

BAR DOG: My daddy was in the 79th regimental band. He serenaded Ulysses S. Grant hisself.

SUSAN: Then you do believe in Freedom of Speech. (*The Bar Dog just stares at Susan.*) Give me thirty minues, Kibby.

BAR DOG: (*After a pause.*) Fifteen.

(*Lights fade on Susan and the Bar Dog and come up on Battau, who is seen struggling as if trapped in a mudhole.*)

BATTAU: Ahh . . . Get me out of here . . . (*Joan enters.*) Help! Get me out of this mudhole. (*Pause.*) My page is dead. I can't move in all this armor. (*Joan walks to Battau.*)

JOAN: Captain . . . at last we meet. (*Battau looks at Joan, embarrassed.*) I'll pull you out. (*She takes some rope and moves closer to Battau.*)

BATTAU: Don't come near me with rope.

JOAN: It's the only way I can pull you out.

BATTAU: You make a rope . . . snake around a man till . . . it chokes him.

JOAN: That's not true. (*Pause.*) I make a rope snake across the Loire.

BATTAU: I heard about that.

JOAN: A very narrow part of the Loire. You could cast that far yourself. (*She gets closer to him, displaying the rope.*)

BATTAU: Don't tie me up. Spit toads, but don't tie me up . . . like a . . .

JOAN: Traitor? (*Pause.*) Here, grab my foot then. For a start.

BATTAU: I heard about your "foot," too. (*Joan stares at him.*) It pulls off, and you grow another . . .

JOAN: I hate to tell you this, but I'm not a witch. It will take a great deal of brute strength to pull you out.

BATTAU: How do you know? (*Pause as Joan stares at him.*) Uh, huh! You know
. . . because you got "second sight." Admit it.

JOAN: I know . . . because I pull my cow out of mudholes all the time. Back
home. (*Pause.*) A cow can't be pulled from behind.

BATTAU: Don't get in back of me!

JOAN: If you pull a cow's tail . . . tug her out that way . . . you . . .

BATTAU: You what?

JOAN: Pull off her tail.

BATTAU: Don't come near me!

JOAN: So I come in at the front.

BATTAU: (*Calls.*) La . . . vour!

JOAN: Why are you calling my captain? I'm here.

BATTAU: (*Calls.*) Lavour!

JOAN: I'll have you out in no time.

BATTAU: Don't take another step . . . Stay away. (*Pause.*) They all got cows.

JOAN: Who?

BATTAU: Witches.

JOAN: I think it's bats they have.

BATTAU: What's the difference?

JOAN: I'd say a lot of difference.

BATTAU: (*Even more suspicious.*) Oh?

JOAN: I hate milk . . . but . . .

BATTAU: But what?

JOAN: Back home . . . when the morning frost is on the pasture grass . . . and
I'm barefooted . . . and my feet are cold, you know what I do?

BATTAU: Fly?

JOAN: (*Comes close to Battau.*) I told you, I'm not a witch. Keep it a secret,
though. (*Pause.*) Don't you want to know what I do?

BATTAU: OK . . . OK . . . tell me. Just stand back.

JOAN: (*She stands back.*) When the cow drops a steaming green cowpie, I run
and stand in it to warm up.

BATTAU: (*In disgust.*) Oggg! (*Pause. He calls.*) Lavour!

JOAN: Major, I'm going to put this rope around your waist. (*She pauses, ties the
rope around her waist, then loops it around Battau.*)

BATTAU: (*Meekly.*) I'm not a major.

JOAN: One thing I learned in the army . . . no man refuses a promotion. (*She
pulls him from the mud. Battau steps out of the rope, trying hard to regain his stature.*)
I'd be more careful if I were you, Captain.

BATTAU: Captain? You promoted me!

JOAN: Strategy. (*Pause.*) And *Captain* . . . don't kill me . . . in case I have to
save you again.

BATTAU: (*Stares at Joan sternly. After a few seconds he smiles.*) Well . . . we both
hate the English, anyway.

(Joan exits. Battau exits. Enter Ben and Susan. Ben is sketching.)

BEN: A beautiful moonlight night.

SUSAN: I'm afraid I don't like moonlight nights. It's when the Indians raid.

BEN: Is that why you can't sleep at night?

SUSAN: I'm not used to hearing tom-toms all night . . .

BEN: And the splashing of oars . . .

SUSAN: And the war songs of braves, Mr. Caleb.

BEN: After ten days on the Miles-Deadwood Overland . . . intimately thrown together by every bump in the road . . . I think we're entitled to call each other by our first names. *(Pause.)* Ben. Please.

SUSAN: Susan. *(Pause.)* Ah, yes, the Miles-Deadwood stage. Five miles an hour except when the horses are frightened by Indians.

BEN: I could see you were having a bad time of it.

SUSAN: I get sick of riding backwards.

BEN: Especially with silly frills poking at you. That Southern belle sat next to you all the way from Eagle Rock to Meeteetse.

SUSAN: When she finally got out . . . I used a ruler to measure the empty space she left. Five feet ten inches! *(They laugh.)*

BEN: Why don't you take the Butterfield? It's roomier.

SUSAN: And the nickel-plated harness shines in the sun.

BEN: And it stops at hotels.

SUSAN: That's the long way.

BEN: Ah, a lady in a hurry.

SUSAN: I hurry when I can, but the West is deceptive. Nothing here is located where it really is.

BEN: The West is a . . . mystery. Trains are spreading civilization into the wilderness . . . everywhere, little depots, eating houses . . . and the old Conestoga wagon rolls along the Boseman Trail and ends mid-journey at a station for modern pullman cars. The nineteenth century and the Middle Ages meet each other daily on the prairie.

SUSAN: *(Takes the sketch from Ben.)* Is that . . . ?

BEN: You. *(He exits.)*

(Susan begins to sand a piece of wood. Joan enters.)

SUSAN: You haven't been around in weeks.

JOAN: I come when I can: my time is short. We're outside Orleans now.

SUSAN: This last stretch of prairie's been pretty rough.

JOAN: We're building a tower. It goes forward on rollers . . . right up to the city walls. The latest thing in military arsenal.

SUSAN: I've got to put a fence rail on the forward axle. The wheel's broke . . . just when I'm so close to California.

JOAN: But all it is is putting old things together. Everything that is, was. Like the machine that flings stones through the air. The wind's been shooting things through the air for thousands of years now.

SUSAN: I've over ten thousand names now. A woman on crutches clomped her way up a muddy street to be the first person in this state to sign up. In one town, a husband beat his wife for signing this. Not just women's names. Men too. They say the legislature isn't laughing at me anymore. They say Washington D. C. might be afraid of Susan B. Anthony.

JOAN: We've got them scared, all right. My captain says the English think I got "powers." They're shaking in their shoes. He brought me a bouquet of wild onions today.

SUSAN: Your captain?

JOAN: With a blue ribbon around them. You know, so I don't get scurvy. (*Pause.*) He throws breadcrumbs to the song sparrows.

SUSAN: Can he fight?

JOAN: Oh, yes!

SUSAN: That's the important thing, isn't it?

JOAN: Yes. (*Pause.*) But . . . now and then I'm breathless when he gets too close.

SUSAN: I'm breathless . . . more than now and then. (*Pause.*) I rode a stage for ten days with a land-surveyor. He reads Dickens and Shakespeare. He sketches. (*Pause.*) We laughed. Ate together. He played a little brass harmonica. (*Pause.*) He's the kind of man . . . who . . . who can sit up all night and whistle for dancing. He can make me forget everything . . . the rally . . . the vote.

JOAN: (*Singsongs teasingly.*)
OH, HO,
GOT A BEAU!
OH, HO
GOT A . . .

SUSAN: What about Lavour?

JOAN: Soldiers walk so funny . . . arched back . . . When Lavour rides, he looks at his shadow. Soldiers always do that. A nice sunny day is their mirror.

SUSAN: You should see a cowboy ride his horse . . . one foot out of the stirrup . . . way over cocky to one side.

JOAN: That's what my first sergeant calls "too much mane and tail."

SUSAN: I saw a cowboy mount his horse at the rack in front of my hotel, ride across the street to the Post Office, dismount and tie his horse, mail a letter, then mount again and ride the horse back across the street to the hotel, get off, tie the horse and go to his room. (*They chuckle. Pause.*) I had a long wait with a prairie farmer at the depot outside Comb Wash, and I gave him my whole speech. About the virtues of women. What our vote means to mankind, etcetera. A good sixty minutes worth. (*Pause.*) When I finished . . . he said: "When I'm feeding the steers and drive the wagonload of hay there and find jist one, I don't unload the whole thing for him." (*Pause.*) A Westerner always speaks by way of his animals.

JOAN: What about that artist land-surveyor who sketches?

SUSAN: Oh, he's different. He reads poetry to me . . . sits close. Oh, I love a man's smell: train smoke, sweat, horses, sunshine. (*Pause.*) Sometimes I think . . . stay with him. Don't go to California. Take his warmth. (*Pause.*) Then I think of all the people who signed my petition. They depend on me. (*Pause.*) And there are the women waiting to sign my petition. And I know there's a truth stronger than the single pulse of my life! (*Pause.*) What are those lights in the hills?

JOAN: Signal fires . . . Deserters trying to get more of my lancers to run off . . . I've got to go. (*She exits.*)

(*Ben enters.*)

BEN: Susan, sit by the fire with me.

SUSAN: Shall we throw on some more logs?

BEN: The white man builds a big fire and stands way back. The Indian builds a small fire and sits up close. (*They sit on the ground and Ben begins to sketch.*) I'll miss our lively talks, Susan. Tomorrow morning, you take a boat . . . I catch a train. There's no guarantee I'll have any good conversation.

SUSAN: Trains are packed with interesting people.

BEN: Pretty ones? (*He shows her his sketch.*)

SUSAN: (*Shyly.*) You've drawn the hair much too full.

BEN: Did you know Choctaw widows mourn by never combing their hair? For the full term of their grief.

SUSAN: What made you come to love the Indians?

BEN: Their fragileness. (*He continues drawing.*)

SUSAN: I don't think Indians are fragile.

BEN: Their race is.

SUSAN: Sioux steal cattle and molest homesteaders.

BEN: There are outlaw Indians just as there are outlaws among us. (*Pause.*) The early French explorers named them "Sioux." It means "Little Snakes." (*Pause.*) They call themselves "Dakotas" now. (*Pause.*) I've met over a hundred different tribes and maybe twenty thousand Indians, and I've never been threatened with any violence.

SUSAN: I should think the Indian is doing well enough. We have federal agencies set up for them. That's more than women have.

BEN: Ahhh . . . but think . . . who's the first lady of this land?

SUSAN: (*After a long pause.*) The squaw?

BEN: Of course. (*Susan smiles.*) The Dakotas have a saying. "No one should go far in the desert who can't sleep in the shade of his arrows." You have to know the desert to understand that. (*Pause.*) A good quiverful of arrows is as valuable as a horse. (*Pause.*) Stick the arrows in the sand by their points and lie with your head in the shade of their feathers. (*Pause.*) Remember that.

SUSAN: (*Smiling.*) I will. (*Looks at sketch.*) I still say you made the hair too . . . full.

BEN: Ordinarily, I'd give you the sketch. But I want to keep it myself. Do you mind?

SUSAN: No.

BEN: (*He touches the hair on the sketch.*) There's a forest in a woman's hair. A calm which isn't silence hides inside. (*He looks at her slowly, then reaches out to touch her hair.*) Why did you cut it? (*A boat whistle is heard.*) The boat . . . (*Pause.*) Let it go by.

SUSAN: I've got to get to California.

BEN: (*Caustic.*) The rally . . . the "big" rally. (*More softly.*) Some day, what you're doing will seem inevitable. (*He looks at Susan affectionately.*) Marry me. We'll study Indians together. We'll build a house . . .

SUSAN: (*Weakly.*) A house?

BEN: With a porch.

SUSAN: (*Dreamily.*) And stone chimney . . .

BEN: A home—not a squatter's cabin.

SUSAN: . . . with baskets full of flowers hanging from the ceiling . . .

BEN: A two-story house . . .

SUSAN: . . . with shelves for books. And muslin curtains . . .

BEN: Your house . . . to grow old in . . . yours! (*Pause.*) You'll win, Susan. You'll win . . . and when you have the rights as men do, who will care about you then?

SUSAN: Oh, Ben, I'm tired . . . I'm so tired . . .

BEN: (*Moving closer to Susan.*) Let me put my face in this hair . . . dark as the eclipse and scented with rain.

(*He puts his face to her hair, then moves slowly to kiss her. After a pause, they break apart.*)

SUSAN: (*Annoyed by her feelings.*) I'm happy. (*Pause.*) Dear God, I'm happy.

(*The boat whistle is heard.*)

BEN: Tear up the boat ticket, Susan. Women will win . . . It's the ordinary course of history.

SUSAN: But I'm part of that history. (*Pause.*) I was chosen. And I promised. (*Pause.*) Every day I see strings and snags of women's hair in the brush . . . all along the trail. (*Backing away from Ben and moving toward the sound of the boat whistle.*) They say . . . women's hair gets caught in the brush. Pioneer women. (*Pause.*) And I keep hearing their silent voices.

(*Pause. Susan moves further toward the sound of the boat whistle. Light fades out on Ben as he speaks.*)

BEN: Susan . . . go with me . . . I have arrows enough . . .

(*The boat whistle is heard again. Susan moves slowly toward the sound as Ben exits. Joan enters and is hurriedly going by.*)

SUSAN: Joan . . . Joan . . .

JOAN: I'm in a hurry.

SUSAN: Mrs. Stanton wrote that the Married Property Bill was passed. Think of it. Women now have a purse of their own. (*Pause.*) What do you mean, you're in a hurry? You just got here.

JOAN: I don't have time . . . They're waiting.

SUSAN: The Committee on Woman's Suffrage that I tried to get into Congress was defeated. (*Pause.*) I need to talk . . . I *need* somebody . . .

JOAN: They're waiting.

SUSAN: Please . . . just a minute. (*Pause.*) A minute! You owe me that! (*Joan remains, but she keeps looking toward the battlefield area of the stage. After a pause.*) The committee I tried so hard to get into Congress . . . wham! Done in.

JOAN: You told me.

SUSAN: Aren't you even sorry?

JOAN: Of course I'm sorry.

SUSAN: What about the Married Property Bill!

JOAN: Good.

SUSAN: Just . . . *good?*

JOAN: (*Looking nervously toward the battlefield.*) Don't you think I'd like more time?

SUSAN: I . . . I need to talk about the small things . . . the little stupid everyday things . . . the things we used to laugh about . . . (*Joan is impatiently looking toward the battlefield.*) . . . I haven't earned a dollar in six days . . . I smell like a smoked side of bacon . . . I can grease a fry pan on my cape . . . I let a dog sleep on my feet to keep them warm. (*After a pause.*) I saw a bride today. She sat in a chair outside the church. And her husband knelt in front of her, and put his arms around her—chair and all.

JOAN: Susan . . . I have to go. (*She exits.*)

SUSAN: (*As she watches Joan go off.*) . . . He put his arms around her . . . chair and all.

(*Boat whistle sounds again. Pause. Susan picks up her pamphlets to continue her journey.*)

SUSAN: (*Singing as she exits.*)
COME ON NOW
COME ON NOW

SEE WHAT'S NEW,
I'VE SPLIT THE SKIRT
SPLIT IT RIGHT IN TWO
  AND THERE AIN'T NO HORSE THAT
  CAN'T BE RODE,
  AND THERE AIN'T NO MAN
  THAT CAN'T BE THROWED.

(*The Miner and Bar Dog enter the Bar Dog's area.*)

MINER AND BAR DOG: (*Singing.*)
  LAST NIGHT I GOT LAID BY THE FIRE
  AS I HUNKERED DEEP DOWN BY THE BURRS,
  I WONDERED WHY MY SWEET YOUNG COWGIRL
  DIDN'T TAKE OFF HER LONG SILVER SPURS.
  SILVER SPURS . . .
  SILVER SPURS . . .
  I GOT LAID WITH LONG SILVER SPURS.

MINER: I want rusted in the boiler. I want the jimjams. I want me so drunk, I'm gonna open my shirt colla ta piss. (*Pause. He pounds with his fist.*) Kinda hooch Indians trade their wives fer.

(*Susan enters.*)

SUSAN: (*To the audience, the Bar Dog and the Miner.*) This speaker you see here now is one jump ahead of the marshal. Stick around. I can get arrested any minute. (*Pause.*) No throwing of turnips, cigar stumps, beets, old quids of tobacco, or lumpblack. (*Pause.*) A rally is going on here in California. Open up your ears and hear me.

MINER: My brother's wife is in this here California rally . . .'n she is left my brother 'n nine hired hands by theirselves with nobody ta holler 'em in at night.

BAR DOG: Women oughta stay at home . . . where they got it easy.

MINER: Mules 'n women are jist alike . . . They don't know whether ya treat 'em good or not.

BAR DOG: Hey . . . you got somethang 'ginst mules? (*Bar Dog and Miner chuckle.*)

SUSAN: Now . . . ah . . . this country's in the middle of a contest for equality . . . a contest that . . .

BAR DOG: Set me up fer a bitin' contest. With a snake. I'll give the critter a handicap. He kin bite me first.

SUSAN: . . . a contest that will ensure the constitutional rights of all citizens.

MINER: Hit's Sunday. Don't you ivver shut down?

SUSAN: I don't have any Sundays . . . Now I know you're decent gents and want to do the right thing . . . and the right thing to do is give a fair chance to all. But the cards are marked. The dice have ten sides. The dealer's dealt us out.

MINER: (*Singsong.*)

Her heart is in New York
But her Butte is in Montana
God how she loves the hard-shelled
   Baptist lemonade.

SUSAN: I know you're decent gents and want to do the right thing . . . and . . .

BAR DOG: Save part of yer breath fer breathin'.

SUSAN: . . . And the right thing is a fair chance . . .

MINER: Ya can't sell a thousand-foot claim on a vest-pocket specimen . . . 'n ya can't sell us on no women votin' with jist you up there.

SUSAN: In the state of Kansas, that good state, they voted for women's suffrage.

MINER: Jest grasshopper yerself back ta Kansas, then. (*Both men snicker.*)

SUSAN: In the state of Kansas . . . if you would consult the newspaper . . . I can give you the newspaper . . .

MINER: Give us limb! We don't wanna buy it—jist rent it. (*The men laugh.*)

SUSAN: In the state of Kansas, the legislature is coming to terms with civil rights for females. In the language of the law that means . . .

MINER: *Limbs* is our language.

SUSAN: (*Trying to continue.*) Civil rights! In the language of the law, that means . . .

MINER: While yer "long-windin' it" up there, gold is sinkin' in the ground by the inch.

MINER AND BAR DOG: (*Chanting.*) Limbs! Limbs!

SUSAN: (*Swings her leg up on a beer keg. Sings.*)

COME ON NOW
COME ON NOW
   SEE WHAT'S NEW,
I'VE SPLIT THE SKIRT
SPLIT IT RIGHT IN TWO
   AND THERE AIN'T NO HORSE THAT
   CAN'T BE RODE,
   AND THERE AIN'T NO MAN
   THAT CAN'T BE THROWED.

(*Pause. Susan moves closer to the Men. The Men have been startled by her song and she now has their attention.*)

SUSAN: Do you know what baseball is? (*The Men grunt in agreement. Pause.*) My brothers were allowed to play baseball. But not me! Because I was a girl and baseball is not "polite." (*Pause.*) So you know what I did? I hid behind the trees and bushes on the farm, and I spied on my brothers. I watched them pitch a ball, then I'd go to some deserted place behind the pasture and I'd throw a hundred speeding baseballs into the fence posts. But I knew I couldn't really be a good player until I got on the team, because baseball is a team sport. When you hide and try to steal knowledge, you have to take second best. (*Pause.*) So I went out in the open, and I got in the game. When my brothers yelled at me, I just stood tight to the base. And I learned to play that game as it should be. And I ran the bases hard. And sometimes we won and sometimes we lost. But we all played, that's the American way.

(*The Bar Dog and Miner are impressed.*)

MINER: (*Extends his hand to her.*) Limpy Bob.

BAR DOG: (*Extends his hand to her.*) Three Deuces.

SUSAN: (*Shakes hands with Men.*) Susan B. Anthony!

BAR DOG: Anthony . . . Anthony . . . (*To Susan.*) You know somebody called Double Ugly? He come through here with some cattle.

SUSAN: Is he here? (*Looking around.*) Ugly? Ugly?

BAR DOG: He done took off. He left this here lariat and gun fer you. He said . . . "Tie 'em up and shoot 'em iffen they don't behave." (*Pause.*) He also said somethin' bout signin' some paper fer ya.

SUSAN: My petition! He signed it! Oh, Ugly! Ugly!

(*Marshal enters.*)

MARSHAL: OK—everybody freeze! (*Miner and Bar Dog run off, leaving Susan, who tries to hide.*) I seen you . . . Susan B. Anthony! (*Pause.*) Come on out! (*After a pause, Susan slowly comes forward.*) So yer the Susan that voted. (*Pause.*) I've chased you so hard I feel like I was run through the syrup-cane mill. I come through mountain snow on a dog sled. Winds was strong and dead trees was fallin' everywhere. Only way I could keep them dogs goin' was give 'em whiskey every mile.

SUSAN: How did you know I was here?

MARSHALL: You went back on your course. Nine times outta ten, a criminal does that. Just like a stalked bear or lion. It's the age-old thang in nature to deceive by doublin' back. (*He takes some bark out of his pocket and begins to write.*) When I make a catch, I record it ta my book . . . 'n if I don't have no paper, I use birch bark. (*After a pause.*) So you're *her.* I lost you fer a while in the Alkali Flats near Frenchtown.

SUSAN: You've been hot on my trail since Horse Creek.

MARSHAL: That's right.

SUSAN: . . .Elkhorn . . . Mount Idaho . . . Squaw Gulch, Woods Flat, Otter Lake, Mother Lode . . .

MARSHAL: . . . Big Hole, Bumble Bee, Yankee Fork, Wilson Bar, Carson

Hill, Walla Walla. I seen their smoke signals. Sioux is followin' ya too.

SUSAN: When I see a column of smoke in the sky, I just send an answering smoke signal back. Indians aren't all that unfriendly, Marshal.

MARSHAL: (*Shocked.*) You send 'em back an answer?

SUSAN: Of course, I don't know what I say. (*Pause.*) If a woman's so stupid and insignificant she can't vote, why take all the bother to haul her back East?

MARSHAL: Seein' a little rattlesnake in yer path . . . ya wouldn't let it move off 'cause it's too small ta bite.

SUSAN: Do you have daughters, sir?

MARSHAL: Five. None of 'em bigamists!

SUSAN: Neither am I.

MARSHAL: None of them for "free love."

SUSAN: Neither am I.

MARSHAL: Woman that comes out ta these parts by herself is half-bigamist, or half free-love, or both, one ta the other.

SUSAN: I can tell you haven't been to my lectures.

MARSHAL: What good is all this done ya? People is jist come out against you more 'n ever. People is jist voted you down again. (*Pause. He hands her a flyer.*) California just killed women's right to vote.

SUSAN: (*Looks at flyer and reads.*) A hundred and ten thousand for . . . A hundred and thirty-seven thousand against . . . It was close. (*After a pause.*) What good does this arrest do you?

MARSHAL: (*Looks at her defiantly.*) I cross many a river with cattle. Sometimes their leader turns back and the whole bunch begins ta swim in a circle. That circle's gotta be broke—or they all drown.

SUSAN: I've got women swimming in a circle. Is that it? (*A pause, then angrily.*) Why don't you people out here ever talk direct?

MARSHAL: You don't buy a horse is got brands on it all over. That's a sure sign it's been owned by a lotta cow dogs 'n ain't been loyal ta inny of 'em.

SUSAN: God only knows what that means. (*Pause.*) Marshal, we've been through a lot together. You're not going to . . . to . . . shackle me, are you? (*She holds out her hands to him.*)

MARSHAL: (*After a pause.*) Hell, no! (*Pause.*) But being a girl ain't gonna save you. Yer under arrest.

SUSAN: I've got good outdoor wrinkles from the sun. Some indoor wrinkles, too. I'm no *girl*.

MARSHAL: (*After a pause.*) You ready, then? (*Pause.*) Jesus, she jist answered the Sioux back.

SUSAN: Ready.

MARSHAL: I hear ya sing, too.

SUSAN: Marshal, you're going to hear my song from here to Rochester.

(*Susan and Marshal exit. Soft battle drums. Joan and Lavour enter.*)

LAVOUR: (*Looks at her tenderly; after a pause.*) Nervous?

JOAN: A little.

LAVOUR: Excited?

JOAN: A little.

LAVOUR: (*Looks at her lovingly.*) I think . . . I'll watch you take Orleans today.

JOAN: *Watch* me?

LAVOUR: (*Teasingly.*) Well . . . I'm tired . . . You know it rained all night. I had to get up early and dig a trench around my tent.

JOAN: (*Smiling.*) Didn't we all. (*Pause. Fondly.*) When I look back . . . I expect to see you, Captain . . . I want to see you . . . swinging that shining sword . . .

LAVOUR: I'll be there.

JOAN: (*Kneeling before Lavour to put leg armor on him.*) You're right. There's always the stink of death in my nostrils. (*Pause; still putting on his leg armor.*) All that can must carry torches . . . and tell the men to be careful of cannon holes—they're filled with water. They're little rivers. (*Pause.*) What is the last count of sergeants?

LAVOUR: Four thousand.

JOAN: Save them for the wall. Use our knights for the sieges. (*Lavour now begins to put armor on Joan.*)

LAVOUR: Follow the drums . . . do you hear me? And stay to the back.

JOAN: I can't do that.

LAVOUR: You must stay to the back.

JOAN: The closer you get to battle, the safer it is. You know that. The dead are always far out.

LAVOUR: Please . . . don't take chances. (*Pause. As he finishes putting on her armor.*) It's such a curse of a war, a bloody curse of a war. I long for the wars of my ancestors. (*Pause. He has finished putting on her armor.*) Please . . . stay to the back.

JOAN: The army needs its infantry. You know that.

LAVOUR: Do you have the map? (*Pause.*) The map I gave you . . . with the terrain . . . the position of the wall . . . with the . . .

JOAN: (*She holds out her two hands and cups them together, palms upward.*) This is my map. (*Pause.*) These lifelines are the gulches and creeks angling to the center of the drawbridge . . . where we assemble the archers. The end of the Loire drops down to a trickle out where my palms meet. Toward those little wrinkles there, the lancers settle in with the stone machine. I cock my thumbs, and they're towers looking down on the land below—our moving towers.

LAVOUR: (*He takes Joan's hands, puts them to his lips and kisses them.*) Please . . . please . . . don't take chances.

(*Lights begin to dim as battle drums are heard.*)

JOAN: My captain . . . will you be the first with me . . . to enter Orleans?
LAVOUR: No . . . this is your history.

(*A Lancer comes onstage bearing a standard, and hands it to Joan. The Archer enters. Joan stops in a victory position.*)

JOAN: If this is my glory, then I grieve for God's. (*She exits.*)
ARCHER: She's over the wall.
LAVOUR: Follow her!
ARCHER, LANCER AND LAVOUR: (*Chanting, as they exit.*) Joan, Joan, Joan . . .

(*Joan returns to the stage to plant her standard. Susan enters.*)

SUSAN: (*Echoing the men's chant.*) Joan . . . Joan . . . (*Happily.*) You took Orleans! (*They embrace. Pause. Susan pulls away.*) I'm going back to stand trial.
JOAN: With your victories.
SUSAN: *Little victories.*
JOAN: Petitions . . . the Marriage Property Bill . . .
SUSAN: Little victories . . . Women can't vote. Maybe they never will.
JOAN: Maybe . . . they will.
SUSAN: I need you. (*Pause.*) Who will brush my hair . . . when it's gray.
JOAN: I don't know what it's like to fight when you're fifty . . . sixty . . . seventy . . . eighty yours old.
SUSAN: I'll miss you.
JOAN: And I'll miss you. (*Pause.*) Reach. (*Pause.*) I reached out for you with this, my oldest arm. I found you.
SUSAN: I turned back. I found you.
JOAN: Reach. (*Pause.*) I had to. (*Pause. Points to audience.*) It's just another prairie. (*Pause.*) You won't be alone. (*Pause.*) The future will help you. (*Pause.*) Take the dark.

(*Susan reaches out to the audience as the lights go down.*)

END

Territorial Rites

Carol K. Mack

Territorial Rites was given a reading by The Women's Project on November 18, 1982 with the following cast:

CATHERINE	Kathryn Grody
SAM	Ron Leibman
MARGARET	Frances Sternhagen
GENEVIEVE	Caroline Aaron

A revised version was given a rehearsed reading on January 16, 1983 at Capitol Rep in Albany, New York and on January 17 at The Women's Project with the following cast:

CATHERINE	Shaw Pernell
SAM	Michael Arkin
MARGARET	Margaret Barker
GENEVIEVE	Cynthia Barnett

Territorial Rites was given a Studio Production by The Women's Project June 1 to June 12, 1983, directed by Josephine Abady, set by David Potts, costumes by Mimi Maxmen, lighting by Frances Aronsen, and the following cast:

CATHERINE	Robin Groves
SAM	Michael Gross
MARGARET	Kim Hunter
GENEVIEVE	Penelope Milford

SET: The interior of a converted barn studio in rural Connecticut. The walls are barn siding, roughly insulated, and far upstage is an old woodburning stove with a chimney to the roof. The rafters are filled with objects that seem about to spill over: stored boxes of family memorabilia, Sam's materials, and old suitcases. A simple working kitchen of fifties' vintage occupies the stage right wall. There is a counter for preparing food that juts out at right angles downstage of the appliances. To the center is a round dining table and a couple of chairs. Downstage left is an old couch. a coffee table, and many colorful ragged cushions. This area is *littered* with papers, magazines, books, objects never picked up such as plastic spoons from last summer's picnics and pieces of petrified food that even the cats have rejected. There are also a few cats. Accumulated bric-a-brac and dustballs are abundant. Downstage left a door leads to offstage bedroom. Upstage left leads to an offstage space where Sam's mammoth Celastic sculptures are stored and worked on. (This work space can be shut off by an offstage door which Sam slams on occasion.) There are two entrances to the barn. The first is offstage from near Sam's work space: the "Breezeway" entrance; the other is downstage right. Construction sketches of the giant sculptures hang on one post of the barn—but at the opening, a ficus tree stands in front of most of them.

There are two windows from which a character might see a corner of the adjacent main house of Margaret Leary, connected by a breezeway, and the trees and hills of Connecticut beyond. But at opening the windows on the upstage wall and over the sink stage right are dark. In the morning they are covered with frost. It is only in the final scene that they are clear and one can see tree leaves outside as the beginnings of Spring are in evidence.

Downstage of the barn, running the length of the apron, is a ramped "outside" path by which you could walk to and from a car or enter the barn through its downstage door. This "exterior" is used several times during the play, and twice the "exterior" and "interior" are used simultaneously.

In contrast to the realism of the interior, its edges, shape, "outside" path and lighting should suggest a "heightened" reality rather than a naturalistic one.

CHARACTERS

Catherine Leary (Cate). 30+. Warm, vulnerable, slightly off-center quality. Fourth Grade teacher and writer.

Sam Ehrlichman. 35+. Humorous, lovable, intense, urban artist. Cate's lover.

Margaret Leary. 57. Brilliant, elegant Medievalist. Uncompromising. In wheelchair due to an advanced degenerative illness (Multiple Sclerosis). Cate and Gen's mother.

Genevieve Leary (Gen). 35. Attractive, flamboyant, comic, but sensitive actress.

ACT I

A Weekend in February

Scene 1—Friday evening, mid-February.
Scene 2—The next morning.
Scene 3—Sunday morning.

ACT II

Scene 1—Two weeks later. Morning to afternoon.
Scene 2—Immediately after.
Scene 3—April 18. The day of Sam's opening.

ACT I

Scene 1

After five P.M. Friday evening, mid-February. Catherine and Sam enter barn and click on light. The interior is washed with warm amber light—the barn windows are frosted and black. Catherine and Sam are carrying bags of groceries; dressed in parkas, boots, caps, scarves and gloves. During the dialogue below, they take off all their outdoor clothing, put the bags down on the kitchen counter, put the groceries away.

SAM: (*Entering following Cate.*) Cate, one more body here is what I don't need. Understand? No more stray cats, no more relatives, and frankly I'd rather have a convention of Holy Rollers than your crazy sister!

CATHERINE: But, Sam, she's not anything like what you read in the paper.

(Catherine, a slight, pretty woman, no make-up, a man's cardigan sweater and something slightly childlike and vulnerable in her face and posture, fills the bowls of catfood and takes them offstage.)

SAM: Attila the Hun never got such press. Why is she suddenly showing up here and how long is she staying?

CATHERINE: (*Re-enters.*) I don't know. I told you, I don't know.

SAM: (*Picks up telegram from counter.*) "Save space at dinner for a herbivore. As always, Genevieve." Ten words. After ten years. Economical.

CATHERINE: (*Looks at telegram while speaking.*) It's eight years and why are you reacting this way? You don't even have to talk to her. Just go work in your studio and ignore her.

SAM: (*Nodding an "it should be so easy" nod.*) Her telegram triggered a couple of events at the front today while you were at school.

CATHERINE: What now?

SAM: Oh, just a few hostile moments erupted here in Nirvana. Would you like some vodka with the news?

CATHERINE: No.

SAM: O.K. I'll give it to you straight: Nurse Brendon has left us.

CATHERINE: On the rocks please.

SAM: (*Pouring her drink, hands it to her.*) Yes. Old Faithful Brendon, resident of nearly three months of nurse abuse, quit at three P.M. today. She had her limit like the others. Lady Macbeth just had to find her spot—that's all. Give her a final *zetz*. (*As Cate turns upstage to go to intercom.*) Don't go for the intercom, please. Your mother's resting now. Warming up her batteries for attack.

CATHERINE: Sam!

SAM: (*A slow grin.*) We had quite a day, teacher. Would you like a little show and tell?

CATHERINE: All right, Sam. What happened?

SAM: It starts early A.M., with the telegram. I head out for my usual run through the tundra and your mother, meanwhile, somehow convinces the garbage man to take away all my gear. I am talking paints, brushes, plaster . . . the whole schmeer. I come back and my stuff's loaded up, ready for the dump. I'm panting, blowing steam outta my nose, bellowing on the top of my lungs and the poor schlep thinks he's caught between two meshuggenehs, so very quiet, he puts it all back and takes off like the Indy 500. Foiled again, your mother dumps on Brendon and phhht!

CATHERINE: I'd better go have a look . . .

SAM: I checked on the Creature right before I went to pick you up. She was sleeping like Dracula.

CATHERINE: All the same.

SAM: (*Stops her with:*) I thought it was gonna be so peaceful here, you know? I thought I'd hear the snow falling and the bats copulating. "A quiet bluff," went the ad—"Rural Vistas"! Nothing in the ad about nurse interviews. (*Sharper than before.*) You know what I love, Cate? Silence. No interruptions. No involvements. Space and *time* and silence! (*To soften it with Yiddish-tinged humor.*) A little music on the side, maybe?

CATHERINE: (*Crossing to him.*) Sam . . . ?

SAM: I lost the whole day today, Cate! If for one day she'd leave me in détente!

CATHERINE: (*Takes his hand.*) I'm sorry. (*He kisses her hand. She turns, making room in a sloppy, impromptu style on the coffee table and dumps the shopping bag of homework papers on it.*) I better grade this stuff before Genevieve gets here.

SAM: (*Looks at lettuce.*) I think I'll put some hot chili peppers in the salad.

CATHERINE: Fine.

SAM: (*Looking in refrigerator.*) Where's my jar of Jalapeño peppers? I think somebody threw out my peppers. No obvious accusations will fall from my lips.

CATHERINE: (*Looking hopelessly at pile of papers.*) Look at this!

SAM: (*Slamming refrigerator door.*) The poltergeist has struck again!

CATHERINE: (*As she goes through mass of papers, something sticks to her fingers and she immediately recognizes what it is.*) Yuch! Covered with snot. (*Wipes hand, sets paper in pile with master sheet to correct.*) There's this one kid in my class who lives with his finger in his nose. I keep a box of Kleenex on my desk but he always uses his homework. (*Checking name.*) That's him! In the dictionary too . . . I was looking up this word last week, "zeugma"? And you know what?

SAM: No, what? (*He feels an irresistible rush of love for her, goes to couch and kisses the back of her neck.*) Hey, to hell with the homework! Shred it. Send all the shreds to the parents. That's *it!* That's it, Cate. You mail out all these shreds like report cards, see? So naturally the parents complain and you get laid off, O.K.? (*Inspired, he climbs onto couch.*) And then we go live forever on this remote Greek island and we grow raisins while you finish your novel. (*He kisses her neck. She smiles and continues correcting.*) Cate? (*She turns and meets his eyes. He does not say what he planned.*) Uh . . . What's "zeugma"?

CATHERINE: It's like a syllepsis. He got it on that page too.

SAM: What's a syllepsis? Don't tell me zeugma.

CATHERINE: (*Using her hands a lot.*) It's a figure of speech where one word modifies two other words but only makes sense with one of them, like . . . (*Improvising.*) O.K. Like, "Her golden hair and panties"?

SAM: (*Delighted by her, thinks a beat.*) Ah, how about: "She opened the door and her mind to the man with the golden hair and panties"?

CATHERINE: I love that. Sam . . . ? I love you. (*She kisses him.*)

SAM: (*Holding her. Teasingly.*) Yeah? If some other guy had answered that ad, I bet you would've held him hostage all winter.

CATHERINE: I'm a sucker for stray animals.

SAM: Thanks a lot.

CATHERINE: (*Hugging him tightly.*) How about you? Would you have found me in the City?

SAM: Tokyo even. Looking up at me over a pollution mask.

CATHERINE: I wonder . . .

SAM: My gentle Cate, my kind lady . . . (*Holding her.*) You know what you are? My muse. No really! I bet you're gonna float up to the rafters one day and hang there with a harp.

CATHERINE: (*Amused.*) Is that what I am?

SAM: You realize what you've done to me? I *feel* everything now! Like when I see you driving the jeep, my heart melts . . . I'm not sure this is even healthy. Hey, what are we gonna do about this, huh? (*Turns her toward him so he can look at her eyes. Slowly.*) You coming to New York with me, Cate?

CATHERINE: (*Quietly.*) Ah, Sam, I love you. But you know I can't leave her . . . I'm not putting her in an institution, Sam.

SAM: (*Hopefully.*) Maybe when Genevieve sees how it is, she'll give you a hand, huh? What do you think? (*Without waiting for answer, with burst of en-*

thusiasm.) I want to show you *sidewalks,* Cate! And bag ladies! And listen, you could rescue maybe a hundred stray cats on a good day! And plants? The streets are full of discarded plants. They don't even give them a *chance.* You'd be like the Green Cross of Soho . . . (*For real.*) Cate?

CATHERINE: (*Disengaging herself, feeling torn and sad.*) Don't count on Gen. Unless she's had one of her monthly epiphanies, but . . . I haven't read any of her new epiphanies in the paper, have you?

SAM: (*Seriously.*) I need you, Cate.

CATHERINE: I'm sorry. (*She crosses to intercom. With receiver in hand.*) Hello? Mother, are you all right? (*Listens, strained.*) Yes. I heard . . . yes. Can we talk about that later? No, she hasn't arrived yet . . . Well, I have Tofu for Genevieve and a salad and . . . oh? No, it's fine, no problem . . . Listen, would you like Sam to come get you? Well, I can't be in . . . all right. See you later. (*She hangs up, goes into immediate action getting dressed, avoiding Sam's eyes.*) Oysters. Mother wants oysters again.

SAM: (*Blandly.*) Maybe she's pregnant.

CATHERINE: Does this month have an ''R'' in it? You think Green's is still open? (*She hurriedly checks watch, gets her boots on, talking.*) If I run, I'll just make it . . . (*Grabs her coat from hook, stops.*) Could you get her in the chair, you think? Or would you rather get the oysters?

SAM: (*Nodding.*) Is that my choice, Cate?

CATHERINE: (*Avoids confrontation by speaking rapidly, getting hat and coat on very quickly, breathlessly vulnerable.*) One of the children said today that he read in the newspaper that, uh, lobsters live for forty years and even when they're old and blind they can find their way back to their homes . . . isn't that something? I hope that oysters don't turn out to have a life history . . . you know? (*Beat.*) We need more Tofu anyway . . . I'll be back in a flash, O.K.? Sam? Look, if you don't want to get Mother, I'll bring her over when I come back, no problem.

(*She exits to exterior. Sam, who's been nodding at her familiar way of handling things, follows her and yells after her.*)

SAM: You know asparagus scream when they hit boiling water? (*Sound: car door slams, motor starts up and headlights go on.*) Not many people know that! . . . Not many people think about lobsters . . . (*The headlights swerve and catch Sam's face as he slams his fist on the wall.*) Oh, Cate! You *had* to take the jeep!

(*As the headlights swerve away, the stage becomes dark and Sam exits after a beat of looking out after Cate. The lights come up again immediately on Margaret. She has on a heavy mohair shawl and a laprobe. She is elegant. She uses her electric wheelchair as if it were a Daimler. M.S. symptoms are only slight tremor in upper body when she is agitated, a hand tremor and occasional spasm which at times makes her drop things. Her mind and sharp humor are intact. She is a ''difficult'' woman.*)

MARGARET: George? Will Catherine be back soon? (*Silence.*) Has she gone to get me oysters? (*Silence.*) George? (*She doesn't look at him.*)

SAM: (*Flatly.*) The name is Sam. Samuel. Sammy even. But not George. Not Harry, not Irving. If you check out the lefthand corners of those sketches, you can confirm what I'm saying.

MARGARET: What difference does it make what I call you? You presumably know who you are.

SAM: (*Slightly amused, shrugs.*) Now that you put it that way . . . (*Crosses to kitchen area.*) You like chili peppers in your salad? Because I think somebody may have accidentally thrown them out. Of course, if it wasn't an accident, it was a felony.

MARGARET: Oh, don't bother about me. I'm just going to have oysters and a thin slice of lime . . . Nothing like the scent of oysters! You know a good evening will follow as snow follows rain!

SAM: Since when does snow follow rain? Never mind. I don't want to start anything 'cause my energy level's a little low tonight. But *first* of all, how could you send Cate into town, now of all times?

MARGARET: It makes Catherine happy to make me happy.

SAM: (*Casually digging.*) Yeah. I wouldn't flatter myself about Cate. I mean, she'll do anything to make anyone happy. Cocktail?

MARGARET: Port . . . (*Watching him pour drink.*) Yes. She's indiscriminately good. (*Taking glass.*) I often tell her, don't cast your pearls before swine, as our Lord said; but there you are.

SAM: (*Raising his glass.*) L'Chaim! Well, here's to the prodigal return and oysters.

MARGARET: (*Drinks in one gulp.*) May I have a tad more? I'm a bit nervous about Genevieve.

SAM: (*Ironic, pouring her healthy refill.*) Nervous? Why?

MARGARET: Such a sudden decision, such a long way. (*Pressing.*) Why *now?* *You* wouldn't happen to know, would you?

SAM: Are you kidding!? Two months before my show! Which leads me to *second* of all.

MARGARET: What are you talking about, Harry?

SAM: (*Enumerating.*) First of all how could you send Cate out in the slush, and *second* of all, when are you going to stop pushing plants in front of my work. I see the marks on this container here.

MARGARET: What *are* you talking about?

SAM: Come on! Tell me that's not a Ficus Benjamina. Between that tree and the garbage man, I'm drawing conclusions. You're trying to tell me you don't like my work.

MARGARET: Well, don't take this personally . . .

SAM: Go on.

MARGARET: (*Distaste palpable.*) It's plastic.

SAM: (*Puzzled.*) Right?

MARGARET: Well . . . with synthetic materials one sets out at a great disadvantage.

SAM: My early stuff was all in squid ink . . . you would have loved it. Unfortunately it's all at the Jeu de Paume now and they have a lot of steps.

MARGARET: (*Ignoring.*) And, you *did* ask . . . Well, it doesn't seem *big* enough, if you see what I mean.

SAM: (*That gets to him.*) Uh. How big is big? I mean, I don't see what you mean exactly.

MARGARET: Well, the George Washington Bridge, for example. Is small. The Ice Age is larger . . . But if you're going to entitle the thing, "Galaxy" . . . well!

SAM: You can call it Rhode Island.

MARGARET: Just look at that Ficus tree.

SAM: Yeah?

MARGARET: Isn't it beautiful?

SAM: Only God can, Mrs. Leary. Only God can.

MARGARET: Is there any more port?

SAM: (*Dejectedly, pouring small amount.*) Sure.

MARGARET: (*Resenting amount.*) To my eyes that tree is beautiful. An egg, is beautiful. And once in a while a genius might have made us believe that something manmade . . . say a window at Chartres. (*Holding her port up to the light with shaking hand.*) Something was as beautiful as a tree. Art was all for glory then, not some gallery showing.

SAM: (*Drinks a long drink of Scotch, smiles.*) I promised not to take it personally.

MARGARET: Of course, as a Medievalist, I'm accustomed to excellence. Still, I've invested in your work, haven't I?

SAM: (*Incredulous.*) Yes?!

MARGARET: Well, you are behind in your rent.

SAM: You're behind in your heat, Mrs. Leary.

MARGARET: I had understood it to be a summer rental . . . it had been my summer studio and never equipped for Winter, but then of course Catherine made all these arrangements.

SAM: Yes. And Cate and I have got it insulated now and made it just about possible for me to work without turning blue . . . You may think Galaxy is small, but it can't be moved until the show. It's captive on your territory.

MARGARET: I meant, conceptually small.

SAM: I got it.

MARGARET: But nonetheless, I am supporting you as I consider the back rental a loan.

SAM: Soon repaid.

MARGARET: I imagine alimony and all that plastic must be costly.

SAM: (*Getting annoyed.*) Yes . . .

MARGARET: How many of that last series did you sell?

SAM: All.

MARGARET: Oh, that's right. I remember now, they went to some industrial compound or compost.

SAM: (*Supplies the word harshly.*) Complex. Executive offices. New design. Won awards for innovative architecture.

MARGARET: A place of commerce.

SAM: They had a big lobby.

MARGARET: So do museums, Harry.

SAM: You feeling unhappy about the prospect of being repaid?

MARGARET: You must be joking.

SAM: You'd rather have a pound of flesh, wouldn't you?

MARGARET: That was *your* compatriot.

SAM: But you'd like yours in the area of my balls!

MARGARET: I'll go back to the house till Catherine returns.

SAM: (*Grabbing the back of her wheelchair.*) I'm saving my balls for your daughter. They're hers to mount as twere. But you better leave them alone.

MARGARET: (*In a white hot fury because he holds chair.*) Do you know when snow follows rain? On that hot July day that Catherine moves out with you. *That* is when snow follows rain. I'm not senile yet, Mr. Rosenburg.

SAM: (*Yelling.*) EHRLICHMAN! SAM EHRLICHMAN AND YOU KNOW IT!

CATHERINE: (*Entering breathlessly with packages.*) Sam! Are you fighting again? Are you all right, Mother?

SAM: (*Panting.*) She won. It's all right. I'm out of shape.

CATHERINE: Sam, why did you . . .

SAM: (*Overrides.*) I didn't start it, Cate, honest . . .

CATHERINE: (*Throwing her scarf and hat on couch trying to "move on" cheerfully, strained and breathless.*) Look at these beautiful flowers, aren't these wonderful colors, Sam? And I have oysters for you, Mother . . . and, let's see, look: a fudge cake! I'm glad she's not here yet. I mean you know how sensitive she is, Mother. And she's used to big receptions . . . (*During above she puts away things and they watch her like a movie.*) and "hype." (*To Margaret.*) That's what they call it where she lives.

SAM: (*In black mood, pours large drink.*) I'm going to do some work.

CATHERINE: Sam?

SAM: (*Starting upstage.*) I've got a lot on my mind. Seems my scale's off.

CATHERINE: What?

SAM: Scale, scope . . . size. Ask Hedda Gabler. (*He exits to upstage work area and slams offstage door loudly.*)

CATHERINE: (*Warningly.*) You know he's under a lot of pressure. And he lost the whole day today.

MARGARET: I find it impossible to become contemplative about polyethelene. Speaking of which, why is your sister coming home?

CATHERINE: (*Sits.*) I don't know.

MARGARET: It's all rather like a horror story, isn't it? A bit of science fiction.

CATHERINE: What?

MARGARET: The plastic morality of my eldest child and all her synthetic friends oozing across the wheatland . . . And then, those Eastern cowboys one sees in the newspapers, all heading West, in search of *something*. They meet in the middle. Then from sea to shining sea we have a landscape by Hieronymus Bosch. There will be such emptiness across our land that nuclear weapons will have nothing left to vaporize.

CATHERINE: (*To stop the torrent.*) Mother, I'm sure you want to freshen up before she oozes in.

MARGARET: I want to eat. (*Wheels to the dining table.*) The oysters, please. (*Cate goes to refrigerator. She puts the box of oysters on counter. Chin up, hears refrigerator door close, then.*) Catherine, I'm sure Genevieve will take one look at me and she'll want you to put me in a "home" as they call those farthest places from.

CATHERINE: For wayward girls or what?

MARGARET: (*Facing her, relentless.*) You know what I mean. A place where they *process* you like a sausage. A "skilled nursing facility" with a surplus of technological equipment and a prearranged outcome. I will never be a package, Catherine, wheeled neck in neck with other human vegetation . . . I am in possession of my aesthetic standards. Less flexible than Sam's. His standards are "popular" therefore relative. They would make Giotto gag.

CATHERINE: Please stop it. Mother. You're getting upset over nothing. And I don't see why you're taking it out on Sam!

MARGARET: I'm sorry. It's a shock Genevieve arriving from the wasteland so suddenly . . . what *does* she want?

CATHERINE: (*Putting oysters and lime on table for Margaret.*) I don't know. But I have missed her. And I am glad she's coming home.

MARGARET:(*Tries squeezing lime unsuccessfully.*) Well, don't put too much faith in her. She's absolutely heartless. She belongs in California like an artificial Christmas tree. That's Genevieve all over. Look under the tinsel, there's plastic. Where will she stay?

CATHERINE: In the storage room next to the studio. (*At a look.*) I'll clean it up. (*Pointedly.*) Our old room won't be vacant long. Only till we find a new nurse.

MARGARET: (*Takes that in.*) You have to be so *careful* these days. Did you ever notice, Catherine, a kind of maniacal quality about Miss Brendon's eyes, her movements?

CATHERINE: (*What now?*) "Maniacal"?

MARGARET: "Still water," Catherine. Yes, I think we're quite lucky she walked out without notice in the *day*time. I think we were all about to be murdered in our sleep . . . She had a quality of repressed rage about her. (*Challenging glance, "Yes, she did."*) Smoldering hostility.

CATHERINE: Vanilla junket are words I might have used.

MARGARET: (*Controlled fury.*) Do I still have the right to choose with whom I spend my waking hours? Or must I grow increasingly indiscriminate as I become progressively incapacitated?

CATHERINE: But what did you say to provoke her to . . .

MARGARET: Provoke *her*. She mispronounced three out of four words reading a text aloud to me in a tone signifying a kind of cretinous stupor. She let me know I was committing at least venial sin by cutting off her access to daily soap opera. And then this *illiterate* talked to me as if I were a two-year-old just because my bladder released prematurely. (*She drops fork due to hand spasm.*)

CATHERINE: (*Stopped in her tracks by this news—picks up fork automatically.*) Then you . . . you've had that problem again. Why didn't you . . . (*Attempts to feed Margaret an oyster.*)

MARGARET: (*Frustrated, lashes out.*) Euphemism got your tongue?! If I can't eat the oysters myself, I don't want them! (*Abashed.*) I'm sorry. Oh, Catherine, I'm not tactful. I do so admire that "diplomacy" of yours. That way with all sorts. But then people without enemies have no character whatsoever. (*Turns.*) There are times one must speak out!

CATHERINE: (*Still thinking about ramifications of symptom. Covers plate with foil.*) Yes . . . of course.

MARGARET: At the university, for example. The faculty loathed me from the start. Small, banal little minds. Put them all in a fish tank. Should I have played games for tenure?

CATHERINE: It's over!

MARGARET: Certainly is! No pension . . . Just, over. (*Wheels downstage to look out window.*) Genevieve must think of this as the summer house. We were happy here once, the three of us. Fit together so nicely, like a triptych.

CATHERINE: She *had* to leave. She needed an audience. But don't you think she's a remarkable actress? I don't mean in the soap opera but in her new film! You've seen the clippings . . . ?

MARGARET: (*Avoiding—looks out fourth wall window.*) Catherine? You know the trees that were planted for you and Genevieve? Hers has grown all crooked . . . the pine. Bent right over. Do you think she'll take it personally?

CATHERINE: (*Amused.*) Not if you don't point it out . . . I thought *hers* was the copper beech.

MARGARET: (*Firmly.*) That's yours.

CATHERINE: I don't think she'll remember. Dad planted them when we were very little.

MARGARET: Yes.

CATHERINE: You never talk about him.

MARGARET: What is there say? He left. Just like Genevieve. Entertainers both of them. Peas in a pod.

CATHERINE: (*Sits near her.*) Sorry I brought it up.

MARGARET: Even God left.

CATHERINE: (*Stops a beat.*) Did He?

MARGARET: Yes. We're quite alone.

CATHERINE: (*Affectionately.*) When did God leave?

MARGARET: (*Like a bedtime story to herself, as Catherine covers her with the mohair shawl and listens attentively, sitting by her like a child.*) Once upon a time . . . Yes, very suddenly. There was one moment in a high mass, when the host was raised, and the souls of the celebrants rose up to the vaulted nave and hovered there. The faces of all the congregants were illuminated by the light that sifted through the rose windows—each panel finished by anonymous hands in the service of God—an enormous, holy stillness fell on the world and *that* was the penultimate moment for God in our galaxy before He moved. (*Looks at Catherine.*) He knew it would be downhill from then on. (*Dim to blackout.*)

Scene 2

It is nine o'clock the next morning. Pale sun streams through frosted windows. Sam is drinking coffee. Genevieve enters from offstage work area. She has huge, restless energy and is often "on" although always vulnerable underneath.

GENEVIEVE: (*Walking around with orange juice.*) I can't get over how incredible your stuff is!

SAM: (*Embarrassed.*) Thanks . . .

GENEVIEVE: No, I mean really.

SAM: (*Nodding.*) Thanks.

GENEVIEVE: It's like magic! Like being inside fireworks! God, it's fantastic. What do you call it?

SAM: (*Ready to go under table with embarrassment; looks for help to Cate, who stands at bedroom door.*) This series is called Galaxy Two.

GENEVIEVE: (*With relish.*) Galaxy Two!

SAM: 'Cause the last show I did was called Galaxy One.

GENEVIEVE: (*Inspecting a technical drawing.*) I mean that is so *perfect!* It's like you worked from the point of view of an astronaut . . . I can see you dangling in space just inside these points of light and like there's only this space and silence and the stars! That must be like what it's like out there, really. I think you should call it "Creation"!

SAM: (*Sinking into his coffee cup.*) That might be, uh, too much of a statement, you know? (*Cate smiles at Sam's sheepishness, and is enjoying her sister. She crosses to kitchen to get some coffee.*)

GENEVIEVE: Yeah, I see what you mean. (*Directly with energy.*) You know when Cate wrote me you were good, I figured, well she loves the guy, you know, so what's she gonna say, he paints like connect the dots? I mean how objective could she be? But you are really exciting! Now, when's the show?

SAM: Next month. (*He starts choking and coughing.*)

CATHERINE: (*Pounds him on back.*) If you're going to ask that kind of question, you should learn the Heimlich maneuver.

GENEVIEVE: Hey, I'm sorry! Are you O.K.? Is he O.K.?

CATHERINE: (*Continuing to rub his back soothingly.*) He's allergic to openings.

GENEVIEVE: You're not worried?! (*Sam looks pleadingly at Cate to end topic.*) But you shouldn't be, you guys, really! They're gonna love it . . . my God, it blew me away the minute I got here. What time *is* it here, anyway?

SAM: Nine.

GENEVIEVE: (*Assimilating.*) In the *morning* . . . I'm sorry about missing dinner and waking you guys up. You and Mother both! Oh boy!

CATHERINE: It's O.K.

GENEVIEVE: She's all right alone like that? I mean . . .

CATHERINE: (*Pouring more coffee, interrupts.*) We have the intercom, and usually we have . . .

SAM: You're just in time!

GENEVIEVE: What?

SAM: For the interviews. Your mom runs through nurses like Kleenex. We had this one lady yesterday. Three months.

CATHERINE: We were just about to canonize her.

SAM: But here we go again! About to choose the victim of the week.

GENEVIEVE: I guess I missed a lot, huh? She's . . . in the chair all the time now? (*Catherine nods, Gen abruptly changes subject.*) Well, anyway, Sam, when I walked in? I mean I was really into *myself* and how the hell I was gonna relate to everybody and WHAM, I am hit by these absolutely magic shapes hurtling in on me from all sides. Wow! (*She gives him her brightest smile.*)

SAM: Thanks . . .

GENEVIEVE: I just want to share how I feel, you know? It's so stimulating. God, I wish I had my loom. I have this loom for mostly therapeutic purposes, but I had to leave it in L.A. Well, I really don't want to talk about anything too down because I'm really biorhythmically at six A.M., you know? I better have some more coffee. (*She stands and walks to the kitchen area.*)

CATHERINE: You want to shower, Gen? That'll wake you up.

SAM: (*Sotto voce.*) I think she's up enough.

GENEVIEVE: (*Cheerfully from kitchen.*) Have you guys ever been in a hot tub?

CATHERINE: Nope.

GENEVIEVE: (*Crossing back to table with coffee.*) Someday you should get one, really.

SAM: (*Agreeably.*) We have a giant kitty litter . . . It's always warm.

GENEVIEVE: (*Taking Sam's hand in hers, direct gaze.*) I hope you *do* realize that I am sincere about your work.

SAM: I do. I do. I just get overwhelmed very easily as Cate knows . . . (*With boyish grin.*) That's probably why she never says anything.

CATHERINE: (*Fondly.*) Tccchh, Sam! It's nearly two months to the show and if

I say *anything* he practically dives under the bed!

SAM: She says positive things all the time. I'm just not used to *effusive!* I'm going to go run it off. (*He starts to clear.*) Finished?

GENEVIEVE: I'm still hungry. You have any of that chocolate cake I missed last night?

CATHERINE: Second shelf, fridge.

SAM: (*As Genevieve goes to refrigerator, mouths.*) She on something?

CATHERINE: No, just depressed.

SAM: Oh!? Well, I'll be leaving you two. I'm going to run, shower, and work in that order and where will you all be the rest of the day when I'm working?

CATHERINE: (*With a small look.*) We all will be out of your way. Don't worry.

SAM: Thanks. (*Kisses her nose.*) It won't be much longer . . . just I have to finish.

CATHERINE: (*Surprised.*) Since when do you apologize?

SAM: (*Shrugs.*) I don't know. See ya later, huh? Gen, can I get you anything while I'm out?

GENEVIEVE: If you see a cute seven minute miler, that'd be nice. (*Sam exits. Genevieve crosses from kitchen eating enormous piece of cake.*) He is just *wonderful!* He's so talented and I love the way he looks at you. Want a bite?

CATHERINE: It goes right to my ass. I thought that was a family trait.

GENEVIEVE: I stand on my head now. I haven't gained a pound since I started.

CATHERINE: (*Smiles, then holding in emotion.*) I'm glad you're here.

GENEVIEVE: (*Lightly.*) I couldn't write more or call, you know? I had to get it together. Then, it got easier to stay away.

CATHERINE: I know.

GENEVIEVE: (*With "cover."*) But here I am!

CATHERINE: *Why?*

GENEVIEVE: You sent me a telegram. (*Digs in her pocketbook, pulls it out.*) Here . . . It says, "Help."

CATHERINE: That was last summer! It's yellowing with age, for God's sake.

GENEVIEVE: (*Noncommittal cover.*) Oh . . . well, I guess I had to think about it, like interpret it.

CATHERINE: HELP? You need a year to think about what *help* means?

GENEVIEVE: (*Coolly.*) I didn't come here to rehash old telegrams.

CATHERINE: (*Refusing to drop confrontation.*) Dammit! I asked you last summer when she started her war on nurses . . . and poor Sam, caught in the middle. I finally find the man I've been waiting all my life for and I . . . *Help*, plain and simple and where were you?!

GENEVIEVE: (*Hates criticism.*) Mostly on the freeway . . . Listen Cate, I'm sorry about the telegram. It takes me a while to make things my *own*, you know, to *respond*, but what can I do now? I mean I'm *here*, I'm not just here . . . I'm *here*. So.

CATHERINE: (*Eagerly.*) Take her home with you. (*At Genevieve's surprised silence.*) Just for a little while, Gen. So Sam and I could have some time alone.

GENEVIEVE: Look, it's like this, for starters since Tom and I split, he's got the house and . . .

CATHERINE: It's been real convenient for you staying out there and carrying on your vendetta so you didn't have to lift a finger to help out.

GENEVIEVE: Listen, there's a lot you don't know. (*Decides not to confide. Changes tack. Moves. Exercises.*) Cate? This place is so isolated and it never was intended for all year round and frankly it is truly bleak here . . . I was thinking she'd be better off in a place where they had some facilities.

CATHERINE: (*Interrupting.*) She'd give up on arrival, Gen. The naugahyde would kill her on sight. She closes her eyes when we go past the Howard Johnson's on our way to town? She hates the orange roofs.

GENEVIEVE: She's gonna have to come to grips with the twentieth century if she keeps getting worse.

CATHERINE: If?! Where are you hiding?

GENEVIEVE: (*Avoiding.*) You said she's in the chair full time now. What else?

CATHERINE: She's deteriorated a lot recently. She's had bouts of incontinence since last summer and the muscle impairment is pretty pervasive.

GENEVIEVE: But with M.S. she could level off. She had years of remission when we were kids.

CATHERINE: (*Trying to get through to Gen.*) She might live even several more years unless an infection carries her off. But Dr. Miller says she'll become increasingly helpless and her mind may be seriously affected. So even if she lives, she'll be a vegetable.

GENEVIEVE: (*Violently after beat.*) Dr. Miller? We have to take her somewhere else!

CATHERINE: (*Steady gaze.*) What's wrong with your home?

GENEVIEVE: (*Cornered.*) I'll run that by you one more time. At this moment it is enemy-occupied! O.K.?! And have you also happened to notice that she has not come out this morning to see me, HUH? She *hates* me!

CATHERINE: No, she doesn't.

GENEVIEVE: (*Compulsively takes more cake, eats.*) Not actively most of the time. It was always like Vesuvius. She'd kind of stare past me, dormant for a while, and then WHOOOOSH. All that hate would just spew up and I'd lie there covered with it . . . like, paralyzed. (*Pleads, justifying.*) That's why I had to get out. Get a distance on it.

CATHERINE: And? (*No response. Cate cajoles.*) You're such a big success now, Gen. You should be over some of this by now.

GENEVIEVE: That's what my shrink says.

CATHERINE: You should be able to at least make up . . . Mother says you hurt her feelings.

GENEVIEVE: She has them?

CATHERINE: It's been so sad to watch . . . since the retirement and now she's almost totally dependent . . . I don't know what's worse. I mean she's lost her platform and she's just trying to keep her *self,* you know? To survive intact.

GENEVIEVE: (*Colder than we've seen her.*) This survival intact translated means: here stands a monolith of parochial opinion, bigotry and selfishness. And you want me to forgive her and love her. (*Losing control.*) My God, it's like there's this ugly wart sitting there and I'm supposed to love a wart? WHY?!

CATHERINE: (*Used to this.*) Because the wart is your mother and you'd feel a lot better. Remember how if you kissed a frog he'd turn into a prince? (*As if to a child.*) Now do you think you *might* have hurt her feelings?

GENEVIEVE: Oh boy, I can tell you teach kids! She always favored you. And you never had to *do* anything for it. (*Jealousy palpable.*) No matter what I did she never cared.

CATHERINE: She used to pick on me much more than you, Gen!

GENEVIEVE: She was just making you perfect . . . and every once in a while she'd look at you like you really got up to her standards. (*Ruefully.*) But me, I never got that hope in her eyes.

CATHERINE: (*Wistfully.*) You never got those impossible expectations!

GENEVIEVE: How *is* your novel going, Cate?

CATHERINE: Oh fine, just fine!

GENEVIEVE: Yeah? How many pages since you saw me last?

CATHERINE: (*Suddenly busy cleaning dishes.*) Gosh, that is a really strange kind of quantitative question, isn't it? I mean I am teaching full time and taking care of Mother and Sam and . . .

GENEVIEVE: Hey, all I asked was how many pages?

CATHERINE: I'd say about, twenty?

GENEVIEVE: Cate, that's two pages a year.

CATHERINE: I look on it as a life work.

GENEVIEVE: But, Cate . . .

CATHERINE: (*Interrupts.*) It's hard finding three hundred and eighty perfect words a page. I get overwhelmed. I'm thinking of switching to Haiku!

GENEVIEVE: (*At that, laughs and hugs Cate, breaking all tension between them.*) Oh boy, I missed you!

CATHERINE: (*Energetically confiding.*) I feel like I'm under seige just getting through a day. How can I write? There are *hairballs* all over. I'm wearing the laundry. All my cleaning instincts zoom in on my novel like a laser. Mother always said, "Pick out those extra adjectives, like fleas, dear! Be merciless. We have too many adjectives in this world!"

GENEVIEVE: (*Sitting on kitchen counter.*) What're you trying to write *about,* Cate? Any good soft porn?

CATHERINE: (*Immediately sorry she confided. Withdrawing.*) You don't really care, do you? Why should some New England quarterly mean anything to someone like you? For one minute there I thought you meant to help.

GENEVIEVE: Hey! I didn't say I wouldn't try.

CATHERINE: (*Looking levelly at Gen.*) Forget institutions, O.K.? And forget specialists. There's nothing they can do.

GENEVIEVE: (*A beat.*) I'll . . . see what I can do, O.K.? You happy?

CATHERINE: (*Reassuringly.*) I'll get her. She's just as nervous as you are. You'll see, you'll have a good reunion.

GENEVIEVE: And you'll ride off with the prince and live happily ever after, have I got it right?

CATHERINE: There *are* happy endings. How could you go on if you didn't believe that? (*She exits to breezeway-connection exit.*)

GENEVIEVE: (*To herself.*) That's a real good question . . . (*She intends to stay, but at the sound of her mother's voice, she exits to Sam's workspace.*)

MARGARET: (*Offstage—to Catherine.*) I used to believe that God was dead . . . (*Appears onstage.*) that He became acutely ill during the second act of a restoration comedy and then went into a final coma during the Industrial revolution . . . (*Reflectively.*) It would take centuries for anything that huge to die. (*Cate looks around for Genevieve.*) Of course I revised my theory later. Now I know God never died. In 1347 He moved to another galaxy . . . Birds migrate, so do fallen angels, why not God? Genevieve left.

CATHERINE: (*Loudly.*) She can't *wait* to see you!

MARGARET: (*Briskly.*) One thing is clear: God isn't here anymore. Would He allow Man to watch television? The answer alone is proof. One has only to think of other galaxies . . . Catherine?

(*Cate has left to find Gen. Margaret senses her absence around the "galaxies" and wheels around to find her gone. But at the same moment, Genevieve enters from workspace, with encouragement from o.s. Cate*)

GENEVIEVE: (*With huge "on" persona.*) Hi, Mother! I'm home! How are you?

MARGARET: (*Wheels past Gen, not looking at her.*) Very well, considering a broken sleep.

GENEVIEVE: (*Hard for her to apologize.*) I'm really sorry about that . . . I'm really sorry about a lot of things. Could we forget about our fight?

MARGARET: You can.

GENEVIEVE: But . . .

MARGARET: I forgot long ago.

GENEVIEVE: (*Reacting to that cautiously.*) See, I really didn't mean what I said exactly . . . I mean like it was so . . . well, like Cate says I hurt your feelings.

MARGARET: Aren't you a bit old to be saying "like"?

GENEVIEVE: (*Stung.*) I don't know.

MARGARET: When the aliens land, they'll speak Middle English. The last text they'll have had time to decode will have been *The Canterbury Tales*. (*Wheeling to face Genevieve.*) I feel sorry for them, spending all that time educating themselves, preparing to land, assuming they'll be able to communicate . . . And, Genevieve, when I'm with you, I identify strongly with their plight.

GENEVIEVE: Ri-ight!

MARGARET: Well. (*Taking in her presence.*) Well, what have you been doing this last decade or so?

GENEVIEVE: I uh . . . just had a big part in a film that . . .

MARGARET: Oh, yes. I heard that you'd taken your clothes off in some new film. As you know, I don't follow the cinema because it is damaging to the cortex.

GENEVIEVE: You must read the newspaper, Mother. Cate must have told you I got some good reviews . . . why didn't you get in touch with me?

MARGARET: Truly I didn't know you cared . . . or remembered. Because you'd have to forget a lot to go taking your clothes off in public.

GENEVIEVE: (*With feeling.*) Well, I did!

MARGARET: Take them off?

GENEVIEVE: Care!

MARGARET: How would we know? What I cannot understand, Genevieve, is why you keep getting married. Why do you bother? The last one was for only two months. It's like moving. (*Pointedly.*) Take me, for example. I hate to move. I like to be absolutely still. This house suits my Benedictine temperament to a T.

GENEVIEVE: Does it.

MARGARET: (*Challenging.*) To a T! I've never been more content. I suppose after your hedonistic climate, it must seem drab.

GENEVIEVE: It would be better in color.

MARGARET: Why are you here?

GENEVIEVE: I thought I should come home . . . (*Improvising.*) Cate asked me.

MARGARET: That would be the first time you did something for somebody else.

GENEVIEVE: She wants me to take you on vacation.

MARGARET: I don't believe it.

GENEVIEVE: (*Jealous of Cate, "telling on her."*) *Ask* her then. She wants a breather with her lover. You've worn her out. She needs to get away from you.

MARGARET: She's being held spiritually hostage by that Jewish person.

GENEVIEVE: You're still at that?

MARGARET: I'm not anti-Semitic.

GENEVIEVE: Let's drop it, O.K.?

MARGARET: They're relativists, all of them. With their liberal passions, their Talmudic on-the-other-hands. Led us straight to nothing. Brain probers.

GENEVIEVE: Turn it off.

MARGARET: (*Going on.*) They got us into this mess . . . that Freud, Einstein, shattering molecules, dreams.

GENEVIEVE: Anyone who leaves the Church just because Mass is in English.

MARGARET: It wasn't that. (*After a beat.*) God moved.

GENEVIEVE: Oh, yeah? Well, if you knew when He was coming back you could develop a following. (*Challenging.*) I told Cate that no matter *what*, you wouldn't go anywhere with me.

MARGARET: Over my dead body, Genevieve.

GENEVIEVE: Well, there's always that! Oh, hey, listen, I'm sorry!

MARGARET: I can't believe this of Catherine.

GENEVIEVE: She can't take you hassling Sam this way. And she's not going to give him up for you!

MARGARET: We shall see.

GENEVIEVE: (*Stunned.*) You're *deliberately* harassing him, aren't you? I don't *believe* this! Don't you know you'll lose? Why not cooperate?

MARGARET: Yes, he'd be content if I sat like a plant and voiced no opinions. He'd probably like to cover me in plastic. The fact is I think he's already done two of the cats.

GENEVIEVE: You should *want* Catherine to be happy.

MARGARET: But I *do*.

GENEVIEVE: (*Trying again.*) Cate thought you would *like* to go to California for a month or two . . . it's warm there.

MARGARET: It's the seventh circle; that's why it's warm. She never thought I'd *like* to go. She's not stupid. It's the beginning of the end—making plans for me.

GENEVIEVE: Don't get paranoid.

MARGARET: I don't know you. I haven't seen you in so long you are literally a stranger. According to your scientists, body cells change every seven years. You are actually somebody else, Genevieve, since last I laid eyes on you. You don't really think I'd go cross country with a total stranger.

GENEVIEVE: (*Giving up, sadly.*) No, Mother.

MARGARET: Well then, now that we know where we stand, we can go on from here.

(*They look at each other unmoving as the lights fade to black.*)

Scene 3

Sunday morning. Catherine sits on the old sofa in a pit of cushions and newspapers: The New York Times *and local papers have been taken apart and heighten the mess of uncleared magazines and papers. Lights up on Catherine who is concentrating on a section of the* Times *as Genevieve enters from upstage pacing angrily around with restless energy. Her pacing does not attract attention, so she sits down and watches Cate.*

GENEVIEVE: (*Finally.*) Can I help?

CATHERINE: The nurses registry in town claims that nobody's available. So I'm checking farther afield.

GENEVIEVE: Have you looked under zookeepers?

CATHERINE: (*Looking at Gen.*) I'm really sorry it went so badly, Gen . . . it's going to take a while.

GENEVIEVE: So what are you circling?

CATHERINE: Right now, if you want to know, I am looking for part-time work.

GENEVIEVE: WHAT?!

CATHERINE: It's been a cold winter and we're running low. Sam can't pay till later and I've . . . got a little spare time.

GENEVIEVE: I don't believe this! Cate, you just told me you can't get through a day!

CATHERINE: We have to make this job offer extremely lucrative. It's R.N. and a lot of reading obscure textbooks, and no "Edge of Night."

GENEVIEVE: (*Sincerely.*) Cate, listen, I said I'd chip in.

CATHERINE: (*Embarrassed.*) She uh . . . won't accept your money, Gen.

GENEVIEVE: She *said* that?

CATHERINE: Last night . . . but she'll . . .

GENEVIEVE: (*Stung, quietly furious.*) Why does she have to know? We could "launder" it through some clean organization. You could tell her you won it at school bingo!

CATHERINE: I'm sorry, I . . .

GENEVIEVE: (*Interrupts, violently picks up* The New York Times.) O.K. here goes! Accountants! Accountants! Accountants! Lord there are a lot of accountants around or maybe there's a major shortage of accountants . . . How about her *own* money, then?

CATHERINE: You mean sell the house?

GENEVIEVE: (*Sarcastic.*) Oh, sure! (*Immediately, digging into paper.*) Wait a minute, I have found you a local dream job: Assistant dipper in a chocolate shoppe. That's two P's and one E and that means real fudge, honey!

CATHERINE: What does Oh, sure mean?

GENEVIEVE: (*Deadly.*) How about the collection?

CATHERINE: Come on, she sold that ages ago.

GENEVIEVE: (*Examines her hands.*) Your town paper is dirtier than *Variety,* did you know that? No, you don't know much. Well, when you were real little, I'm talking thumbsucking and the little white shoes? I was a precociously observant kid. At *that* time I was older than you, although for the press, let's understand I'm now younger.

CATHERINE: And?

GENEVIEVE: And our lady of the chair owned in her blessed name one humongous collection of Medieval art.

CATHERINE: Hype has seeped into your brain, you know that? She was just on the faculty and she . . .

GENEVIEVE: She had a *load* of Gothic crap. You remember ths bronze reliquary in the shape of an arm? (*Demonstrates.*) It was like this piece of knight from the elbow to the fist. Jesus, you couldn't give that stuff away in L.A. unless some freak had an underground *crypt* or something! God, don't you remember *any* of it?

CATHERINE: Sure . . . when I was really little I used to stand on the couch and look out one window and there were shelves across the window with small glass bottles—they were pale gold and their necks were iridescent. I used to sway back and forth to watch them change color.

GENEVIEVE: Early Roman glass, and you were a holy terror. They had to keep putting them higher up so you couldn't get at them. You even put pennies in the reliquary!

CATHERINE: She used to wear a cloisonné medallion—I think it had a unicorn on it and stars . . . But that was long ago.

GENEVIEVE: (*Steadily.*) Yeah?

CATHERINE: I can't possibly believe that Mother wouldn't say anything, I mean knowing what the situation is and . . .

GENEVIEVE: Have you ever *asked* her?

SAM: (*Enters briskly making machine-like noises, "vroom-vroom," from breezeway connection in running clothes, scarf, hat, and pushing Margaret in her chair.*) Look guys, I'll be back in half an hour and I am planning on working the rest of the day . . . I'm feeling this terrific *energy* so I would really appreciate it if . . .

CATHERINE: (*Tensely.*) We'll be out of your way, O.K.?

SAM: Hey, O.K.! Well, top of the morning to you, Mrs. Leary and regards to the cow . . . don't thank me, it was nothing.

MARGARET: (*Tensely to Genevieve.*) Good morning. (*Both Gen and Cate look at her a beat.*)

SAM: (*With immediate evaluation.*) Well, *I'm* off. I know you'll want to be alone, each of you! (*Exits to exterior and off.*)

CATHERINE: Mother, would you like tea?

MARGARET: (*Briskly.*) I think there's still some Earl Grey. If not: Indar.

CATHERINE: (*From kitchen, searching.*) Tetley?

MARGARET: Tetley is fine, dear. I wouldn't want to be any trouble. (*To Genevieve.*) Anything interesting in the papers? I see you've been through them.

GENEVIEVE: (*Intently.*) Cate was looking for part-time work.

MARGARET: Don't forget the lemon, darling! (*To Gen.*) *Was* she? Did she find anything interesting?

GENEVIEVE: (*Crossing her arms.*) Meat-hauler . . . But she'd have to join the teamsters.

MARGARET: A paying tenant would straighten things out in short order! (*Catherine crosses from kitchen with teacup.*)

GENEVIEVE: (*Clearly.*) But I was telling Cate that you may still have a few pieces (*Margaret takes cup.*) of the collection.

MARGARET: Of course.

CATHERINE: You never told me.

MARGARET: Did you ask?

(*Suddenly Margaret's hand goes into spasm and she drops the teacup on the floor.*

Genevieve is very still and Cate mops it up quietly and neatly. Margaret covers with:)

Do get some Earl Grey when you have a chance. That tastes like rust.

CATHERINE: All right. (*She pauses on way to kitchen counter.*) I thought it had all been sold a long time ago.

MARGARET: Almost. Piece by piece.

CATHERINE: I'm just . . . surprised there's anything left.

MARGARET: Enough to continue spartanly to my scheduled end.

CATHERINE: (*Not able to emotionally absorb new information.*) Mother . . . you knew I intended taking on part-time work. Sam's back rent has to wait till after the show . . . and you don't want Genevieve to help.

MARGARET: (*In a white rage underneath.*) Let *him* take the part-time job! Let him pay his rent! I'm not pushing myself off schedule for a second rate artist!

CATHERINE: (*Shocked.*) Mother.

MARGARET: (*Wheels downstage furiously.*) ''And there is nothing left remarkable!'' Nothing impeccably crafted. Mediocre all of it.

GENEVIEVE: Oh man, your vision is so damn parochial!

MARGARET: But it's *mine.* As is the remainder of this collection. And Sam is a decadent man.

CATHERINE: Wait a minute . . .

MARGARET: Technologically dependent as *you,* Genevieve, with your microphone and your cameramen and your celluloid. Cut from the same cloth.

GENEVIEVE: (*In a rage.*) Technologically dependent—me!? What about you and your machine here? If we were men, and you weren't crippled, I'd punch your teeth in!

CATHERINE: Gen!

MARGARET: (*Literally wheeling on Genevieve.*) I'm not ''crippled''! And you're not talented!

GENEVIEVE: (*Loses control, shouting.*) Who're you to say who's talented? You never created a thing! What have you done? Teach? Intimidate a bunch of college kids? All you do is say ''No''!

MARGARET: (*At Genevieve who is storming out.*) How dare you come back and interfere? *Sellout!* You have no standards!

(Genevieve slams offstage door. Catherine runs after her. Shaken, she turns, looks at Margaret in silence.)

MARGARET: She's set you against me now.

CATHERINE: I don't understand how you could . . .

MARGARET: (*Interrupts, pleading for understanding.*) She wants me to use up everything. Then where will I be? At her mercy. And we both know what she'd do.

CATHERINE: You owe her an apology, Mother.

MARGARET: (*Guilty under Cate's steady gaze, stubborn.*) She's just successful. Success is not talent. It is a by-product of common taste.

CATHERINE: (*Shaking her head; quietly.*) People have great respect for Sam's work. For his concept of space and his use of new materials. (*Looking directly at Margaret.*) But out of feeling for *me*, I don't think you should have said that.

MARGARET: Sam should be taking that part-time job, you have your writing!

CATHERINE: (*Coolly.*) That's up to me, isn't it? Mother, if I can get Gen back here, will you apologize to her?

MARGARET: For you . . . (*Directly.*) But I won't *go* anywhere with her, Catherine. You can see she's volatile, dangerous . . . and she hates me.

CATHERINE: No . . . (*Turns at exit, thoughtfully.*) How do you know I'm talented, Mother? You haven't read anything I've written in years.

MARGARET: I trained you to be relentlessly objective. Gave you the highest standards. Anything that satisfies you must be excellent.

CATHERINE: (*Picks up a paper from coffee table.*) Here. It's a Haiku:
"The old house vanished
Then the rose was swept away.
Now nothing is left."

MARGARET: Very nice. Simple.

CATHERINE: It was written for our nuclear protest by Noah Portland, Grade 4L . . . seventeen syllables. (*Looks at Margaret. Angry, hurt and defiant.*) I admire Sam's work and Genevieve is wonderful. Don't shut her out this way.

MARGARET: Her mentioning the collection to you was a deliberate provocation. Rather like the snake creeping into Eden with news of worldly pleasures. (*Significantly expectant.*) It would be an act of faith on your part to resist.

CATHERINE: (*Direct and angry.*) It would have been an act of faith on yours to have told me. To have trusted me . . . I'm feeling a bit used at the moment. (*She turns to exit.*)

MARGARET: Catherine? . . . Perhaps I lied to Genevieve. Perhaps I don't want her to think I'm at her mercy.

CATHERINE: (*Turns, intently.*) Is that the truth then, Mother? There's nothing left?

MARGARET: Yes. That is the truth. But don't tell Genevieve.

CATHERINE: I won't tell her, Mother, if you remember that you've promised to apologize.

MARGARET: You were both so sweet when you were little . . . you were like Rose Red and she was like Snow White with your translucent skin and soft innocent lips . . . you looked like angels.

CATHERINE: There were three of us. She's not the snake. (*Catherine exits with a last look at her mother.*)

MARGARET: (*Alone, thinks silently.*) Yes . . . Goodbye, Catherine. (*Wistful.*)
"The old house vanished
Then the rose . . . "

(*Lights dim to black.*)

ACT II

Scene 1

Early March. Two weeks later. Morning light shafts in the barn.

CATHERINE: But I can't under*stand*, Gen, all you have to do is stay in the room with her for more than two minutes!

GENEVIEVE: A terrific old game. Christians and Lions.

CATHERINE: You're not giving her a chance to apologize. You can't go on like this.

GENEVIEVE: (*Gently.*) I know. Cate, I'm sorry. It's time for me to cut out.

CATHERINE: I need you.

GENEVIEVE: Yeah, well it's all timing. Like you need me just when I need you just when she needs you and not me. Cate? (*She walks away nervously.*) Listen, I know you believe everything you read in the papers, but maybe you noticed the clippings I sent lately were all seen-with and no new films. No soaps, *nothing*. I mean I don't know when it started but, I just got so—*terrified*. I couldn't go out there. I turned up late for appointments. A lotta money going out and not much coming in . . . and then Tom? He really *does* have the stupid house and I haven't any work right now 'cause when I have to go out there I vomit. Isn't that wonderful? And you can verify this by making a couple of calls . . . (*She crumples onto couch, not looking at Cate.*)

CATHERINE: Why wouldn't I believe you? . . . I'm sorry. But Gen? You always bounce back . . . If you did it before, you can do it again. You've been so successful!

GENEVIEVE: Oh yeah.

CATHERINE: But you went out and *did* it!

GENEVIEVE: The defector. The big sell out! Let me tell you something, Cate.

It's uncharted territory out there. It's real scary.

CATHERINE: She doesn't mean "sell out." She just meant you made lots of money . . . But Gen, how else would you measure that *kind* of success?

GENEVIEVE: I just heard a curl in your voice.

CATHERINE: But I *admire* you! (*She takes out a book from under the litter.*) Look! All your clippings.

GENEVIEVE: But I'm like a pariah around here. She won't even take my money.

CATHERINE: What did you *expect* when you left that way? (*Gen shrugs.*) Did you get what you wanted? (*Gen shrugs.*) Well what *did* you want?

GENEVIEVE: (*With a shrug.*) I don't know. Recognition, adulation, trophies, happiness, love, limousines. Everything! What do *you* want?

CATHERINE: I *have* everything I want.

GENEVIEVE: You do?!

CATHERINE: Almost . . . I mean it would be nice to finish a page. And, uh . . . Sam can't take this much longer! He's . . . never mind.

GENEVIEVE: I'm making things worse by sticking around.

CATHERINE: Please . . . you can't leave this way!

GENEVIEVE: Oh boy, I remember that look! I remember the time I was pulling the wings off this really terrific looking beetle. I thought maybe I could peel them off like decals and wear them. You found me with these wings in my hand, you got that same look in your eyes. Like Sweet Jesus, why'd I get her for a sister?

CATHERINE: You always think I'm judging you.

GENEVIEVE: I can't carry her out of here on my back screaming! Damn, what about *her?* Don't you think she should offer to help out?

CATHERINE: She . . . seems to think we wouldn't take care of her if she were dependent on us. She's trying to control her future.

GENEVIEVE: And yours, kid. You shouldn't have to hold down two jobs. You really do get yourself stepped on.

CATHERINE: It won't kill me.

GENEVIEVE: It won't help your book along. Damn it, she *owes* you something.

CATHERINE: Gen? Maybe she really doesn't have it, you know? And she doesn't want to admit it. That's what I think. I think this property is the last of it.

GENEVIEVE: (*Realizing.*) She told you that, didn't she?

CATHERINE: . . . yes, but look, Gen, after all she hasn't seen you in years and you can't ex . . .

GENEVIEVE: (*Interrupts.*) You're such a baby. You believe the best of everyone, Cate. It puts a hell of a lot of pressure on us! We all feel guilty when we step all over you.

CATHERINE: Sam doesn't step on me.

GENEVIEVE: No? He just takes it for granted you work time-and-a-half while he does his thing.

CATHERINE: He's got a deadline.
GENEVIEVE: I forgot. You're doing a life-work!
CATHERINE: Why don't you stay out of my business, Gen?
GENEVIEVE: O.K., sure!
CATHERINE: I don't see you as an example of How To Anything!
GENEVIEVE: (*A long angry look, then:*) That's 'cause you haven't seen me at what I'm best at!
CATHERINE: What?
GENEVIEVE: *Packing!*

(*Blackout on sisters. During blackout there is much crashing about. There are sounds of objects slammed down on floor. There is the sound of a motor starting up and a car leaving. There is the sound of a refrigerator door opening and slamming shut, of ice being removed from tray into container, of a suitcase being kicked across a floor, of ice and liquid in a glass. The sounds, all amplified, become quiet sounds as the lights come up again and it is later. The sun is streaming through the windows, lower and more directly as the afternoon is progressing. Genevieve has "packed" and then thrown her suitcases around. There is clothing sticking out of the cases and the totes are sloppily crammed with stuff. Genevieve is pouring Scotch for herself in kitchen area. She has had a few. Sam enters from his offstage work area. He has been drinking also and is still drinking. He watches Gen down a Scotch and pour another.*)

GENEVIEVE: (*Seeing Sam, holds up glass as toast.*) Skoal! To absent friends and enemies. (*She drinks.*) Am I in your way here?
SAM: (*Not very aware of her, tipsy, sits.*) S'O.K.
GENEVIEVE: I'm in *everybody's* way, so let me know if you want to work, O.K.? It's just now that I've packed, I'm not sure where to go . . . You're sure I'm not in your way?!
SAM: I'm not working, I'm drinking.
GENEVIEVE: Oh.
SAM: In a sense I am also working.
GENEVIEVE: Well . . . where'd they go anyhow?
SAM: Cate took your mom to the doctor.
GENEVIEVE: Really? Why?
SAM: Routine . . . I don't know. Routine. Would you like to know how you can work when you're not?
GENEVIEVE: Sure.
SAM: This is something I have perfected over the years . . . O.K.? First, I call everyone I know and they've got their tapes on. So I talk to their tapes for a while and I drink a little, and I cook every raw thing we've got, see, and then I drink a little more. Now I'm finished working. I'm just drinking.
GENEVIEVE: So you don't mind.
SAM: What?
GENEVIEVE: Me, here.

SAM: Nah. (*Thinks.*) Finally a little silence and I can hear it ticking. Maybe I'm used to combat . . . maybe my adrenalin has stopped flowing. I can't feel my pulse.

GENEVIEVE: (*Offering Scotch.*) More?

SAM: Thanks. (*Silence.*)

GENEVIEVE: (*Holds her glass up.*) Here's to Mummy with her heart of stone.

SAM: (*Intently.*) The only person I know who could freeze a meatball with a look. (*Strikes him funny.*) She could market that, you know? Wheel into kitchens all over America and freeze food.

GENEVIEVE: And homeowners!

SAM: (*Realizing a momentary ''truth.''*) Your mother may be living proof that cryogenics works!

GENEVIEVE: Listen, this is *true*, Sam. There are times when euthanasia has to be practiced in self-defense.

SAM: Nurse Jekyll?!!

GENEVIEVE: What?

SAM: Are you ready to pull that plug? I'm looking the other way.

GENEVIEVE: (*Playing British nurse.*) Close your eyes and count to ten, Doctor . . . There! Done.

SAM: Gone? (*Radio voice—using Scotch bottle as microphone.*) All right, for you listeners out there: brain death occurred at six P.M., nearly sixty years after death of the heart!

GENEVIEVE: A miracle! Kept alive for almost sixty years without a heart!

SAM: And went undiscovered until the autopsy.

GENEVIEVE: (*Spontaneous idea.*) You know what I want to do, Sam? I want to read your fortuna.

SAM: My ''fortuna''?

GENEVIEVE: Yeah, I learned how from an Italian hermit.

SAM: No shit. Do I have to do anything?

GENEVIEVE: No, just give me your hand. Here goes.

SAM: What do you see?

GENEVIEVE: (*Looking intensely.*) Paint.

SAM: Oh.

GENEVIEVE: (*Fascinated.*) So many colors! Look at that. Let me see the other . . . wow! You know what I've always wanted? . . . Like I've always wanted to be painted all over with something edible and then get it all licked off.

SAM: No shit? You want some cake?

GENEVIEVE: When I was about five, I saw this picture of a painted Indian? And I thought how does he get that paint off and right then this *idea* comes to my head.

SAM: You remember it.

GENEVIEVE: Oh God! Yes! See, I drew this picture of this Indian lady who was supposed to be his wife and she's all painted the same way and I explained

how he got her paint off and how she got his paint off and they ripped up
the picture!

SAM: Pretty precocious!

GENEVIEVE: It was one of the major traumas of my childhood. I worked it
through though.

SAM: Good. You worked out everything?

GENEVIEVE: No. I used to be scared of men, see? But then I got older and I
wasn't scared of them anymore. But I was scared of commitment. And
marriage. Terrified shitless of marriage. And I had to work *that* out . . . it
was a priority fear, like death, you know? But then what happened was I
got scared of men again.

SAM: (*Sits near her.*) I'm getting depressed, Gen, that's very sad.

GENEVIEVE: Oh, it's O.K. now. Only now I have to meet the right man and
know that he's right and that it's not because of my fear of commitment
that I think he isn't right. Like Tom was wrong. Even if I had it all
together, he would've been wrong.

SAM: I'm feeling very old, Gen . . . could you read my fortuna and tell me if
I'm dying?

GENEVIEVE: O.K., O.K. Hey look at that. There is this wide streak of ter-
rifically good karma coming your way! Sam, when's the opening?

SAM: (*Jackknifing over.*) Oh God, my stomach. The word went right to my
stomach!

GENEVIEVE: I'm sorry! (*Kneeling over him.*) I'm always saying the wrong thing.
I'm so sorry!

SAM: I'll be all right in a minute. Don't talk . . .

GENEVIEVE: (*Noticing his ear, his hair, close.*) O.K.

SAM: (*Aware of her too; withdrawing slightly.*) I'll be all right . . . I'm fine. Fine.

GENEVIEVE: That's exactly the way I felt before a show.

SAM: Really?

GENEVIEVE: (*Nodding, has been bottled up.*) It got so bad, Sam . . . even filming
. . . *anything* now. Oh my God, hold me, Sam!

SAM: (*Rocking her.*) I'm sorry, I'm sorry . . . you all right?

GENEVIEVE: (*In his arms, slightly tipsy, free associating, very vulnerable.*) Makes me
feel so safe . . . like being in the wings of one of those big angels, you know.
Giant golden wings. You know the story of Cupid and Psyche? He used to
come to her in the dark and he left before dawn so she never got to see him.
So she lights a lamp one night to see him when he's sleeping and the hot oil
drips on him and he splits . . . now *why* didn't Psyche know a good thing
when she had it, huh? She's lying around in those wings all night, right?
Like so what if he turned out to be a *pelican* . . . I mean if she loved him.

SAM: (*Smiles, amused by Gen, gives her a hug.*) You O.K.? You feel better?

GENEVIEVE: Oh yes . . . much!

SAM: (*Looking at her, suddenly intense.*) I'm just realizing something . . . listen,
Gen, *here* you are. I can touch you, I'm holding you, and we're together in

time, *now!* But before you came, when I saw you on that screen, Gen? Your breasts were up there the size of bathmats! But my hands can cover them . . . think about that! How scale can change. Like what's *true?* What's true? Those giant nipples are forever and they're going to go on like Humphrey Bogart's smile . . . which we can see when we close our eyes even though we never met . . . never were even on the same street together . . . *That* is a miracle!

GENEVIEVE: Bathmats! . . . I never even went to the screening. How was it?

SAM: It was an O.K. film . . . But you were wonderful I was really impressed.

GENEVIEVE: Really?

SAM: Excellent . . . Gen, she says my work isn't big enough. But see, I'm *in* it, that's the point. I mean, if I stood where I really am, I'd be dealing with a whole different point of view. She's been getting me crazy!

GENEVIEVE: She doesn't know shit. It's *your* galaxy, Sam, and she's jealous. That's what.

SAM: (*Very aware of her physically.*) You think?

GENEVIEVE: Trust me on that . . . I know . . . Sam? What're you thinking?

SAM: Cate thinks I'm perfect.

GENEVIEVE: She's gotta grow up.

SAM: I'm thinking she's too good for me.

GENEVIEVE: (*Touching his face.*) Me too. Always expects too much . . . Ever since I can remember.

(*Lights fade to black on Gen's last line. Lights up on "outside" ramped area as Catherine pushes Margaret across the apron in the wheelchair. She is wearing a poncho and holding an umbrella over Margaret. They have come from offstage car.*)

MARGARET: (*In the middle of conversation wtih Cate.*) You're *sure* you didn't see them, Catherine?

CATHERINE: No, Mother. But I was *driving.*

MARGARET: (*Insistently.*) Well I saw them. An unusual amount. If you see more than an ordinary number of dwarves on the streets, it means a change of fortune.

CATHERINE: I never heard that.

MARGARET: It's not a saying. Just an observation. I have lived longer than you.

CATHERINE: In the rain, too.

MARGARET: They were carrying umbrellas. Normal size umbrellas. That's how I spotted them. It may have been a tour group.

CATHERINE: Are you feeling comfortable?

MARGARET: What was Dr. Miller whispering to you, Catherine?

CATHERINE: Now, *that,* I know you imagined.

MARGARET: You've just transposed your pronoun . . . Catherine. You're not concentrating.

CATHERINE: The doctor said that you ought to be in a place where more sophisticated help is available to you. Maybe we should all consider . . .

MARGARET: He *did* then, whisper. Words of change . . . and then I saw all those dwarves!

CATHERINE: You are going to rest now. We'll talk later.

MARGARET: (*Settling down, sadly.*) My own body is abandoning me . . . betraying me piece by piece. (*Exiting with Catherine.*) Ah, Catherine. What would I do without you?

(*Catherine enters the barn from the breezeway entrance and the interior barn lights go up full. Catherine takes off her wet poncho and shakes it out and hangs it up. She notices Gen's luggage. She notices the empty glasses and empty bottles and other stuff strewn around, and then she notices her sister's scarf and coat. She is puzzled. She calls out: "Sam?" There is silence. She walks to the bedroom door and tries the knob. It is locked. Surprised, she knocks on the door. "Hello?"*)

SAM: (*Enters from bedroom door, closing it behind him.*) Hi!

CATHERINE: Hi, Sam . . . you all right?

SAM: Not really . . . had a little too much to drink.

CATHERINE: I see . . . how come?

SAM: I don't know. It all kind of got to me, you know what I mean?

CATHERINE: The last piece.

SAM: I just can't . . . I don't know. You want to go out for a walk?

CATHERINE: It's raining.

SAM: Oh . . . I don't mind. I really could use some air.

CATHERINE: Well go ahead.

SAM: I could use some company.

CATHERINE: Oh. O.K. I'll change. I'll just be a minute. (*She walks toward the bedroom. He stops her.*)

SAM: Why can't you go as you are?

CATHERINE: (*Confused by the urgency with which he stopped her.*) Um . . . actually I have mud on my shoes and I'd like to change out of my skirt and put on some jeans 'cause it's raining. Is that O.K.?

SAM: No. Cate, for me, just this once. Just let's go, now.

CATHERINE: What's the *matter* with you, Sam?

SAM: (*Shrugging.*) I'd just like to go out for a walk, now. Without a big production.

CATHERINE: I'll be one minute.

SAM: Please . . . Cate. Don't go in there now.

CATHERINE: (*Truly alarmed at this point.*) Why? Sam, what's wrong?

GENEVIEVE: (*Coming out of the bedroom.*) It's nothing. It's just me. I think I must have passed out. (*Cate looks from one to the other.*)

SAM: She passed out, that's all. And I guess I did too.

GENEVIEVE: Could you do me a favor, Cate, and stop looking at me like that?

(*Blackout.*)

Scene 2

As lights blackout on Scene 1, the sound of a vacuum cleaner starts immediately. It continues as the lights come up on Scene 2. As the lights come up, Catherine emerges from the bedroom pushing a vacuum cleaner. She has wrapped a scarf tightly around her head to cover her hair. There is a huge outdoor garbage can in the center of the floor.

Genevieve enters in a different outfit and looks as if she's been crying. Cate has been crying too but her expression now is frozen over. Genevieve stands silently and watches her sister's activities. Cate continues to vacuum, taking the cushions off couch and doing them and finally, when she turns off the vacuum cleaner, she immediately goes to kitchen area and begins taking everything out of the cupboards. Cate clears every magazine, cushion, plant and debris from the stage by the end of this scene.

GENEVIEVE: (*Increasingly frightened by the robot quality of the cleaning.*) Gee, I didn't know it was spring. Like I haven't seen one robin even . . . Cate? (*No response.*) Well, I guess you know what you're doing. (*Looks at kitchen table.*) Is that mouseshit or caraway seeds? (*No response.*) How about sign language?

CATHERINE: (*Flatly.*) When are you leaving?

GENEVIEVE: Listen . . .

CATHERINE: When?

GENEVIEVE: Oh, Cate, listen.

CATHERINE: Bye, Genevieve.

GENEVIEVE: A little creature comfort . . . nothing major.

CATHERINE: Leave.

GENEVIEVE: You're worse than her.

CATHERINE: She.

GENEVIEVE: You are. Unforgiving, rigid.

CATHERINE: Whatever you say, your stuff's by the door.

GENEVIEVE: Cate, you're being . . .

CATHERINE: (*In even tones.*) I like this vinyl cleaner. It is quite powerful. It's better than our previous brand. This, in fact, is the most satisfying thing I've ever done. (*As Gen moves closer.*) Please leave now.

GENEVIEVE: (*In tears.*) I'm sorry, I'm really sorry, it was just a momentary impulse thing and if it *had* gone any further it wouldn't have meant shit. (*Silence.*) But it *didn't,* honest!

CATHERINE: (*Facing Gen, sounding like Margaret.*) Never in your life have you acted with any regard for the consequences of your actions. Never! You are like some very old flower child and it is really unattractive to be a dried up flower child. Worse than your irresponsibility is the fact that you have never in your life had any cause outside your *self*. It is no wonder that we are sick of all your so-called marriages. Who wants to mop up after a middle-aged three year old?

GENEVIEVE: (*Like a whipped puppy.*) I said I was sorry!

CATHERINE: That's not enough! You were sorry for the beetle, too, but it was goddamn dead! You always mess up, Genevieve, and then you say you're sorry. I've had it up to here with you forever. So just *get* out of my life!

GENEVIEVE: (*Immediately, with underlying emotion held in.*) I'm pregnant. I figure you should know that since you've been adding up my fuckups, here's another one to add to the list. The baby's due in six months, and *that's* why I came home. So if I decided to have it, you and the Loch Ness monster could hold my hand. (*Bitterly.*) But see, Sam's the only one around here with *feelings!* You're so goddamn emotionally constipated, you'll never write anything. You're too scared to live, how can you write? Sam has humanity and real passion in him! So he gave me a couple of hugs. So big fucking deal! (*Exit upstage, offstage exit.*)

(*Catherine is very still for a moment. Then she continues to clean. But now, as she cleans and stacks dishes, and throws things into the garbage pail, each plastic spoon is a memento and tears begin silently. Sam enters from his studio and stays out of Cate's way in the kitchen area. He opens refrigerator and discovers that all the food is on counter. He gathers some peanut butter and bread and makes a sandwich, all the time intensely aware of Cate who keeps her back to him so he won't see her cry. He tries to eat his sandwich and finally tries to speak to her indirectly.*)

SAM: So Rabbi, the lady vouldn't anyvay speak to me, if I got on my knees. She vouldn't let me apologize even. So vaddaya think? I *love* her, but *that* she don't believe . . . I should try again? (*Changes tone.*) In my whole life I never felt so *sad*, Cate. You know what I mean "sad"? Like the sun went out. It's like everything's grey and I landed back in Kansas and I'm never gonna see Oz again. I feel . . . like what's the point of anything, of the show or getting up in the morning . . . You hear me?

CATHERINE: (*Coolly, dumping more objects.*) Tell the Rabbi that I'm thinking about the time I walk in on you and it's *serious*. Tell him if this is what it's like when you love somebody, what's it like when you don't? You have a rotten track record.

SAM: That was all before *us*. (*Catherine looks at him coldly.*) I told you the truth about Gen.

CATHERINE: One available female, Sam. And New York's a vertical city. I'm thinking of the opportunities per square block. It's mind boggling.

SAM: (*Throws sandwich in garbage pail.*) I hope those were caraway seeds . . . It's funny, Cate. I'm thinking different. I'm thinking maybe this show could do good and I get to start over. Set up with some kids and hunker down and

CATHERINE: Don't start that now!

SAM: (*Intensely.*) But now I'm thinking so clearly. No blocks, no nothing. Just I want you. I want the diapers and the hearth and you in the mornings.

CATHERINE: (*Bitterly.*) Wait, Sam, it will pass.

SAM: Listen. I'm never going to say again you're painting me into a corner. I'm pleading with you—give me another chance.

CATHERINE: (*Close to tears, furious.*) You expect me to believe you now? Fooling around with *Gen?* You think I'm going to just cave in at the little boy smile and the easy promises?

SAM: It's a big responsibility having somebody totally believe in you and depend on you, I mean when you haven't ever been absolutely reliable before. And it makes you want to run for your life or something . . . Maybe I did it on purpose.

CATHERINE: (*Caustic.*) Don't ''analyze'' it. (*She starts offstage with box of plants.*)

SAM: Hey! Where're you taking those plants?

CATHERINE: Out.

SAM: They'll die!

CATHERINE: (*At exit.*) They were half-dead when I found them. All of them, half dead just like you.

SAM: What are you talking?

CATHERINE: When you answered the ad, desperate and blocked and all burned out, were you ''Out of touch with all human feeling?'' end quote? And was it a productive stay for you, Mr. Ehrlichman, because I love your thank you. (*Continues cleaning.*)

SAM: (*Watching her as she cleans.*) I'm thinking, Cate, maybe it isn't *me* after all . . . I know I said no marriage, no kids for a while. I laid it right out there. Maybe that made me safe, huh? 'Cause now I'm saying let's do it. Let's make the whole commitment and you're saying: no thanks. Maybe all along you didn't want any of it and you figured I'm the perfect freelancer.

CATHERINE: Pretty convoluted, Sam. Almost Byzantine.

SAM: Is it, Cate? You get rid of me and you get to stay safe at home!

CATHERINE: I want a clean start. No plants, no cats, no body. When are they picking up the Galaxy?

SAM: A couple of weeks.

CATHERINE: Good. I don't want any residue.

SAM: Don't worry. The Galaxy goes with me, Cate. You stay here with your twenty pages and every five years I'll visit you for the next paragraph!

CATHERINE: You'll be surprised how quickly my work will go with a little space and silence of my own. (*She closes a carton of stuff and it pops open. She looks exasperated.*) This is your stuff. I don't have any rope.

SAM: (*Getting angry.*) I'll get some. Do I have a deadline? I mean how much time do I have to get my stuff out?

CATHERINE: Take as long as you want. Only just don't try to con me anymore, all right? No more jokes.

SAM: (*Realizing he's losing her.*) If I didn't know you were in there, Cate, I'd say somebody's walking around impersonating you, just a bitchy look alike, not my Cate . . .

CATHERINE: Go away, Sam.

SAM: Look, I didn't murder anybody. Didn't even . . .

CATHERINE: Please! (*She exits with the carton.*)

SAM: (*Following her.*) I'm going . . . but, Cate, . . . someday you're going to have to forgive me for whatever you think I did . . . I'm only human. I never pretended I was perfect . . . in fact I clearly warned you I was an irregular. O.K., I'm going. But I'm not saying goodbye . . . I'm going to wait for you, Cate. You can't stop me from waiting!

(*She slams offstage door, car door and there is the sound of a motor starting up. Sam turns downstage to take a last look around and then starts to exit and crosses paths with Genevieve. They are both embarrassed by accidental meeting and sad. He exits silently. Genevieve has come to retrieve a suitcase. She is pensive as she throws a few things out, looking for her own totebag, which she finally finds and picks up near kitchen counter. She picks up beer bottle to have a drink. Margaret enters from breezeway-connection entrance, agitated.*)

MARGARET: What's going on? Sam won't tell me anything . . . what's happening here? Where's Catherine?

GENEVIEVE: I don't know. I'm leaving, Mother. (*Holding in all anger.*) Look, I'm sorry if I provoked you.

MARGARET: I hear you've spit out your gum. I take that as an act of contrition.

GENEVIEVE: (*This is "who" I am.*) People ask me for my autograph. Do you realize that?

MARGARET: People . . . well, I promised to apologize.

GENEVIEVE: (*Intently.*) People what?

MARGARET: Don't know much. That's all. I told you years ago, Genevieve, marry a professional man, live in a suburb, then do your hobby. It would seem more remarkable in suburbia than in history.

GENEVIEVE: You can't stand it, can you? That I made it!

MARGARET: You do have a mutant vocabulary.

GENEVIEVE: (*Anguish close to surface, twists bottle into her hand.*) Why?! I don't know why I had to come back to this horseshit. I really don't know! You know you really don't make a difference . . . you don't . . . (*She stops, suddenly, and winces with pain.*)

MARGARET: (*Alarmed.*) Genevieve, what did you do?

GENEVIEVE: (*Takes a deep breath, holds up her hand, palm out, bleeding.*) Blood.

MARGARET: For heaven's sake.

GENEVIEVE: Notice *me?!*

MARGARET: Get some soap and water on that at once.

GENEVIEVE: You drove my father out and you drove me out!

MARGARET: Your mind is a bog of melodrama. Genevieve, will you get that hand out of my face?

GENEVIEVE: You drove us out with your impossible standards. We didn't want to leave you. ·

MARGARET: "We!" You really are your father's child. Are you going to sit there dripping blood, or are we going to talk to each other.

GENEVIEVE: (*Covering her hand with dishtowel.*) What did I do to make you hate me?

MARGARET: (*Almost touching Genevieve's hair.*) I don't hate you, Genevieve. You're my firstborn. How could I hate you . . . I do resent that you chose to revile everything I taught you; to spite me.

GENEVIEVE: The world's changed. Nobody even thinks about flying buttresses! Nobody cares at all about anything you think is important.

MARGARET: Don't you think I know that?

GENEVIEVE: You drove my father out when I was only ten . . . I needed him.

MARGARET: I know you thought he was quite a hero . . . even then, you took his side. The pair of you always laughing together, he'd swing you about the room with that boisterous energy of his . . . that (*Stops.*) But that night when he threw me about in a different sort of mood, you were fast asleep.

GENEVIEVE: What are you talking about?

MARGARET: Your father had a rather slummy character. All surface. No substance. Extraordinarily charming. But he had roaming hands and eyes and worst of all a sloppy mind. It was *that,* his own recognition of his mediocrity, that started the drinking—drove him downhill. (*Turns. Wheels away.*) That man could not commit himself to logical argument or follow through any idea. He'd wheedle out with his charisma. The younger students especially were charmed by this . . . "spontaneity." He was very handsome. When we first met I was completely overwhelmed by him. I was then a doctoral candidate. I was his first student but certainly not his last. When he finally abandoned us, my family generously said, we told you so.

GENEVIEVE: (*Crosses to her.*) How could we have known? I was only ten. Cate was five . . . Why didn't you tell us before?

MARGARET: The faculty all believed, as you, that I drove him out. I was never "popular" but they had no excuse to get rid of me. I continued on annual contracts. There were three of us to support till you left.

(*Catherine enters upstage, stops upon seeing them together, and remains motionless when she overhears the conversation.*)

GENEVIEVE: I *had* to leave. (*No response.*) But I . . . won't you ever forgive me?

MARGARET: (*Sadly.*) I will never *rely* on you.

GENEVIEVE: What will you do if Cate goes?

MARGARET: Well, as you so kindly pointed out to her, I still have the collection . . . or part of it.

GENEVIEVE: You *do* have it then, she thought you didn't. Didn't you *tell* her . . . ?

MARGARET: (*Impatiently.*) It hasn't the value you place on it.

GENEVIEVE: But you said it would be enough to . . .

MARGARET: (*Snaps, interrupting.*) Yes. It probably will, according to Dr. Miller. (*Looking at Genevieve directly.*) You were just born when I bought those pieces. I was making a name for myself in the world of early Gothic art and truly I was an *enfant terrible,* advising collectors, museums . . . There was a huge auction. I was present in an advisory capacity. I had just a bit of money, and with it I bought a few exquisite objects. I was sure they would be your legacy . . . my best guesses paid for your education.

GENEVIEVE: You think I've wasted that too. You think I've been disloyal since I was born!

MARGARET: Genevieve, I have carved out my life with rigorous discipline. It is painful for me to watch you simply *reacting* your way through like so much flotsam, drifting from harbor to harbor.

GENEVIEVE: I've held you responsible for so long. You must be very lonely.

MARGARET: Don't confuse me with one of those slummy people in your scripts. I have music and solitude . . . there's sloppy thinking behind a word like lonely.

GENEVIEVE: (*Holding back tears.*) No thinking. Only feeling . . .

MARGARET: (*Wheels away, can't deal with it.*) I'm planning on dictating some new essays this . . . (*She sees in her line of vision that Catherine stands upstage very still.*) How long have you been there, Catherine? Eavesdropping is a breach of civilized behavior. One expects it of servants, not blood.

CATHERINE: (*Ice.*) There is an applicant for the nursing position waiting in the living room. Her name is Miss Pugh. She is an exceptionally tall Black woman who is deaf in one ear and because of her height, her ability to turn the other ear, and her cold disposition, she is impervious to insult. She doesn't like television or people. One might think from her first appearance that she was a killer, but still waters do run deep. And so I am going to tell her that she is hired. (*Turns to leave.*)

MARGARET: (*Clearly to Catherine, undaunted.*) Catherine, I have only lied to you twice in my life. One was about the collection . . . and the other was the tree: Yours *is* the bent old pine!

CATHERINE: (*Equally clear, from pain.*) But Mother, I have never lied to you at all.

(*Blackout.*)

Scene 3

April 18, the day of Sam's opening. Lights up in the barn. The garbage pail is gone as are all objects and bric-a-brac that covered all surfaces. The coffee table is cleared and is white and gleaming. There are no plants, or cushions or books in sight and the place is immaculate. The windows are now clear and through them one can see a few branches with new leaves and soft green haze in the background.

Catherine enters from the bedroom, her hair pulled back tightly in a bun, and wearing a neat looking cotton pants suit. She adjusts a ribbon at the collar of her blouse; goes to a shelf to get her attache case, puts it on coffee table and clicks it open. She takes out a small notebook and pencil. She notices a smudge on the table surface and wipes at it.

Genevieve starts across the "outside" ramp downstage with a gargantuan bunch of flowers, some of which drop unnoticed as she walks. She is dressed in a lightweight loose shift and is more obviously pregnant than before. There is a sense of voluminous presence between her enormous bouquet and her large self crossing to the downstage door. She finds it locked. Undaunted, exits and rattles the upstage offstage door. She then uses a key. Cate, hearing the key turn, stiffens, thinking it is Sam. Cate does not turn to look as Gen enters and looks around, taking in the austerity with a sadness registering on her face. She looks at the back of Cate's head.

GENEVIEVE: I just wanted to tell you I agree with everything you said about me and I brought you a couple of presents. (*Silence, no response.*) The first is this piece of advice: don't mess up your life, Cate.

CATHERINE: (*Not turning, flatly.*) I thought you were Sam. He has the only key.

GENEVIEVE: It wasn't well worded. I mean, if you climbed to the top of some remote mountain and the wise man said: Don't mess up your life, you'd probably push him off.

CATHERINE: (*Turns to look at Gen, evenly.*) I . . . didn't know about the baby. It took me by surprise.

GENEVIEVE: Me too.

CATHERINE: (*Cold.*) Under the circumstances, I'm sorry I spoke to you that way.

GENEVIEVE: I thought a lot about aborting it. When I first came home I was trying to decide. When I left I had decided and I had it scheduled this last month in New York and then . . . when I was in the waiting room I had this epiphany . . . (*Catherine turns away.*) No, honest, it was my last true epiphany. (*Sitting tentatively on edge of couch as if near a wild animal that might bolt.*) I finally realized that I had always had this incredible desire to be connected. I guess that's what I've been trying in my own way . . . just to be connected. Only this time, Cate, it's different. I have a yearning to have those little baby fists curl around my hair, tug at me . . . even now, I'm always thinking about this cord that my life passes through and joins his. And it makes me feel safe. Like I am so powerful!

CATHERINE: (*Restrained.*) It's a boy, Gen?

GENEVIEVE: Yeah. Tests. Cate, I don't want to sever any more ties or disconnect ever again, so I made up my mind finally . . . I'm going to go for it.

CATHERINE: (*Stiffly.*) I've been feeling sorry all month about what I said.

GENEVIEVE: But I deserved it. I got like carried away sometimes, needing
somebody to hold onto, somebody, anybody to need me . . . or else I was
like hang-gliding all the time, you know?

CATHERINE: (*Withdrawing.*) I know, but I'd rather not discuss that if you don't
mind.

GENEVIEVE: (*Suddenly embarrassed.*) Is there anything to eat around here or did
you boil everything?

CATHERINE: (*Rises.*) Sit down. I'll get you something. (*Goes to kitchen.*)

GENEVIEVE: Cate? You don't still believe about me and Sam?

CATHERINE: Yogurt?

GENEVIEVE: (*Unhappily.*) I'd rather have something less healthy. Anything
unhealthy? (*Watches Cate.*) See, thing is I'm a terrible drunk. I'd like to be
one of those people who say, ''Where am I? What'd I do? Who are you?''
But the thing is I remember everything all the time and this time nothing
happened. The moment kinda *passed.*

CATHERINE: (*Contained, returns with plate.*) It was inevitable. I just expected too
much from him and everyone else.

GENEVIEVE: He's as good as they get, believe me. And he adores you.

CATHERINE: (*With crystalline energy.*) You ever notice how Sleeping Beauty
wakes up and the prince carries her away on his horse, and Cinderella gets
to the castle, and Snow White gets wisked off and then it's happily ever
after? You never hear from any of those ladies again, do you? I have given
this a lot of thought and you know what I think? I think they kill them.
Because there *is* no happily ever after. So they have to shut them up. Toss
their bodies in a moat and let the dragons eat them. And assholes like me
still believe in happy endings! (*She puts plate down heavily.*) I kept this fudge
in the freezer. You'll have to suck on it!

GENEVIEVE: (*Awed by her sister's unexpected fierceness.*) Oh listen to me, Cate,
whatever you do, you can't *stay* here!

CATHERINE: (*Rigidly contained.*) I've accomplished quite a bit this past month
in solitude. I have spent much uninterrupted time writing. Miss Pugh has
kept Mother in hand without incident and I put the novel aside and began
working on rather intricate sonnets.

GENEVIEVE: (*Bangs the fudge on the table.*) My second gift is Sam's telephone
number . . . don't look at me that way. He gave me the number for you.
Don't you even know what day it is? Don't you want to wish the guy luck?

CATHERINE: I'm sure he's in the gallery surrounded by women wishing him
luck. He's very appealing. Don't you agree?

GENEVIEVE: From the fudge I thought maybe you'd forgiven me . . . (*From
real depths.*) I'm sorry, Cate. I've been through hell.

CATHERINE: Me too. And I also had an epiphany. I realized that I wanted to disconnect. I don't want to be your confessor or Sam's muse, and I'm sick of being everybody's milk and cookies!

GENEVIEVE: But this isn't the answer. (*Looks around.*) It's like a cloister.

CATHERINE: (*"Protesting too much."*) The children are on Spring recess and it is especially peaceful. I think you are just jealous that I am content; you've always been jealous of any happiness I've found!

GENEVIEVE: Oh *right!* I have always wanted to live like a nun in an egg. You've undoubtedly noticed my secret craving for a pristine life. It's too damn messy to *live,* isn't it, Cate? (*Turns Cate around.*) You know what you are doing? You're turning into mother!

CATHERINE: And what's wrong with that? She's a brilliant woman and a scholar.

GENEVIEVE: She was a total wipeout in life! A failure.

CATHERINE: She is eminent in her field. She's no failure.

GENEVIEVE: She never lived at all! She wouldn't compromise one bit with normal human limitations. And look at you. If life isn't always noble you won't play! You get a couple of scratches, you hide in your shell!

CATHERINE: (*Eyes filling.*) I'm teaching children and writing poetry and . . . I feel . . .

GENEVIEVE: (*Won't let her off hook.*) Yeah?

CATHERINE: (*Dissolves, ripping paper to shreds.*) Oh, I *hate* iambic pentameter. I never used to hate it . . . some days? Some days like everything I say I say in fives! And I, oh shit!

GENEVIEVE: Go on.

CATHERINE: I feel empty. Sometimes with all the scraps of paper in the silence I feel like a ghost—just surrounded by dead things—I feel a hollowness that is just . . . I don't know, I don't know . . . I *try* writing.

GENEVIEVE: (*Hugging her.*) Listen, you've gotta live first, then *after* is when you write.

CATHERINE: (*Lying in sister's arms. Cries.*) I remember when Sam came here last spring the sun just washed through the room and everything was brilliant. The flowers came up like flags and the colors almost hurt your eyes . . . it must have been Sam seeing the country for the first time . . . it must have been me feeling such *joy* . . . and now . . .

GENEVIEVE: Oh, Cate, you're not going to make the same mistake she made, are you? Look at me. Do you really want to disconnect? (*Catherine shakes her head "no."*) O.K. then ready for the third present? I owe you, Cate. I'm willing to stay here. It's up to you. Hey, put these flowers in some water, huh, before they all die. (*Pushes flowers at Cate and exits.*)

(*There is a sudden banging on offstage connecting breezeway door, upstage, as if something large is crashing against it.*)

CATHERINE: (*Walks offstage.*) Hello, Mother.

MARGARET: (*Agitated, wheels past, entering.*) I don't know why you insist on locking up during the *day!*

CATHERINE: (*Absently crosses to counter with flowers.*) I'm sorry.

MARGARET: I'd like some Port. Have we any Port? Where'd you get those flowers?

CATHERINE: (*Looks at bouquet.*) They're for Spring . . . (*Pours two glasses of Port.*) Let's toast to Spring, Mother. Everything's looking gentle again . . . all the new leaves.

MARGARET: (*With energy, sipping Port.*) I do love what you've done to this place, Catherine. So clean! We should have a painter touch up the marks on the walls. Then it will be quite perfect . . . like an egg.

CATHERINE: (*Stops, a pulsebeat.*) Yes . . . it is very clean. Like an egg.

MARGARET: Catherine? Do you feel all right?

CATHERINE: (*Holding glass up.*) Today is the opening of Sam's show. Shall we toast to that?

MARGARET: You saw for yourself the man wasn't serious . . . Would you rather have gone on till you grew older and then have him leave you for some fawning undergraduate?

CATHERINE: (*Hears the slip.*) What are you talking about?

MARGARET: A short time of happiness, a long time of pain. I know his type.

CATHERINE: (*Understanding, sadly.*) Do you?

MARGARET: My one mistake.

CATHERINE: Perhaps that wasn't your mistake.

MARGARET: You're the crown of my life; I couldn't bear to think of you abandoned . . . Anyway, you have work to do. You have your own standards to uphold. It may be a struggle, but in the end, it's worth it *not* to compromise.

CATHERINE: (*Looks intently at Margaret.*) Is it? In the end?

MARGARET: Catherine, listen to me, I've made an important decision! (*Wheels around, speaks almost gaily.*) I've decided to travel before I die. To go back in time to China, India. Crete!

CATHERINE: (*Absently.*) Really?

MARGARET: We shall leave as soon as I've investigated the monsoons. (*Cate stares at her.*) Perhaps as soon as school lets out. That is my decision. I'm going to sell the house and what is left of the collection. Genevieve has written offering to chip in and this time I've accepted. You'll stop teaching. Take a leave of absence. We'll set off as soon as possible. First we'll stop at Lourdes on the off chance that there's anything to it . . . then of course, Chartres, and we'll start travelling back in time till . . . well, who knows. We'll have to travel quite slowly of course, but then Catherine, you've always been patient. I'll dictate my essays to you and you'll get them ready for publication. There's not much time left. You must realize that. (*Pause.*) This last month—you have forgiven me . . . ?

CATHERINE: (*Crosses to her mother.*) Yes. (*She kisses her mother.*) Mother? I love you very much but . . . I have to leave.

MARGARET: (*Pulling herself in with difficulty.*) It occurs to me, Catherine, that certain species may choose extinction. The world may no longer suit them. The condor for example . . . The dinosaur. Perhaps it was a prescient beast. Found it impossible to go on!

CATHERINE: (*With bittersweet fondness.*) I won't be leaving you behind. I just have to find my own way.

MARGARET: (*Denial, wheels away sharply.*) Such a cranky mood you're in, Catherine, you are a cranky old bear today. What you need is a completely new landscape. Please do think some more about it. China will help.

(*She wheels to exterior ramp while Catherine walks to table where Gen has left Sam's number. She picks it up, looks at it, smiling wistfully. Then she goes to telephone and sits to dial. Receiver in hand, dials, speaks in a whisper at first when she hears the voice on the other end.*)

CATHERINE: Sam? . . . Hi, Sam?! . . . Yes. Hi! . . . YES, really, HI! (*She laughs, levels tone a bit.*) Sam, I uh wanted to wish you a lot of luck today . . . What do you mean what's today, Sam. The opening . . . Sam? You O.K.? (*Smiles, listening.*) You're under the bed right now? (*She laughs but there are tears too.*) Yes. Yes . . . I know you do. (*Wary, looks down.*) I guess about three and a half hours . . . Oh come on, Sam, you can't . . . O.K. I'm coming . . . I'll bring a spatula and get you to the show . . . (*Her face turns solemn.*) No, Sam, I won't be staying. (*Listens, closing her eyes a minute.*) But you were *right.* You'd only feel crowded again . . . I'm sorry, Sam, it wouldn't work . . . I have to be by myself for a while. (*Stands, with her own old gesticulation but finally this is her way of explaining.*) Listen, Sam, I'll make you a promise, when I know I can live without you I'll come live with you, O.K.? (*Listens.*) I don't know right now . . . But you said you'd wait . . . O.K. (*Meaning now and then.*) I'll try to hurry . . . Yes! I love you.

(*Lights dim to small circle on Catherine's face and then come up "outside" with a warm, golden light. Margaret is "outside" at downstage barn door. Exterior.*)

MARGARET: (*Calls to interior.*) Catherine? (*Weakly.*) We're going to have to get somebody in to weed the flowerbed . . . Catherine, can we talk? *Please?* (*Genevieve enters across ramp in the sunshine.*) Oh . . . it's you, is it?

GENEVIEVE: At the moment I'm all you've got.

MARGARET: (*Almost a whisper.*) Catherine?

GENEVIEVE: She has to go.

MARGARET: To Harry?

GENEVIEVE: Maybe.

MARGARET: (*Sadly.*) Ah . . .

GENEVIEVE: (*With a surge of sympathy.*) I think you lost the battle, old beastie

. . . Now what did your fabulous knights do? They picked up their standards and moved on. (*She picks up the light afghan lap blanket from the wheelchair.*) As I recall, the standard bearer would take the shredded banner from the field and . . . gently fold it for another battle. (*She folds the blanket as Margaret sits, weakly, unable to look at her.*) In a way you've won the tournament, though, haven't you?

MARGARET: How?

GENEVIEVE: You want Cate to carry on your impeccable standards, and write her books? I think she'll do it now.

MARGARET: (*In a dead voice.*) Where will I be?

GENEVIEVE: Why, with me, of course. Where did you think? Not a word, please. I know you think I'll feed you pet food. But I won't. I'll fly in oysters with a thin slice of lime . . . because then you know a good evening will follow as snow follows rain.

MARGARET: (*Looks at Genevieve.*) Catherine told me about the baby.

GENEVIEVE: It's a boy.

MARGARET: Very like you to be sure of the sex and not the lineage.

GENEVIEVE: (*Restrains herself.*) I'm sorry.

MARGARET: It doesn't matter. My genes are dominant. (*Hard for her.*) I thought it rather courageous of you to go forth alone.

GENEVIEVE: (*Tentatively.*) But I have you . . . ?

MARGARET: (*Hard to ask.*) Shall we stay here?

GENEVIEVE: If you want . . . until the baby. Then you're coming with us. (*Inspired.*) You know I've decided *exactly* where to put you, Mother. In a few years when I go back to acting I'll put you in my dressing room. You'll be my mascot. You'll keep hassling me like only you can. And I'll totally forget my stage fright. (*From a deeper place, risking, asking for forgiveness* now.) And one day, when I'm sick to my stomach, you'll hold my head . . . and you'll feel my pain, and like you'll say: Hey, you're not half bad, kid. I'm even beginning to like you. (*Silence as Margaret absorbs that. The rest is like a rocking.*) Maybe the three of us will go on tour. The south of France . . . China. And I'll just push you both along, sing you lullabies.

MARGARET: (*Moved.*) Oh, Genevieve.

GENEVIEVE: I know you don't like this century, Mother. But here we are! Like "it's where it's at, you know?"

MARGARET: (*With a hint of amusement and the slightest concession.*) "Where it's at" . . . I'll have to remember that for when the aliens land. After all, they should try to keep in touch . . .

(*During above, Catherine emerges from bedroom, her hair loose, in trenchcoat, shoulder bag over shoulder; she puts flowers in vase of water, throws out paper and she holds on "exterior" Margaret and Genevieve like a camera for one long beat. Then she walks offstage as the lights fade to black.*)

END

Heart of a Dog

a performance piece

Terry Galloway

Heart of a Dog, a theatre piece, was first performed by Terry Galloway on June 1, 1983, at The Women's Project. It was directed by Suzanne Bennett, with set by Maxine Willi Klein, lighting by Joni Wong, costumes by Mimi Maxmen, and sound by Jane Pipik.

Night. The interior of a room, the peeled-paint kind with salvaged almost exotic furnishings. Nothing's fussy, just slightly off kilter. It's pitch black until a match is struck and a pipe, cigarette or whatever the woman cares to smoke is lit. A lifesize replica of the RCA Victor dog sits in one corner.

When my mother's mother was a young woman she lived in a place in Texas called Snake Canyon. It wasn't called Snake Canyon for nothing. She lived there way in the middle of nowhere with her husband and four children. One morning she got up to see her husband off to work as usual; and then she went in to check on the baby.

My mother says she remembers waking up for some reason and there was her mother standing in the doorway—barefoot, still in her nightgown, her hair still down.

The baby was lying just as still, a little death bubble coming out of his nose.

My mother says her mother didn't say a word, didn't make a sound. She just picked that baby up and ran; she ran, just as dawn was breaking, barefoot through Snake Canyon.

(She turns on a light.)

That's the kind of bedtime story my mother always tells us when we go home. And now is it any wonder that I'm up in the middle of the night expecting . . . expecting what?

(The alarm clock rings and flashes. She's slightly startled.)

Hah. Good scare. *(She stops the alarm.)* It's midnight. And I'm not famous yet. Shit. But what do you care? You love me anyway, right? Sure you do. Well, come on. (*She makes a coaxing sound.*) Here dog! (*A kissing appeal.*) Look, dog! (*She holds up a bone.*) A measure of God's grace and it's all yours if you just crawl over and slobber all over me, huh? . . . Nope? . . . How very un-dog-like. Let me get a better look at you . . . Ahhh. So. It's a wolf at the door. Well suit yourself. Me? I like bones . . .

bones, mother, is how you scare me. Like the silence
of Snake Canyon when your own mother ran barefoot—
in her arms your infant brother (death's blue
bubble from nose to lip still unburst).

bones, mother, is how you scare me. Like the jazz
you sang in all those nightclubs in Berlin—
the red dress heating up your skin as the boys
watch, sweating and smoking (your own thin
handsome soldier among them).

bones, mother, is how you scare me. Like the night
you stuck your bridge out, playing the toothless crone—
terrified by how suddenly beauty aged, we begged
you to be beautiful again (none of our own
young faces quite as beautiful as yours).

bones, mother, is how you scare me. Like the thought
of you with your father's eyes weeping his death—
all the imagined future husked to the flesh.
bones, mother, is how you scare me.
As familiar to me as this flat blue Texas sky
and the story of your own mother who ran barefoot
through the silence of Snake Canyon.

That's a poem I wrote for my mother on Mother's Day. A box of choco-lates, a knot of flowers and a card with skull and crossbones. She laughed. (*She laughs a melodramatically wicked laugh and places the bone in front of the dog.*) That's the last of that. The cupboard is now officially bare—one bone and (*accessing*) one beer, fleshless and lukewarm. Shall we party? Toss caution to the winds? Break it out, crack it open, 'ere it shall wither pluck the red rose?!! Let's! . . . If I may do the honors: (*On her knees to the gods.*) We are grateful to be spared the attentions of your appetite and thankful for the bones of those less for-tunate. (*She takes a long swig of beer.*)

You ever see that movie about the Giant Ants? . . . They came from beyond and landed at night.

There'd be this shot of a wooded road—the moon fat and casting shadows.

This guy would come whistling by and then he'd hear something—NENENE-
NENENE like a pulsing machine—NENENENENENE—and he'd stop,
a puzzled look on his face. NENENENENENE louder and louder; he was
never afraid, just confused—what was that sound? NENENENENE-
NENENE; and then a shadow would cover the moon and he'd look up and
see—

I never looked but my sister did and screamed her guts out.

We must have seen that movie a million times when we were kids in Berlin
and life was less fearful. And we used that sound whenever we'd play scare
NENENENENENENENENEEEEEK. (*She has frightened herself.*)

I wish there was something to eat. Let me rummage around. (*She starts looking and muttering to herself.*) If only I could get practical we wouldn't be in this
mess. Hiding out till the miracle comes. I'm too damn romantic is what—if
it's not Princess Charming it's the saviour of the oppressed. And where's Em-
ma Goldman when you need her? Remember all that fire and purpose?!

ASK FOR WORK. IF THEY WILL NOT GIVE YOU WORK ASK
FOR BREAD. IF THEY WILL NOT GIVE YOU BREAD, *EAT THE
RICH*!

(*She sits.*) Ahh! Potato chips! Just as well. There ain't no riches near this
dump. (*Tastes.*) Stale. Shit . . . That it should come to this. Who would of
thunk it . .

My great grandma and great Aunt Eve, they could predict. Or just see
something in the shadow of the future. They were twins, dog, and they lived
to be 93 and died within three months of each other. And they'd been there
right before that baby died. They'd travelled by train through the night; and
when they got back to Burkburnett, they put their bags down in the hall and
they made a pot of tea. And my Great Aunt Eve looking at the tea leaves said,
"Ava, don't bother to unpack those bags. Somebody just died."

This reminds me of staying up all night long on the holidays and all the
women in the kitchen telling stories—stories about who lived and how they
died and what they wore and everybody doing the different voices.

You like mysteries, dog? Those were our favorites. Like how my Daddy had
this dream about Roosevelt dying and when he opened the paper next morning it was just like he had dreamed. My family believes in those things—visions and dreams.

I had visions, too. When I was nine I could hear the voice of God and leave
my body to fly with the demons. I'd be sitting on the back end of a car looking
up at the stars and all of a sudden I'd be six feet away looking at myself looking
up at the stars.

But that's a cheat. See, you're looking at a modern medical accident. That's
a story my mother isn't fond of telling.

When she was seven months pregnant with me, she developed a kidney infection. It must have been serious because they pumped her with antibiotics
and waited for the lights to dim. But she lived, I was born and all was bright.

But my life had been irrevocably changed.

Nine years later, down came the visions. Eventually they burned themselves out. But when we left Germany and moved back to Texas they found that it was, and I quote: "A chemical imbalance caused by the introduction of drugs to the fetal nervous system" that had left me not quite blind as a bat but definitely deaf as a doornail.

Even then I could feel a draft: the door to a kinder world was swinging closed. Slam/Click/Locked! Brrrrr. There fed the freak.

It was a fat little pig child with a roundhead haircut; It wore these thick pink cat-eye glasses and cracked Its two front teeth playing games of death; It had just started Its period and Its boobs had popped out; It wore a hearing aid the size of a small transistor radio that rode between Its breasts like a third one. Every step It took was a clamorous humiliation—BOUNCE BOUNCE BEEP BEEP BLEED BLEED! *It* was *me*. And I froze.

They shipped me off to the Lions Camp for Crippled Children hoping for an early thaw. That summer I won the swimming award! Hardly fair considering I was the only one who could do much more than float, but everyone won something, right?

There was a grand ceremony and awards were pouring out. Kids were clumping up on crutches, braces and artificial legs; being wheeled up in wheelchairs, pushed up in wheeled beds and drawn up by pulleys. So when it came time for me to accept my award, I limped all the way up to the stage!

Ah, it wasn't unrelentingly grim. We had our jokes. You know the blind man in the china shop joke? You've heard it but you're in the mood to hear it again. How nice! Ok, so this blind guy goes into a china shop and there's this table loaded with priceless crystals, antique watches and clocks, invaluable collectors' items. The blind guy picks up his cane and starts beating the shit out of it—WHAMWHAMWHAM! The proprietor runs up screaming, "What the hell do you think you're doing!!" The blind guy says, "Oh, just looking."

(She laughs at her own joke.)

My best friend that summer was a fourteen-year-old girl gone from the waist down. We were just like that. *(Crosses her fingers.)* I'd race her bed down this steep incline to give her some speed. My first summer romance. *(Crosses her fingers.)* Just like that.

I always wonder what happened to her. Children like that don't live very long. But if I ever found her again what would I say? What could anyone possibly say? *(She goes to the typewriter.)*

Dear Friend,
    I know just how you feel.
But remember, nobody's the real thing.
I mean just look at me—no ears, weak eyes, teeth broke,

fat butt and *these legs!* No, I do not have beautiful legs
not even here in New York City.

But remember this honey when it all starts getting
you down—People love their freaks! Didn't you know that?
And of course it helps to have a beautiful face (which I do).
And how are things in Texas anyway, beautiful?
I can just imagine. I mean my parents were worried too
that I might not ever find my rightful place. You know—
no ears, weak eyes, teeth broke, fat butt and these legs!
But it's different somehow out here. You'd never believe it
but *people love their freaks!*

As for me, well ever since I took up the old trombone
my status changed: suddenly this—no ears, weak eyes,
teeth broke, fat butt and these legs—suddenly, they're
in demand! And of course it helps to be a wizard on the old
trombone (which I am). But you've gotta remember honey
when it seems too much to bear—*people love their freaks.*
I'm speaking from experience here.
People love their freaks.

Well the band's just starting up so I gotta go,
but I'll write you swethbeart real soon. And no
I'll never forget those beautiful afternoons
when I pushed your wheeled bed along the banks
of the Rio Grande and moved your head tenderly to the side
so you could see across to the Mexico of your dreams.
Our kisses were the purest love I've ever had.
And I'll never forget them or you my darling
even though this busy life pushes me even now
to the Four Corners.
No, I'll never forget them or you.
And I'll write. I promise. Real soon.

It's a doggy dog world. (*Extends her hand.*) Wanna bite? That reminds me, I
could sure use some advice. Can you help me, dog? Tell me, would there be a
right way or a wrong way to end it all if all had ended? What is the proper eti-
quette of suicide? The one woman who ought to know already took her last
leap out of polite society. I wonder what she would have had to say about it
. . .

(*She takes on a dumbell voice.*) Dear Ms. Vanderbilt, how how can a . . . a . . .
(*she looks for a likely object and finds*) a cheese grater be used to aid one's self
departure? Questioningly yours.
(*Ms. Vanderbilt replies.*) Cheese grater across the wrist (*she demonstrates with
vehemence*) is definitely the wrong way. Cheese grater along the vein (*another*

demo) is . . . quicker.

(*Dumbell voice.*) Dear Ms. Vanderbilt, thank you for your advice concerning my method of self demise. Now having chosen I find myself with nothing to wear. Any suggestions?

(*Ms. Vanderbilt.*) On this occasion of self liberation, one is free to dress according to one's own wishes. But as a general rule, whether stark naked or formally attired, always wear your pearls!

(*Dumbell voice.*) Dear Ms. Vanderbilt, I'm all dressed up and ready to go! But now I'm having trouble finding an appropriate exit line. Can you help me there?

(*Ms. Vanderbilt.*) A final word about final words—whether written or spoken they are always better done in French. "Vous me faites deguealer, au revoir!" sounds infinitely more refined than "You make me puke, good-bye!" Don't you think? Follow these simple rules of self departure and you will have the satisfaction of knowing that you have died as you have lived. And that now, as always, dying well is the last revenge!

I can't believe I did that! (*She licks the blood off her wrists and unselfconsciously smacks her chops.*) That must be why people kill themselves. They can't stand the ways their own minds work, their own blackened souls, their own perverted lusts. Ahhh, but of those matters who is left to say? It's always Dracula who breaks the long silence to speak . . .

I am not entirely without a soul.
I have expressed much tenderness.
My lips gliding with such control
over the soft temptations of a lovely neck.

I have deliberately restrained the disturbing fangs—
my smile kept carefully even and small.
And even as the night has bent me tighter
in a mesmerizing pang,
I have lowered the intent
red eyes.

I have known despair not
completely one of hunger: the gaunt
incapable figure, wrapped in a somber cloak,
walking the black streets. And the stars
so inescapable.

And even I—seeing the human ruin
in evidence about me, seeing the useless charms
they carried to deflect me—even I, in these moments

when not even the waters reflect me; even I have wished,
as the night pales, for a white view of the morning.

(*She leans in for the kill and breaks out singing.*)

Oh your father is dead/And your mother is sick!
And your wife is a drunk/And your kid has one leg!
And your brother is dead and your brother is dead
And your brother is dead and your . . . your . . . (*She falters.*)

What has possessed me! A mystery, isn't it?

You know where the heart of the world's death wish is? Berlin! That's where I grew up—right along that line drawn by soldiers. All the Americans there used to pretend that there had been no war and there was no wall! But the kids—we knew different; we knew radio. The station was American, right? All murder, mayhem and rock 'n roll. We used to sit on our parents' bed and eat lemons and after the news we'd listen to "The Mystery Hour." Then we'd go out and play spy.

We lived right by the Grunewald, the Green Forest. See, there was our Berlin and that other Berlin and the Grunewald was right in the middle. And in the middle of that was a graveyard. We'd crawl under the wire, hunker down in the weeds and watch the mourners pass by. The coffin would be on this horse drawn cart and they'd beat this big drum BOUMM BOUMM BOUMMMMM!!! We loved it! And then we'd go play funeral. Or mystery . . . One of us was always the one who died; one of us was the one who did it; and a third, usually me, was the one who had to find out Who/Where/What/and Why? Wanna play, dog? Ok. *BANG! You're dead!*

(*She turns on the radio. "Mystery Hour" theme music begins. She transforms into a male detective, the hero of her own radio show. All other character voices are on tape.*)

JAKE: Don't be afraid, sweetheart. This time of night the island's full of noises. It's 4:25 a.m. and the shadowland they call Berlin is sleeping like a baby. A baby shark. And sharks don't sleep. Neither do I. I just circle and wait. Me? Call me Jake. Call me the next time you're in trouble. Trouble's my business. I'm Jake Ratchett, Short Detective! (*Emphasizing blare of music.*)

Yeah, you heard straight, sugar—gumshoe, a private eye, a hard bitten dick! The Russkies don't like me, the GI cops don't like me, but all the kraut hookers let me ride half fare.

I'm a tough guy on a tough case. I've heard every sad tale this city has to tell. I've even told a few of my own . . . This one is about a rose. That was her name—Rose, (*the voice of Rose Harlotte, very American, singing a German torcher*) Rose Harlotte. It must be 24 hours since I met her but I remember it like it was yesterday. (*Her voice fades.*) Some dames ya don't forget.

It all started with death and a phone call—(*The ringing of a phone. Jake answers.*) Ratchett.

WOMAN'S VOICE: A crasee maddog killer's got my zent, so I'm as goot as deat, but here's zuh schcoop: a zertain Zirze zinging a zertain ziren zong zaw zomsing in zhe zity she shouldn't haf zeen. She knows too much ant not enoff ant a little knowledge iss a dangerous sing ven zhe zomebody you zaw zaw you see ant zhe zomebody she zaw zaw her see. I've zait all I can zay, but here's von last sing—she's deat and zo's anybody else who gets in his vay if you don't stop it before it's tsoo late!

JAKE: Lemme get this straight. A certain Circe singing a certain siren song saw something in the city she shouldn't have seen. She knows too much and not enough and a little knowledge is a dangerous thing when the somebody she saw saw her see. She's dead! And so's anybody else who gets in his way if I don't stop it before it's—

CRAZY MADDOG KILLER: —too late! (*A shot is fired. A scream. Sound of body falling with a thud. Then the CMDKiller laughs his CMD laugh and hangs up the phone. Sound of the buzz of a vacant line.*)

JAKE: My kind of case. (*Hangs up the phone.*) I didn't have much to go on but I went anyway. I hadn't gone far when (*heavy footsteps begin*) it sounded like maybe (*footsteps continue*)—but I couldn't be sure. (*The footsteps fade.*) I ducked into an alley to give em the slip but—somebody else was waiting for me!

ZULFIA: Ach! Ist du—

JAKE: Ratchett.

ZULFIA: Der schnoop?

JAKE: Da same.

ZULFIA: My name iss Zenzless, Her Ratchett, Zulfia Zenzless. Ant I zaw zomeone zee zomesing she shouldn't haf zee. Ich weissnicht fiel but I do know—

CMDK: —nothing! (*Shots, scream, body falls and hits as the CMDK laughs his crazyMD laugh.*)

JAKE: Another senseless slaying! (*Sirens.*) I didn't have time to play patacake with the cops. I found a door (*a thump as he bumps his nose*) and opened it. (*Door opening on nightclub sounds. Rose Harlotte singing in the background.*) And there she was! An angel of paradise tricked out like the devil and singing my own heart's truth! (*The song ends.*)

MC: Let's have a hand guys and GI's for that all American songbird— Missss Rossseee Harlotte!! (*Applause.*)

JAKE: When she took her bow she caught my eye and gave me a look that made my skin sizzle. (*Sizzling sound.*) Whatever she knew I wanted to know it! I slipped through the crowd—EXCUSE ME, BEG PARDON, GET OUTTA MY WAY—and made my way backstage.

GOON: Wadeaminute, pipsqueak! Whadda ya think you're doing? (*Ratchett throws a punch, goon groans and falls with a thud.*)

JAKE: I didn't have an answer. I knocked on a door. (*Knocking.*)

ROSE: Who's there?

JAKE: It's me.

ROSE: You?

JAKE: Yeah.

ROSE: Ah. Come right on in. I've been waiting for you. (*Jake opens the door.*)

JAKE: She was waiting for me alright. (*Series of fast gunshots.*) Ya missed.

ROSE: My mistake.

JAKE: Pretty cool. But you'd melt in my arms, sugar, if I read you right.

ROSE: Be careful little man. I've got a lot on my mind and a gun in my hand.(*There's a slap, a thunk and a gasp as Jake whallops the gun out of her hand and takes her in his arms.*)

JAKE: Our lips fed hungrily on each other. (*A growling animal sound as he chews the air madly. Then he breaks the "embrace" still panting.*) A kiss like that tells me a lot. But not nearly enough. Play it straight with me, kid—I wanna know what it is that I know 'cause I know—

CMDK: —too much! (*Shots. Rose screams. Rose falls.*)

JAKE: Rose! Rose! (*Rose is gasping for breath.*) Don't fade out on me! No! (*She coughs.*) Who did this to ya, Doll? (*More coughing.*) Who? (*Coughing and unintelligible attempts to make sense.*) Rose? . . . Rose? . . . (*Rose gives death's long sigh.*)

JAKE: She wilted in my arms like a limp bouquet. (*The sigh ends and the Crazy Maddog Killer's laugh becomes full force and echoes, echoes . . . *)

So that was the end of that story. And here I am, all alone in the city they call Berlin. Somewhere I might find some answers if only I could think of a question. But now, more than ever, life seems nasty, brutish and short. (*He walks out. Sound of rain falling and Rose Harlotte's voice echoing.*)

(*She turns off the radio, turns back around and starts taking off her make-up.*)

When my Uncle Kenny died he was so thin the needles went right through him. My mother's always been a night person, but it wasn't until he died that she started staying up all night and sleeping out the afternoons. He died at five in the afternoon. She remembers leaving his room and thinking, "Ohh, I'll never be able to love this time of day again."

He was her favorite. And they say I'm just like him only I'm older now than he was when he died. The older you get the more you say that. Yeah, we're alike alright—nailbitters! Kenny used to bite his nails to the bloody quick. Then he got this job at a stable scooping up shit—those nails grew out quick! It just goes to show you dog . . .

Don't get too settled in your ways.
It could change in a minute. On a dime.
That's all history's talk about the chimes of midnight.
I don't like to think about this. Where's my pipe? Where's the whiteout?
Where's the beautiful all fulfilling dame who's expected at any minute
and maybe, after she's got my tongue caught in her teeth
deep in her throat, maybe . . .

So tell me, what is the beautiful? The usual balance of the strained?
The savage intellect and the timid heart? The gentle hand and
the utterly pragmatic life? Where's the average? Do you know the strain
of trying to find and maintain this average? If only
I could be average and unafraid! If only I could sleep all day
I would I sure would, but . . .

gee, there's so much last minute business to do. Look,
I didn't want to be this, this isn't what I wanted to be
this isn't how I wanted things to turn out, it's just that this
is what I and it became. No, it's not like I had another whole
different thing in mind, it's just . . .

Who's to blame?
Sure something in me let this thing go on too long
but it's just that see, I like to be polite and believe
that the beastie won't wont wontwontWONTWONTWONT
    WHOOOOWHEEEEEEE!

I want to die in the arms of love.

Kiss me. Quick.

(*Holds for a beat or two. Then breaks.*) Not quick enough! . . . I remember when
we left Berlin. The wall had gone up and we had to get out fast. It was the dead
of winter, in the dead of night. We had to take a train across the Russian sec-
tor and as we came to the border the train slowed and I woke up. I poked my
head out into the corridor and through the window I saw this string of lights
marking the border; and the Russian guards, their rifles slung over their
shoulders, wearing those fur hats that look like animals. The snow was six feet
high! Glittering under that string of lights . . . glittering . . .
    Jump over that wall kraut! Hey you fuckenze deutch? Ohh you know me!
You know me! I'm an Americaner and a whore. Same difference! (*A braying
laugh.*) Only here I call myself an artist! You know doggy-boy, you and me
and artists we all got one thing in common—we spend a hell of a lot of time
licking ass! (*Brays again.*) Speaking as an artist, I tell you that wall must be do-

ing something right, 'cause those Berlin boys! Whoweeee! The last one I had
he fucked my so hard my parents came! (*She breaks that role.*)

In the long run we are all faithless; in the long run we are all dead, ya? Who
knew enough to be afraid? Do you know who was there when we were, hound
dog? Elvis! He looked just like all my uncles and he was in Berlin for the worst
of it. That made things alright somehow, not as scary. I mean there's a difference saying: "THE LINE HAS BEEN DRAWN; IT'S HIGH NOON;
AND THE FATE OF THE EARTH RESTS ON MY SHOULDERS" and
singing (*she sings*) "OOU! OUUU!/HEY! HEY!/I'M ALL SHOOK UP!"

Yeah, he was right there when you needed him. Mrs. Jackson, our
neighbor, she was a staunch Baptist but he was her boy. That boy made
Mamas out of all those women with a blue rinse or plaster shrine . . .

>   And so he went away, my sweet soldier
> to Germany without a war to fight.
> That had something to do with what happened later
> I just know it did—all dressed up and nothing to do.
> And his hair! Those lovely curls! I wept!
> Put them in an envelope marked "HIS"
> the letters all curly, in red.
> My best hand in the color of love.
>
> He was his mother's son but my true prince.
>
> What woman wouldn't love those eyes that had seen it all
> and nothing just the same? So what if he was wild?
> What man isn't, tell me that? What man doesn't
> like a high, a brawl, a girl on either arm, a gun with perfect aim?
> He loved it all. And me. He loved me once. I'm sure of it.
> And would have stayed here, safe here in the damp cleft of my legs.
> I'm sure of it. Even to this day I'm sure of it.
>
> I play that one song over and over again
> until I understand just what he means. I ask him
> "Darling, do you love me tender still?"
> And there it is, plain as day—"And I always will."
>
> He sings it. It's got to be true.

Of course she might not have been that sentimental. She was the same little
old lady who wanted to become a member of the Hell's Angels. She went up to
this brother and said, "Honey, the boys at the bar done told me, if I wanted to
become a member of the Hell's Angels I was gonna have to talk to you. Well, I
wanna. And here I am." The Angel looks her over and says, "Granny, you

don't look like our normal candidate for the Hell's Angels. I'm gonna have to ask you a few questions." She says, "Ok. Shoot."

ANGEL: You got yourself a bike?

GRANNY: Got me a Harley I ride and total at the same time.

ANGEL: You handle your liquor?

GRANNY: Can down a fifth of Jim Beam quicker than you can say spit.

ANGEL: What about your sex life? You like men?

GRAN: Like em ok. But I like to alternate my currents.

ANGEL: One last question—You ever been picked up by the fuzz?

GRAN: Picked up by the fuzz? Nooo, but I've been flung around by the tits a few times.

Now, now. Such contradictions are possible. Look at world events. Look at yourself. Look at me—even when I'm by myself blood is shed. It's the old NENENENENE eating me up. I'm primed to fear this world. It's Texas and Berlin and horror movies and radio and modern medicine and Earth, Wind, Water and Fire . . . and the Mickey Mouse Club. Do you know how the Mickey Mouse Club ended every blessed show? *"THE CLOCK ON THE WALL SAYS IT'S TIME TO GO."*

I was going to SoHo one afternoon to have lunch with a friend when I saw this page of *The Times* about *The Fate of the Earth*. So when the subway got to Penn Station I got off, bummed 20 bucks and took off for Philadelphia so I could die in the arms of my true love. But I knew by then not even love could save me. Nothing between me and the world! I went crazy with fear! "The sky will fall! The sky will fall!! Squaaaaaak!" Finally they carted me off to Gracie Square Nut Hospital. You know Gracie Square? That's where Edie went when she went nuts. The nearest I'll ever get to fame.

My ward was the safest place in the world. But full of surprises. I could leave the room for a minute and when I came back in God knew who would be there. (*She leaves and comes back in wearing a robe.*)

Hello everybody. My name is Sherrie Loose. And I would just like to thank my therapist for allowing me to perform here tonight. Thank you Dr. Katz wherever you may be. You see, she thought it would be good therapy for me because I'm—a ventriloquist. (*She brings up her hand which is wearing a wig.*) And this is Mr. Hand.

MR. HAND: I can talk!

SHERRIE: He can talk! And we can even talk with me keeping my lips still. (*She does. It's unintelligible.*) But we can't be understood very well.

MR. HAND: Not at all.

SHERRIE: Mr. Hand and I are ever so excited to be here tonight because we are going to perform a trick for you that we learned in the ventriloquist book.

MR. HAND: A trick!

SHERRIE: We're going to eat and talk at the same time.

MR. HAND: Eat and talk at the same time.

SHERRIE: Now these are *real* potato chips!

MR. HAND: Real ones!

SHERRIE: Are you ready, Mr. Hand?

MR. HAND: I am ready!

SHERRIE: Am I ready?

MR. HAND: You are ready.

SHERRIE: Are we all ready?

MR. HAND: (*Shrugs.*)

SHERRIE: Ohhkay! (*She stuffs the potato chips down her Mr. Hand's "gullet" as she screams in his voice "We can tallkkk and eattt at the samme time." The chips will fly. Then back to her own voice. "And we can even sing and drink beer at the same time." She pours a bottle of beer down Mr. Hand's "mouth" while singing a few bars of "Singing in the Rain".*) Mr. Hand and I love each other so much. But sometimes Mr. Hand goes a little crazy and he starts banging his head against the table and screaming! (*She starts banging her hand against the table and screaming.*) And the only way to get him quiet is to hit him with a hammer. (*She hits her hand with a hammer a few times. Mr. Hand is then quiet.*) And then we both cry. Because it hurts me more than it hurts him. Right, Mr. Hand?

MR. HAND: Ohhh, yes!

I thought an act like that would make me famous. I thought boy if anybody sees that they'll put me under contract! But when they saw it they put me under heavy sedation. I tried to tell them, "Look, I'm not crazy really. I'm just afraid!" Then they had to ask me what I was afraid of and I had to tell em—"Everything!"

I pick up a daily paper and there's a fifteen year old saying, "I have accepted it—that there could be an end to time." A hell of a lot more frightening than Margaret Fuller accepting the universe.

And these nights when I dream, I dream my whole life—in each detail. And when I wake up I can't remember how old I am. I think I'm 12! No, I'm 16! No, I'm 23! No, I'm 29! No, no, no! The thought of it makes all my life seem (*she snaps her fingers*) just like that.

Ever been to the Museum of Natural History? Left you fearing for your bones didn't it, pup? when I was standing by the monkey case there was this little girl next to me full of indignation: "You mean they *killed* him just so we could *see* him?! *Gross!*" I was in perfect agreement. We certainly are children of our times . . .

I am a child of my time yes, perfectly
at home here in this apologia to the dead

here among these without eyes without ears
with only that illusion of breath only
the skin saved
stretched and cured pulled taut
back over the old bones.
Yes.
I am a child of my time yes.

The white wolves poised—a last
unselfconscious leap—transfixed now forever
there in the twilight's still gleaming.
The eyes of the white wolf
like the eyes of the brown bear
like the eyes of the striped cat
like the eyes of the spotted deer
like the eyes of the red fox
(the little girl named them all
counted them all on her fingers)
the eyes of the dead.

The last light in the eyes of the dead
is the blaze that stalks them forever
like the fox always almost upon its prey—seen
only in madness, only in blindness in fear
crouched like an animal smelling its own blood
as its own blood's thick scent swells; smelling
its own doom, it follows the line of sense until
all senses fail. There's the frenzy of knowledge!
There!
Yes. We are children of our time yes.
Perfectly at home here.

my heart beats beats eats at me at me my heart eats at
me beats beats

but ART makes me feel serene
even staring this in the eye
I see the fine eye for diorama there
behind the glass case
trapped killed skinned remounted replaced
within their natural habitat.
God Shield me from that Holy Face.
Art makes me feel serene
But it's mad, Master, us posing like this to please you.

Don't. Eat. Me. Heart. Don't.

Every minute I get through in this place
ahhhh! What a relief!
And oh so help me Lord and let the tongues lash me
I owe every blessed minute to you!
And oh so help me Lord and let the tongues lash me
I bow to thee my face I shield from thee
I'm belly up, O Merciful God!
Don't. Eat. Me. Heart. Don't.

Oh Merciful God
if only SHE would twist my buzzer
right now I'd drop this idiot chatter
with the unseen. Unseen? Here? Totally unperceived!
My heart may be in my throat but believe me baby
I'd calm down just like that monkey in the case
I'd calm down in the arms of a baby just like you
you sweet little number let me nuzzle while
you love me love me love me to death.

Art makes me feel serene but isn't it mad
posing like this to please you?
"Don't here! Here! Here! We're perfectly at home here!
Our time. Our time. Yes, yes, yes, yes, yes!"
I might as well save my breath—
No! Wait! I'll calm the idiot tongue. Wait!
It's this:
    the slant of light, the slant of your own mind,
the slant of those cat's eyes. Unblinking.
See. Those animals.

Remember my Great Aunt Eve, the one who had visions? She had them all
her life. When she was young they said she was nervy, when she was old they
said she was senile. But she was right every single time. It's not always the cold
eye that beholds—it's the Grandmas and the Cassandras and the dear old
Auntie Nukes.

And the others? The ones without visions—just Big Plans for the world? A
quiz! Quick—what's the difference the military and bucket of shit? The
bucket! (She laughs.) Heyy, they don't scare us! We're tough! They lay a hand
on us, grrrrr! We bite it off! Lemme eat em! We'll show em! 'Cause life may
be tougher than art, but grrrrr! art is tough!

Grrrrrrr! Art's tough!

It's got a grin so wry and sexy
designed to make your wicked body sweat.
But grrrrrr!
(That's a threat)
It'll haul your ass you eye it crossways.
Take your head shake.
Shake too hard snap!—
Black!
Grrrrr!
It's tough.
Sometimes it's not so quick but
likes to tease. Bite out just a little
of your neck. Wet your ear enough to
cause a freeze. But move—
and move it quick.
Once it's got your pussy you
are through.
It drags youUUUUUUuu (gravel makes a road out of your shin)
it drags youuuuuuuuuuu! And grrrrr! till you give in.
"Uncle!" You're shouting "Uncle! Art, ain't you pleased?"
It gets up with a heave and lets you breathe
then Boom! Uh! It's on you once again.
"Uncle!" Still crying "Uncle! Can't you forgive?"
It lifts you easy on its daddy knee
and starts to ride youuuuuu
starts to ride ouuuuuuuuuuu!
It bucks you high! You got to laugh!
It bucks you high! You got to laugh!
Then Boom! Uh! It's on you once again
grrrrrrrr!
Brrrrrr. Be careful with that thing
that thing is tough. And got a rich man's ornery
appetites. And knows you from your inside to your right.
It knows youuuuuuuu. Ouuuuuuuh that grin!
It promised all!
But if it don't make you young it makes you old
(before your time.) It makes you dead.
Grrrrrrr! Grrrrrr! Grrrrrrr!
It's tough!

I could sure use a beer . . . empty . . . gone. And all for effect. (*She looks around the room. It's a wreck.*) Was this always my future? What in the world did my mother mean for me to make of it? All those dark hints at the mysterious . . .

When she was in the hospital with that kidney infection, she was propped up in bed reading a movie magazine, when all of a sudden she felt me turn in her belly; and then her feet went cold and colder; and the cold moved up and up until it almost reached her heart. She knew then that she was dying. She reached to buzz for the nurse. And then she couldn't move.

"Mrs Galloway! Mrs Galloway! What is it? What is it?" The nurse couldn't find a pulse. She ran for the doctor.

My mother was thinking, "If only he will open those windows"—there were these huge French windows—"If only he will open those windows."

And the doctor looked into her eyes. And he opened the windows. And her pulse began again.

That's my favorite story.

And you? What's the matter with you? You haven't even touched your bone. Look at this—primitive! compelling! good for your gums! You ought to read some of Edward Hoagland's books about Africa. There's this great story about some English photographers and the native guides setting up camp by a river. From over the hustle and bustle come bloodcurdling screams! They rush to the river's edge and there's one of the natives being eaten by a crocodile—CHOMP! MUNCH! THRASH! CHEW! and the legs kicking wildly out of the mouth like some sick cartoon. There's a horrified silence. And then all of the natives laughed! Well when I read that, I laughed too. But maybe that's just something in my own nature or the nature of Africa. . . .

I have never paid much attention to landscapes, believing
them too changeable. Only the immutable (long dead) light
of heaven is faithful: its stars fixed, reflecting
not their own fiery centers but the soul's
divine perfection.

Could I be blind
and deaf to the world's breach of quiet
around me I would be: silent, picking at my own depths;
A spiteful love of life, and always with memory
attached to the brain's thick hide like parasite.

I read that in Africa, Fear—
like the insatiable God—compels laughter
from the natives when It bares Its teeth. Inexplicably
to the mannered Englishman there is laughter when a pair
of black legs, kicking disappear into the jawing crocodile.
Yes. We are lucky to escape.

But that is Africa.

We would be lost in Africa among
the unpredictable beasts. We would be lost
in Africa. Could not pluck meaning from the
unexacting jaws, or solace from the river's sucking edge.
Back here among our own dangers we much prefer
our quiet habits—condescending to alite, like
the accustomed parasites,
on the insensate hide of God.

You know it's getting late when the talk turns to God. I won't keep you up much longer, but I'm curious, dog . . . doesn't anything scare you? keep you up nights? trouble your heart?

Have you ever been in love—with a cat? duck? pig? the alien that is inexplicably dear? How did you and I meet anyway? Would you call it love at first sight? You're not perturbed by my lack of body hair, are you? You're so sensitive to some things it's chilling.

Could you really sniff out the approach of an atomic bomb the same way you sniff out a storm? Would you warn me or simply hide your nose in your paws and eat away your last moments before oblivion?

Why do you persist in chasing trucks? In challenging other larger dogs?

Does your heart bleed?

In the end I am not your master but only the hand that feeds you. How does that affect the degree of love?

Do you love me?

(*More to herself than anyone else.*) Need I ask?

END

Candy & Shelley Go to the Desert

Paula Cizmar

Candy & Shelley Go to the Desert was produced by The Women's Project on the mainstage of the American Place Theatre as part of a festival of one-acts, opening on March 21, 1984. It was directed by Carey Perloff, with set by Johniene Papandreas, lighting by Jane Reisman, costumes by Judy Dearing, with the following cast:

CANDY	Mary Catherine Wright
SHELLEY	Lisa Goodman
RON	Christian Baskous

Characters:

Candy, a young woman, not quite 30, formerly from Indiana, now locked into the Big Apple.

Shelley, a young woman, not quite 30, native of New York and still there.

Ron (The Biker), a young man from Michigan.

Time: The present. August.

Place: The desert.

SCENE: *The Desert. A sparsely traveled desert road, no more than two lanes, about 80 miles south of Elko, Nevada—just off I-80. The location is specific, but it need not be. One hell-hole in Nevada is pretty much the same as the next. Onstage are typical desert furnishings: washed out sandy clay soil, sage brush, pebbles, a large rock, a few nondescript cacti, a beer can, a lot of sky—dusty, but cloudless. Off in the distance are jagged, lifeless rock formations, cracking out of the ground. A boulder centerstage is large enough to live on—but in the heat and light of this August day, it creates nothing as humane as shade. We hear a car with a growling muffler approach and screech to a halt offstage. The driver lays on the horn, throws a door open, and slams it shut.*

CANDY: (*Offstage; shrieking.*) Get outa the car! What did I say? Get outa the car! Come on! Come on! Get out! (*Candy appears in the distance.*) Run . . . get away from the car. Get. Away. From. The. Car. NOW! (*Candy runs off again. We hear a bit of commotion, sounds of struggle.*)
SHELLEY: Hey. What . . . Stop it . . . Candy . . .

(*Candy and Shelley come running crazily onstage; Candy has Shelley's arm in a tight grip.*)

CANDY: Come on . . . run . . . let's go. Behind the rock!
SHELLEY: You're hurting my—hey, what's wrong with—rock? Rock?

(*Candy pushes Shelley down behind the rock—they face the audience.*)

CANDY: Get down quick!
SHELLEY: Oh. Rock. (*Starts to stand up; Candy pushes her back down.*) Candy!

CANDY: Now stay down and keep quiet.

SHELLEY: What? What's going on? Candy?

CANDY: Shut up. It's gonna blow up.

SHELLEY: What is? What—

CANDY: Shhhh!

SHELLEY: What's my making noise got to do with—?

CANDY: Shhh! I'm warning you.

SHELLEY: Candy—

CANDY: Things travel out here.

SHELLEY: What's gonna blow up?

CANDY: Things travel further out here. You know about brain waves. They magnify. They can blow something up like remote control.

SHELLEY: I see.

(They sit quietly for a while; then Shelley gets up and starts to walk toward the car. Candy grabs her and pulls her down.)

CANDY: Are you crazy?

SHELLEY: It's hot out here.

CANDY: Where are you going? Are you nuts?

SHELLEY: I want my sun visor.

CANDY: *(Hissing.)* Stay away from the car. *(Beat.)* The car.

SHELLEY: Right. The car. It's a terrific car, Candy. Not a convertible, but—great car.

CANDY: Shelley. I stopped the car—I saved your life in the process, by the way—I stopped the car because it was going to blow up. Am I making myself clear? Loud noise? Boom? KA—POWWWWW. Got it?

SHELLEY: Okay. Okay. I got it. That's nuts.

CANDY: The two little red lights on the dash were blinking on and off and there was smoke coming out of the hood and a loud hissing noise like a time bomb.

SHELLEY: Classic paranoia.

CANDY: How do you explain that?

SHELLEY: I thought you were the Dairy Queen or Radish Festival Goddess from Saints-Preserve-Us Indiana. Am I right, am I right?

CANDY: *(Beat.)* I am from Indiana, yes.

SHELLEY: Well, I was born and raised in New York City and can't drive to save my life but even I know that when a car is overheated steam comes out of the radiator and the little red gizmo light lights up. Didn't you used to run into this sort of thing with your tractor?

CANDY: I don't have to respond to that, thanks.

SHELLEY: Maybe the fertilizer fumes were harmful. They've probably done studies—

CANDY: I have never been within ten feet of a tractor in my life except at the automotive show once a year with my uncle Albert.

SHELLEY: Well, you don't have to get so bent out of shape.

CANDY: You think that's all it was?

SHELLEY: Huh?

CANDY: The radiator. Overheated.

SHELLEY: Oh, sure. I mean, cars are human, too, you know. It must be 110 degrees out here.

CANDY: 113. The radio said. You were asleep. And missed another turn-off—Route 452. Where is it?

SHELLEY: Why do you ask such things?

CANDY: Oh well, that's a relief—it was just overheated. (*Shelley gets up and heads toward the car again; Candy grabs her leg and holds her back.*) Shelley! You'll be killed!

SHELLEY: Will you let go?

CANDY: The hissing noise—the time bomb—the exploding gas tank, they do that, you know—you haven't explained that part.

SHELLEY: This is really crazy. Hello, leg. (*Shakes herself loose and gets back up again.*)

CANDY: Wait! Don't leave me!

SHELLEY: You're acting like we're in a Linda Darnell movie.

CANDY: Just . . . stay a minute.

SHELLEY: I've gotta have my sun visor.

CANDY: In a minute.

SHELLEY: I'm gonna fry out here. I'm not used to all this fresh air. Jeez.

CANDY: I'm afraid.

SHELLEY: I'll be right back.

(*Shelley gets up and heads for the car; suddenly there is a tremendous boom; Shelley dives behind the rock and they cling to each other.*)

SHELLEY AND CANDY: EeeeeeeeK! Aaaaaaaagh!

CANDY: (*Starts to cry.*) I told you! It blew up! I told you! (*Loud sniffles.*) Now what are we going to do?

SHELLEY: (*Also crying.*) I don't know.

CANDY: You would have killed yourself for a lousy pair of sunglasses. I saved your life.

SHELLEY: My visor blew up, too. I'll melt. Oohhhh.

CANDY: And we were always such good friends and I've known you since I moved away from home and we always share everything and understand and I saved your life and now we're just going to die out here.

SHELLEY: Candy—Candy—nobody knows we're here and they'll find us years later. Probably some poor innocent little Boy Scouts out on a cook-out. They'll find our skeletons and they won't even know who we are.

CANDY: Oh no, not some poor little kids.

SHELLEY: It's creepy here. This is a place for the creeps.

CANDY: Well, no. I don't think that's it.

SHELLEY: It's too big. There's no ceiling to hold my head on tight. I could start—my mind could start to—I could—oh, it's too—too—real. (*Flinches suddenly and bounces to another part of the rock.*) EeeeeeeeeeK!

CANDY: What?

SHELLEY: Get it away! What is it? It's killing me! Oh, I hate it!

CANDY: Where?

SHELLEY: It's alive. Get it away! Kick it.

CANDY: I want to see.

SHELLEY: Get rid of it!

CANDY: It's a lizard. Oh that's cute.

SHELLEY: Tell it to leave. Scat. Shoo!

CANDY: Shelley. One does not tell a lizard to leave. Anyway, where would he go? Besides, you get rid of one, 3200 more just show up to replace it. It's an old Indian custom—Apache, I think.

SHELLEY: Oh! Oh! I—Candy, he's dead! I murdered it!

CANDY: They shed their skin. It's molting.

SHELLEY: If so, this one got confused and molted everything.

CANDY: Oh.

SHELLEY: Why did I ever let you talk me into this stupid trip?

CANDY: You needed a change. I could tell.

SHELLEY: They're killing me. Every rock and rattlesnake and El Rancho Big Boy Breakfast.

CANDY: The open road, Shelley. Think of it.

SHELLEY: They're eating my soul. I'm going to walk out into the desert and let them devour me all at once. (*Shelley stands and starts to walk out into the desert. She does a double take—rubs her eyes.*) That's funny. I must be hallucinating already. The car blew up, but it's still there. It's a mirage. It's like Castaneda or something.

CANDY: Don't go near it! It's . . . it's too WEIRD.

(*As if in a trance, Shelley walks offstage to the car; Candy starts to peek over the rock, thinks better of it, and takes cover again.*)

SHELLEY: (*Offstage; she starts cackling hysterically.*) HA! Bombs away! (*From off-stage, Shelley tosses an object over the rock; it lands at Candy's feet.*)

CANDY: (*Scrambling away from it.*) What? Get it away from me. Are you nuts? It's— (*Beat.*) Why, it's an orange juice container.

SHELLEY: (*Entering with a large overstuffed purse or bag and Candy's knapsack.*) Exactement.

CANDY: What a good idea. I'm thirsty.

SHELLEY: Good. Then you won't mind licking orange juice off the luggage.

CANDY: Huh?

SHELLEY: Elementary, my dear Candace. Orange juice—Tuesday. Thrown into backseat. Hot sun. Four days in the car, the heat of the desert beating down through the rear window. Friday afternoon—that's right now—ferments and eureka! Explodes!! The time bomb, at your service.

CANDY: Oh. This—this was making the hissing noise.

SHELLEY: But, *mais oui*.

CANDY: (*As if tickling a baby.*) Oh, so it's little self-ums was just letting off steam, wasn't ums?

SHELLEY: Pressure.

CANDY: Like ittle bittle root beer bottles, if you shake em up too much.

SHELLEY: Whatever you say.

(*Shelley empties the contents of her purse; it is full of useful items for the city dweller—paperbacks, magazines, mints, a can of mace, a whistle, etc., plus drenched maps. She puts on her visor—dripping wet with exploded orange juice—and mirror sunglasses and stares out into the desert, looking completely alien. Without even looking at Candy, she removes a tube of heavy sunscreen from a pocket and hands it robot-like to Candy.*)

SHELLEY: God.

(*Candy very unself-consciously puts blobs of the white sunscreen on various parts of her face—a particularly large gooey blob sits on her nose, and white gunk outlines her lips. While she is doing this, Shelley sighs loudly. Candy fishes suntan lotion out of her blouse, rubs it all over herself. Shelley sighs. Beat; she sighs again. Beat; she sighs once more.*)

CANDY: Will you stop that?

SHELLEY: (*Sighing.*) Stop what?

CANDY: That! That stupid sighing.

SHELLEY: I'm not sighing.

CANDY: Yes you are. (*Candy sighs.*)

SHELLEY: You're the one who's sighing. (*Shelley sighs.*) Well. Now what? Bridge anyone? Toasted bagel? (*Beat; Shelley sneezes loudly.*) What am I doing out here? I can believe you doing something dumb like this, but me? I can't believe that I, of all people, let you talk me into such a dumb stupid idea.

CANDY: Well you might as well relax. Cause you did. (*Shelley sneezes.*) Oh, I can get such a good tan out here. Even. All over. Sun just everywhere, just reflecting off everything. No shadows. Mmmmmmm, this is nice.

SHELLEY: (*Sneezes.*) Listen to me. I'm allergic. There's no pollution. None of the bacteria I'm used to. I could die out here. You know, when the early explorers visited native tribes in the Americas, the Indians started keeling over left and right from foreign flu bugs.

CANDY: Mm-hmm. You better take off your sandals or you'll have tan lines on your toes.

SHELLEY: You can't survive without your own bacteria. You can't take a fish out of water.

CANDY: Water. What a good idea. Maybe there's an oasis out there.

SHELLEY: No, there would have to be coconut trees. Gee, a macaroon would be good. I'm starved. Mmmmm. That's what I want.

CANDY: If you would have let me buy that ice chest at that K-Mart in Ohio you could eat right now.

SHELLEY: Macaroons don't need an ice chest. Oooh, a cinnamon roll with raisins. Hot from the oven. A steak. Blood red.

CANDY: You're a vegetarian.

SHELLEY: A steak. And nachos. A pepperoncini salad. Onion soup with melted cheese. Fried eggs. A hot pastrami sandwich with sauerkraut. And lasagna. That's what I want. (*Candy moves into an odd position—for maximum sun exposure.*) Scratch that. Scratch all of that. Watermelon. Yeah. (*Shelley sighs, then sneezes. Candy holds her arms and legs at weird angles to catch the rays.*)

CANDY: Mm. I know what I want. Yeah. I want hot sex. Hot hot sex.

SHELLEY: In this heat?

CANDY: Hot desert sands, a hot desert breeze, vapors, and a hot hot hot young man.

SHELLEY: (*Sneezing.*) I think I'm really getting sick. I'm getting dizzy.

CANDY: A biker, maybe.

SHELLEY: Got any decongestants? Cough syrup would be good.

CANDY: Biker, mmmm, yeah.

SHELLEY: (*Checking her pockets, purse, Candy's knapsack, etc., for something to use.*) Even a Kleenex. (*Squirming around, she brushes up against another mini-corpse.*) No! No! Here's another one! It's a lizard graveyard. What are they doing? What are they doing?

CANDY: One hot hot biker.

SHELLEY: You know, probably if we got in the car and took off, I'd feel a lot better.

CANDY: Or a lot of them. Hubba hubba.

SHELLEY: (*Sneezing, starts packing up all their things.*) Well, now that you've had a little rest from driving, we should get going.

CANDY: Yeah. He'd pull up on his hot hot machine. Or they would.

SHELLEY: I promise to follow the map better this time—we'll just drive up-town until we hit I-80, then turn right. That's east, got it? Uh, like taking the FDR up to the 59th Street Bridge. See?

CANDY: Ooooh. Bikers like those guys with the shrunken heads on their helmets that we saw at that last Foster's Freeze. Ooooooo-eeeee, Varrrr-rooooom. Varrrroooom.(*She sits up, grasps "handlebars" and "kicks the bike in-to gear"—as if she were really on a cycle.*)

SHELLEY: Uh, Candy, catch my drift there? Like, we'll go home.

CANDY: You wanted to see the Pacific Ocean. Varooooom RRRRRooom.

SHELLEY: I'm sure it looks just like the Atlantic. Just the same except it's on the wrong side when you look at it.

CANDY: Never saw a biker eat a vanilla cone with sprinkles before.

SHELLEY: Candy. Look. It's about time we admitted that this so-called get-away-from-it-all experience is not working out. Maybe the Bahamas this fall—a nice condo on the water, I think.

CANDY: All those sprinkles, he kind of closed his eyes and . . . oh.

SHELLEY: We'll go back to New York and take a subway up to the Bronx Zoo or something.

CANDY: Mmm. And then that one teeny drip of icy . . . white . . . frozen . . . custard . . . cream just one drip on his chest, kind of melting down over his—

SHELLEY: Candy, let's go.

CANDY: Mmmm. He had a real good tan and a lot of terrific blonde hair on his chest, did you notice that?

SHELLEY: Yeah, but he was peeling. Let's go. We've gotta get somewhere civilized before dark.

CANDY: I'd lick it off.

SHELLEY: Candy. I need to go now. I shouldn't 've left. I want it all back. My home. We've gotta go. Candy.

CANDY: There are winos outside your apartment and you pay far too much for it.

SHELLEY: I know. My newsstand. They count on me. They probably had one too many copies of the *Times* today.

CANDY: You were living in hell.

SHELLEY: (*Sneezing.*) I'm sick.

CANDY: I am on vacation. I am trying to enjoy myself.

SHELLEY: I am going crazy. I am. Let's go. I'll do anything you want.

CANDY: No . . . come on, think of it. A steamy biker boy. Spikes on his hat. Thighs all swathed in leather.

SHELLEY: In this heat?

CANDY: Relax. They've got us where they want us. We're at their mercy now. They're just waiting 'til we get a little weaker, then they'll swoop in for the—

SHELLEY: Ha ha. I know you're kidding now. Well, time to leave. This was very relaxing. Ready? Candy, my mother needs me. I've gotta—

CANDY: You are delirious. Now listen Shelley. You know I always do what I say I am gonna do, always and forever, and we said we were gonna get away from the city and see something different and that's that. We gotta do it. Varoooom. See? They're coming. Hear their bikes. Rrrrrroooom. Ratatatatata.

SHELLEY: Please. We've had enough. You've got to take me home now. You've got to. I'll be good. I swear it. I'm sorry I made you stop at that Union 76 trucker place in Iowa. I know you didn't want to.

CANDY: Ooooh. I am ready for you, Mr. Desert Man.

SHELLEY: (*Trying to drag Candy to the car.*) Come on. Look, I'm sorry I made fun of the corn dogs. I've just never seen anything like that before.

CANDY: (*Singing the Little Eva song.*) Chains! My baby's got me locked up in chains . . . and it ain't the kind . . . that you can see . . .

SHELLEY: So . . . so here's the plan. I'll go to the car. I'll get in and sit down and you'll come over there in a second or two and we'll drive off. Simple. I'm sorry you have to drive all the way. I'll . . . I'll pay for all the motels going back. Okay? Look, it's just that I never learned to drive stick shift, that's all. Hey . . . we'll drive along and I'll really learn this time. You work the pedals, and I'll shift. Right? (*Candy continues humming the song, while deliberately and sensuously basking in the sun.*) Candy. Listen to me. This is the kind of place where lunatics bury hundreds of sunburned tourists in the sand after they chop them into little pieces and set fire to their baby oil. People carry axes out here.

CANDY: Ohhhh. Motor boy.

SHELLEY: Please. Candy please.

CANDY: Ohhh ohhh take me.

SHELLEY: Please— (*Candy continues humming, then stops abruptly. There are sounds of bikers off in the distance.*) Oh god they really are coming now oh no.

CANDY: Wow.

SHELLEY: Snap out of it. This is serious now. (*Shelley fans Candy with a copy of* People *magazine.*)

CANDY: Wow they really are.

SHELLEY: Anything, Candy. I'll do anything.

CANDY: Wow I didn't really think they would really—

SHELLEY: Anything. Hurry. I'll give you back your purple sweatshirt and I won't make fun of your pillow from American Airlines anymore. (*Beat.*) I'll let you pick the radio stations. (*Sounds of motorcycle get louder and louder.*)

CANDY: Wow. Dozens of little specks, all heading this way.

SHELLEY: Oh no.

CANDY: Gee. And there's more behind them.

SHELLEY: Candy!

CANDY: Wow. Like an ant farm. (*Beat as Shelley sighs and gasps in rapidly escalating panic.*) You know, I will make a deal with you. Just to be fair.

SHELLEY: A-a-anything!

CANDY: I'll give up my bikers if—well, after all, we've been friends for how long now?

SHELLEY: Anything! I don't know! Uh, ten years! Hurry! LOOK! (*Shelley points to the approaching bikers.*)

CANDY: Oh god no! (*Shelley starts to drag Candy toward the car.*)

SHELLEY: Come on!

CANDY: (*Stops abruptly.*) Wait a minute. Wait. There's just one thing I want.

SHELLEY: Tell me. Fast!

CANDY: Did you sleep with Roger?

SHELLEY: What?

CANDY: Tell me.

SHELLEY: Candy.

CANDY: They're coming. They're almost here. I can smell them.

SHELLEY: (*Beat.*) Yes. I did.

CANDY: Aha!

SHELLEY: But you had already stopped seeing him.

CANDY: Seeing him! Seeing him! In my mind I saw him all the time. At night before I went to bed I saw—

SHELLEY: Okay. Okay. You had stopped, you know, sleeping with him. You broke up!

CANDY: Some friend.

SHELLEY: Please, Candy, can't we just talk about this at some nice safe Howard Johnson's in Nebraska? Come on, the little specks on the horizon are turning into nasty growly men on big dirty machines.

CANDY: So you did.

SHELLEY: We'll be murdered. Raped.

CANDY: Doesn't matter now.

SHELLEY: I can't stand it! (*The bikers are practically right on top of them now.*) I'm too young to die.

CANDY: Maybe I'll just walk off into the des— (*Shelley tackles Candy and pushes her behind the rock, out of view.*)

SHELLEY: Oof. I'm too old for this. (*The biker sounds swell and peak, then the bikers pass. Motorcycle engines begin to fade in the distance. Shelley peeks up over the top of the rock—we see only her head. She sighs; sneezes.*) All clear. (*Shelley climbs on top of the rock.*) Candy? Hey! You can come out now! Ooooh! You're right. This sun is nice. Mmmm-mmmm. (*Shelley takes some of Candy's sunscreen and smears it on her nose, then rubs Candy's suntan lotion all over herself. She sits, soaking up the sun. Looking off in the distance.*) It's moving! It's moving! It's—Candy, wow, it's some kind of furry animal or—oh, look at him go! You don't like those silly bikers either, do ya, pal? You said it, fella, buncha noise and hot air, that's all they are. (*Without Shelley noticing, Candy stands up on the other side of the rock, turns and begins to walk off into the desert. Shelley stares at her feet.*) You know, Can, you're right about tan lines. (*She takes off her sandals.*) WHO needs em? (*She tosses the shoes aside, then inspects where they have landed: another lizard stiff. She picks the body up.*) You guys, you guys, this is really starting to break my heart now. Is this some kind of trans-species death wish or what? Oh, what can I do for you little awful things?

(*Shelley gingerly gathers up the lizard bodies and arranges them, somewhat reverently, on a ledge of the rock. She makes a little design out of them—lizards all in a circle, or a diamond or whatever—and then makes a marker for the "grave" out of pebbles or decorates it with flowers made out of lichen or sage brush. She could even make a little fence for it out of*) *twigs.*)

SHELLEY: Maybe you won't be lizards next time. Maybe you'll come back as mountain lions or wild horses or who knows? You could have your own talk show. Now the rest of you guys out there, stay well. (*She settles back down on the rock.*) Hey, Can? You should've had a hat on in this heat. People never go to the desert without a hat. No wonder you got so upset. Over Roger. My god. What a waste. (*Beat.*) I'll lend you my sunglasses. That'll be good. This is nice suntan lotion. Mmm. Smells like almonds. There's a poison that smells like almonds—what is it? Arsenic? Maybe strychnine. They always mention that in my Agathe Christie's. Nero Wolfe's too. So I always know when someone mentions almonds there's some clue. Ooh, feel that healing, baking, soul-satisfying heat. Mmm. Candy! You really should come out now. Ti-ime. Bikers all gone. Went bye bye. Candy. Come out come out wherever you are! Can. Come on now. This trip is not going to be any fun if you don't talk to me.

(*Shelley peers over the rock and sees that Candy is not there; she scrambles down off the rock.*)

SHELLEY: Oh no! Oh no! Oh no oh no oh no oh no oh no. Candy! Oh no. Candy! (*Shelley runs off into the desert, disappears offstage. Calling from off- stage—growing further away:*) Cannn-dyyy. Cannn-dyyy. (*In a moment we hear a rustling sound. Shelley appears, dragging a half-conscious Candy. Shelley props her up under the rock.*) Candy. Speak to me. Say something.
CANDY: Where am I?
SHELLEY: Oh hell, she's got amnesia.
CANDY: I walked off into the desert and—hmmm. I must've passed out or something.
SHELLEY: Something.
CANDY: You saved my life.
SHELLEY: That's ridiculous.
CANDY: Well, you did. (*Beat.*) I'll never forget it.
SHELLEY: Why? Just tell me why? Why did you go off in this sun? Not because of Roger. Couldn't be. That's too stupid.
CANDY: Roger? Now I remember. I'll never speak to you again.
SHELLEY: Oh come on. (*No response.*) We're best friends. (*No response.*) It wasn't my idea. It was his. I mean, it just happened, there was a certain thing, a certain feeling.
CANDY: Oh. A feeling.
SHELLEY: It happened and then it passed. (*No response.*) You hadn't seen him in a month. (*No response.*) Besides, you always told me he had funny feet and you didn't like the way he said "howdy boys and girls" all the time. Candy, I saved your life.

CANDY: I saved yours, too. From the bomb that was orange juice. So we're even. Fuck you.

SHELLEY: Look, I wouldn't ever want to do anything to hurt you, or hurt your feelings, you're the one I want to help through the hurt, not hurt, I mean, there's hurt out there and we can be hurt, know what I mean?

CANDY: No. Do you?

SHELLEY: I'm your friend. Why didn't you tell me how you were feeling—

CANDY: Cause everyone knows that a friend is the one person you don't have to tell cause they know how you feel and you're supposed to know that, so there.

SHELLEY: I didn't know you cared about him. You said you didn't. (*Beat.*) I should've known you were just saying it. Candy, I'm sorry. What can I do? Tell me. (*Candy does not respond.*) I'm the lowliest homeliest pebble. I'm the stones under your shoes. I should be shot. Can. Can, tell me. I could make it up to you. I could. Tell me what can I do? (*Shelley, truly upset, tries to reach out to Candy. Candy pulls away.*) You know, nobody. Nobody cares for me the way you do. Nobody. *Tout le monde.* (*Beat.*) I really want to thank you for this trip.

CANDY: Oh stop being so patronizing.

SHELLEY: No. Really. Sitting on that rock a minute ago, I had a feeling—

CANDY: Oh, a feeling. How nice. The same feeling you had when you screwed Roger?

SHELLEY: I had a feeling. There I was baking away and— (*She climbs on the rock.*) Here I am, I'm baking away, and suddenly my brains are starting to slip into place. I'm starting to see things. It's the sunlight, I think. I can see clear back to the Mississippi, and over, and across, and all the way up to the coast. I can see years even. And I didn't see them before, so I don't know what they mean, but if I look long enough—

CANDY: Sure, you'll be able to see that that green shag carpet of yours is really tacky.

SHELLEY: I'm serious. You know I am. In the city—you know this—in the city I work day and night just to keep food in the catbowls. Day in. Day out. Last week, last week, Sylvia at work gives me a new mug with rabbits on it. Immediately I fill it with caffeine and wire myself to the ceiling. I spend my days up there. Nights, I go home from work, check the mail box. The mail is always awful. Just indictments of conservative middle class life from obscure nonprofit organizations. On my salary, I haven't even made it into the middle class yet, so why are they picking on me? Appeals, appeals, sometimes in triplicate, using bulk mail rates, from the concerned psychotherapists union or anarchists international. I mean, that's all very nice, I'm glad they care, I send them five dollars, I'm glad to be helpful, but I'd really rather have a letter. So then I make some awful dinner—either junk food or stuff from the health food store, it all tastes the same. Then I call you. That's the best part of the day. I force myself to do the dishes first, so that after I call you I don't have anything awful to do anymore. One night, I call you and you say, let's go to the desert. Let's go have a lot of space, a lot of air, a lot of room to be free. Let's. So we go. And I climb up on this rock and start to see a lot of things. And then you—you get mad. You take it all away. I guess I understand why. But I never thought I was doing anything wrong. So I'm sorry. (*Beat.*) Things'll be different now, huh? Yeah. (*Beat.*) It really didn't mean anything, Can. It just happened.

CANDY: Is that supposed to be some kind of confession? Pretty feeble.

SHELLEY: No. It's just that this is today. Today is us. Right here, right now, you and me. Oh god, what's wrong with me? (*Beat.*) So. When did you find out? Right after it happened? Last week when we decided to come out here? Last month? Did you figure we'd be trapped in a car for oh so many thousand miles and we could confront each other? Maybe you planned all along to leave me here. (*Beat.*) Roger told you, didn't he? That scum.

CANDY: It wasn't Roger.

SHELLEY: You're just protecting him.

CANDY: So?

SHELLEY: So? So you fell for him, he didn't fall for you, he used you, he left you, you deserve better, and he's not even good in bed.

CANDY: Maybe not the first time. Maybe not for one time, but for—forget it. I don't want you telling me how many times. I don't want details.

SHELLEY: So there are other men, worthy of your loyalty and protection.

CANDY: I loved Roger. I felt close to him. He was special.

SHELLEY: I'm your friend. You've loved me. You've felt close to me. You've said I was special.

CANDY: So?

SHELLEY: So why don't you protect me?

CANDY: I have. Go away. It's different, anyway. Him and me. You and me. It's not the same thing at all.

SHELLEY: Yeah. You're right.

CANDY: Besides. You are now not my friend.

SHELLEY: No. Maybe not. (*Shelley stands on top of the rock.*) Oh, I feel like I'm way out there. Out beyond where we can see. That's where I think I am. I have more of a real connection with myself being way out on the vanishing point than I do with myself being here. (*Beat.*) This was your idea. I won't ever be the same again. We should probably go. I think I could even drive the car. I bet I could. Funny. I guess we'll go back now which is a shame because finally, finally I could almost see going on. Driving right up to the edge of the Pacific. Now I don't suppose we'll do that.

CANDY: No. You spoiled it.

SHELLEY: Right. I forgot.

CANDY: It's just as well. I'm better off now. Everything is more clearly defined. Now that I don't have to answer to you anymore I can do anything I want. Maybe be a torch singer in a nightclub. Maybe find a husband and grow peanuts. Who knows?

SHELLEY: I don't know.

CANDY: Well, whatever. It will be exciting. That's all I know.

SHELLEY: That's good. I want it to be exciting.

CANDY: I don't have to be famous. I'll settle for a cult following.

SHELLEY: Oh, don't settle for anything but the best.

CANDY: I was being serious. You, of course, can only make fun of me. I was thinking of my future. What I want. Without having to worry about someone else. I was feeling something exciting.

SHELLEY: Sorry.

CANDY: I was thinking of hopes. You wouldn't know anything about that. Last week, I called you. The summer heat finally blew itself out. I was ready for something. It had gotten hot, so hot, like it does always, it builds and builds and I start to go stark raving mad. Mad. Every year. Some time around mid-August, in the city, I can't help myself, I start to question what I'm doing there—there are better climates. A week goes by, I start to question existence itself. Period. The city is psychic Bombay. I seriously consider just hanging it all up and becoming either a junkie or a dentist. Then one day it's beautiful, a slight breeze, the buildings all carved out of light, real honest and true blue sky. Like last week. It seemed like a good time. I knew what I was doing.

SHELLEY: And you called me.

CANDY: Yes. And we decided we could get away from it all cause it all would be there when we got back, only better.

SHELLEY: Yes.

CANDY: And then I ran into Roger and he was in love.

SHELLEY: Oh?

CANDY: With you.

SHELLEY: No he isn't.

CANDY: I don't want to talk about it.

SHELLEY: He isn't. He can't be. I haven't even talked to him in over three months.

CANDY: Who needs to talk?

SHELLEY: Oh stop it.

CANDY: We'll go now. It'll be getting dark.

(*Lights begin a very slow fade, from now to end of play, lighting the stage first with various and changing shades of lurid sunset colors—the kind you only see in the west.*)

SHELLEY: Okay. Wait. This feels terrible, this between us. What can I do? I'll do anything to fix it and make it better.

CANDY: Who can trust you?

SHELLEY: Please. Candy. Really. Anything. Name something.

CANDY: Tell him you never want to see him again?

SHELLEY: Yes, of course.

CANDY: Nah. Too easy. Tell him I'm the one who left the Rilke sonnets on his doorstep, not you?

SHELLEY: Yes. Naturally.

CANDY: No. It was dumb of me. Might as well make you look like the sap. Tell him you're marrying some guy from your home town?

SHELLEY: New York is my home town.

CANDY: What do you say?

SHELLEY: Fine. Okay. Only don't let me ruin your life.

CANDY: No. No, you least of all, should ruin it.

SHELLEY: That's right. There are other, far more worthy opponents.

CANDY: So you are an opponent then?

SHELLEY: No! Oh no! Just a figure of speech. No, I just mean save your strength for a truly dangerous—

CANDY: As if you aren't.

SHELLEY: I'm not. There are hundreds of real disasters. Well, take out here. There are wild animals and things. Bears maybe. Porcupines.

CANDY: There aren't bears here.

SHELLEY: Really? Oh. Well life really is full of disappointments.

CANDY: Now that's something to be afraid of.

SHELLEY: Oh yes, our life is full of threats like that.

CANDY: Those are the real killers.

SHELLEY: Like thieves in the night.

CANDY: Some masquerading as friends.

SHELLEY: Now don't start.

CANDY: So we'll go.

SHELLEY: Yes. Absolutely. And we are friends. You said so.

CANDY: Not yet. Maybe in Wyoming.

SHELLEY: So you don't hate me. (*Shelley heads offstage to the car.*)

CANDY: Maybe. I don't know. (*We hear Shelley open a car door, then slam it shut. Candy looks.*) Don't sit on my sweater! Look what you're doing. Look what you're doing.

SHELLEY: My legs stick to the vinyl.

CANDY: Sit on your own. (*Candy rushes offstage.*)

SHELLEY: The map is drenched! I can't find the highway. It's washed out.

CANDY: Give me that. I'll find it.

SHELLEY: Oh my god.

CANDY: Relax. We'll just get a new—oh Jesus.

SHELLEY: (*Overlapping with Candy.*) Quick. Get it started. Run him over—run him—fast!

CANDY: (*Overlapping.*) I can't. It won't start. It won't— (*The engine chugs, turns over. We hear a startled male voice: "Heyyy." The car sputters, lurches, stops.*)

SHELLEY: (*Overlapping.*) Get him! Just hit him. Run him down, it's the only way.

CANDY: It won't start—the red light—

SHELLEY: Shit! The radiator! (*Yelling at "him."*) Get back! Get back! I'm warning you. I'll throw this— (*We hear a thunk.*)

CANDY: You'll kill him—he's getting back up. Throw it again.

SHELLEY: Get back! (*The juice container lands onstage.*)

CANDY: There's two of us. We'll hurt you. Oh, Mary, mother of—

SHELLEY: Let's go! (*We hear doors slam. Candy and Shelley run onstage.*)

CANDY: Where do we—?

(*Shelley stops to pick up the juice container. Candy stumbles over her. They get up and turn to see Ron the biker, now onstage, standing in front of them with one hand in a ward-off position.*)

CANDY: Oh boy.

SHELLEY: Do you want us to put our hands up or something? (*Shelley, still covered in sunscreen and sunglasses, hands Ron the container.*) We'll just keep our hands up here so you'll know that we're scared, I mean, peaceful. Uh, me Shelley, me peaceloving.

CANDY: Shut up. This isn't a movie. And he's not an Indian. He's a—oh god—biker. Jesus.

(*Ron doesn't respond. He carries both their purses, plus the orange juice container. Basically, he is more afraid of them than vice versa. He thinks they might be crazy—or at the very least, dangerous.*)

SHELLEY: See, if we would've left when I wanted to—

RON (THE BIKER): Uh. Shut up. (*Ron goes through their things.*)

SHELLEY: You can have all our money. Uh, sorry there isn't much.

CANDY: It's all in traveler's checks. We could make them all out to you.

SHELLEY: Don't be silly. Bikers don't have bank accounts.

CANDY: So?

SHELLEY: So how would he cash them?

CANDY: Why, we could go with him.

SHELLEY: What a good idea! Why don't we all drive to the bank? We could get the money in quarters—you could play the slots! Double it in an afternoon.

RON (THE BIKER): Shut up.

(*Ron, a little woozy from the heat and from Shelley's blow on the head, checks all the linings of their things, looking for something dangerous. As Shelley comes closer to him, he holds her off, threatening her with the orange juice container.*)

SHELLEY: It was only a suggestion.

CANDY: Shut up.

RON (THE BIKER): All right—what do you have? Knives? A shotgun maybe?

CANDY: Huh?

SHELLEY: If my memory serves me, this is the man of your dreams.

CANDY: Stop it. (*To Ron.*) Oh, not you. Her. Uh, you do what you want. I mean—oh god. That's not what I mean. Uh . . .

SHELLEY: That's right. Gang up on me. (*Ron has completed his search of their things—stares at them.*)

RON (THE BIKER): You two are strange.

SHELLEY: True.

RON (THE BIKER): You know, you two should be careful. You could hurt somebody.

CANDY: Huh?

RON (THE BIKER): That car is a dangerous weapon with you two in it.

SHELLEY: Oh. That. Look. We weren't really going to run you over.

CANDY: Nah. We knew the car wouldn't start. It was just a gas! Get it? Car? Gas? Oh, forget it.

RON (THE BIKER): How do you explain this? (*He holds up the juice container.*)

SHELLEY: It's just orange juice. Maybe you were thirsty. I just have bad aim.

RON (THE BIKER): I don't know what to do with you two. You could hurt me.

SHELLEY: Us? Think nothing of it. I mean, put that out of your mind.

CANDY: Yeah. We're harmless.

RON (THE BIKER): Stay away from me.

CANDY: Sorry. I was just trying to get into the shade.

RON (THE BIKER): There isn't any and you know it. Not for hundreds of miles.

CANDY: I see what you mean. (*Ron, slightly dizzy, leans against the rock. He then sees Shelley's lizard graves.*)

RON (THE BIKER): So . . . what? Are you some weird cult or something? Is it potions? Is that what you use? Maybe you're collecting nutsy stuff out here to cast some kind of crazy spell—is that it? Or . . . or poison.

SHELLEY: Poison? Like almonds?

CANDY: Shut up.

RON (THE BIKER): So. That's it.

CANDY: No. We're just a coupla regular kinda gals.

RON (THE BIKER): Sure. Sure you are. Look. I need some gasoline—hey, get back.

SHELLEY: We passed a station about 20 miles back. Chevron. I could give you my credit card. Just head that way.

RON (THE BIKER): Don't get cute.

SHELLEY: Just trying to be helpful.

RON (THE BIKER): You got a gas can or anything? (*They shake their heads, no.*) What's wrong with your heap? It's not outa gas, too?

SHELLEY: Radiator.

RON (THE BIKER): Gee. Too bad. There isn't any water out here.

SHELLEY: So we noticed.

RON (THE BIKER): Hey. I'm sorry you're having problems—whoa, keep over there. But, uh, listen. I've got a siphon, and I'm, uh, just gonna help myself to a little gasoline—I only need a gallon. Uh, here's a couple bucks, that should cover it. Wait. I'll put the money on the rock. And, I'll send a tow truck out to get you once I've gotten a head start.

SHELLEY: A head start? You running from the law or something?

RON (THE BIKER): No. Are you?

CANDY: Don't be silly.

RON (THE BIKER): Are you sure?

CANDY: Oh, come on—do we look like—

RON (THE BIKER): Uh . . . uh . . . get your hands up. Stay back. Now, uh listen ladies, this has been very interesting, meeting you out here in the middle of nowhere and all, but I've got to get going and I don't want any trouble, so just keep away while I get the gas, it'll just take a minute, I'm going to freckle if I don't get outa this sun pretty soon.

CANDY: What're you gonna put the gasoline in?

RON (THE BIKER): (*Holds out the juice container.*) This.

CANDY: But that's our bomb.

SHELLEY: Ssshhhh.

RON (THE BIKER): You really are strange. (*Ron starts to exit to car.*)

CANDY: What'd you do with your shrunken heads? Shelley, ask him what he did with the heads.

RON (THE BIKER): (*Overlapping, to himself.*) Oh, man, have I got to get out of here. (*To Candy.*) Are you talking to me? Look. I'll just take a minute. Then you can go back to whatever weird ceremony is going on out here. Just forget you ever saw me. (*Ron exits.*)

SHELLEY: Oooooh. Motor man. He's really here.

CANDY: Stop making fun of me. See, I should never think things. The abstract always gets me into some kind of trouble in the concrete.

SHELLEY: I am getting the hots.

CANDY: I said, cut it out.

SHELLEY: Why? He's a turn-on. (*Beat.*) I'm not making fun of you. Stop thinking of yourself. Well, okay, he was your idea in the first place, you take him on. (*Ron appears.*) Oh hi. We were just talking about what to do with you.

RON (THE BIKER): Please. Just leave me alone.

SHELLEY: So. Do you have your gasoline?

RON (THE BIKER): No. There's a hole in the jug.

CANDY: Yeah. We blew it up.

RON (THE BIKER): (*He staggers; the heat is getting to him.*) Look. I don't know who you two are, or what you're up to, but I'm getting sunstroke. Now, I want to just lie down for a moment, under this rock, and please, just leave me be and don't turn me into a lizard or anything. (*Ron sits under the rock, takes a goatskin bag from inside his clothes and drinks.*)

SHELLEY: Wow. What's that?

CANDY: Can we have some?

RON (THE BIKER): I'll . . . I'll hold it while you drink. You can have more when I wake up. Don't try to take it while I'm asleep, or—well, something. (*Ron gives them each a drink.*)

CANDY: I can't place it.

SHELLEY: Grape. No raspberry.

CANDY: Kool-aid!! (*Ron eyes them suspiciously; arranges the goatskin under him and settles into sleep.*)

SHELLEY: Comfortable?

CANDY: I've got a pillow in the car.

SHELLEY: Oh, it's plastic—he wouldn't want that.

CANDY: I could cover it.

RON (THE BIKER): Please . . . leave me alone . . . (*Shelley sighs.*)

CANDY: I think he's asleep.

SHELLEY: Already?

CANDY: Must be tired from all that biking—those machines must weigh a ton.

SHELLEY: Candy, he balances the thing, he doesn't carry it.

CANDY: Still. (*Beat.*) He's got nice eyelashes.

SHELLEY: They're okay. I wonder why he doesn't shave his head.

CANDY: Or wear it real long.

SHELLEY: Must be the latest thing.

CANDY: We should make some shade.

SHELLEY: Yeah.

(*Candy and Shelley climb onto the rock over Ron; they take off their blouses. Underneath they are wearing halter tops—perfect for gardening or an ice cream stand on a boardwalk. They extend their legs, draping their blouses over knees and toes, making a canopy for The Biker.*)

SHELLEY: Now what?

CANDY: Now we wait.

SHELLEY: I guess. (*They are silent a moment—the silence is very strange.*)

CANDY: Jesus.

SHELLEY: Yeah.

CANDY: Hey! We could play cards!

SHELLEY: Oh. Good idea. Do we have any?

CANDY: I got a deck with my car insurance. Free.

SHELLEY: Great.

CANDY: I think I left them at home. (*Another strange silence.*)

SHELLEY: Are you sleepy? We should nap, maybe. Conserve your strength. Go ahead. You sleep. I'll keep watch.

CANDY: Watch what? (*Another eerie silence.*)

SHELLEY: Jeez, Can. Uh, do you think—

CANDY: Shelley stop.

SHELLEY: Huh?

CANDY: Whatever you were gonna say. Stop.

SHELLEY: What?

CANDY: What were you just about to say?

SHELLEY: Uh. Uh. Now I forgot.

CANDY: Cause whatever it is, if you say anything that's scary, I'll just—I mean, it's too quiet out there. What were you gonna say?

SHELLEY: Uh, I think it was about—

CANDY: But if it was something creepy you should just keep your mouth shut. What was it?

SHELLEY: Hey! Take it easy.

CANDY: Oh. Yeah. Yeah. Right.

SHELLEY: God. Look at us.

CANDY: I can't see.

SHELLEY: Yeah. The light bothers my eyes.

CANDY: No. No. What I see, well, maybe I don't really see what's there, maybe I just see what I think. And I can't stop thinking.

SHELLEY: Yeah. What should we do?

CANDY: I don't know. (*Beat.*) Are we here? (*Beat.*) You know how some people dream of being famous, and some want to, I don't know, achieve nirvana or something? Well, to me, the ultimate most incredible thing would be to simply disappear in a vapor and emerge as someone else—someone I'd want to become this time around. You think that's religious maybe?

SHELLEY: Someone amazing. In control. Yeah.

CANDY: Yeah.

(*As they talk, the twilight becomes its most vivid. Ron lies there, eyes open, but resting, lulled, watching and listening, under his "canopy."*)

CANDY: Madame de Pompadour.

SHELLEY: Not her.

CANDY: Freud?

SHELLEY: Unh-unh.

CANDY: Mae West. Mae West when she was young. Right. In that movie where she tames the lions. That scene . . . oh, that scene . . . I mean she is sitting there, about ready to kiss Cary Grant . . . well, she does kiss him. It's mmmmmmmmmm, it's a good kiss. (*Mimes the kiss.*) She gives him one hard long kiss and then she just leans back, throws back her hair, and just breaks into a song, like it's just pouring out of her body. (*Mimes the kiss, then leans back sensuously, tossing her hair; the kiss flows into "The Birth of the Blues."*) Mmmmmmmmm, ooooooh, they say some people long ago . . .

were searchin for a diff'rent tune, one that they could croon— (*Stops abrupt-ly.*) I think that's the song she sings. No. Maybe it isn't. I couldn't be her anyway. I'd be afraid of her.

SHELLEY: No you wouldn't.

CANDY: I don't know.

SHELLEY: You could handle it. You and I—we could handle anything.

CANDY: No, I don't think so.

SHELLEY: Come on, we can handle anything.

CANDY: Nope. Not me. This is you we're talking about.

SHELLEY: Oh. I guess. Well, sometimes.

CANDY: Yeah. You can.

SHELLEY: (*Beat.*) Really? (*Beat; softer; realizing.*) That's not who I am.

CANDY: Oh. (*Beat.*) Yeah, I know.

SHELLEY: You don't want to be Mae West.

CANDY: No. (*Beat.*)

SHELLEY: Candy. There is some reason why we came from who we were then to be here. To where we are going.

CANDY: Yes. I can see the distance we've traveled.

SHELLEY: Yeah. Oh feel it out here. Red sky at night—

CANDY: Sailors' delight. (*Beat; they gaze out into the desert.*)

SHELLEY: (*Appreciating this.*) A person's really alone out here. (*Beat.*)

RON (THE BIKER): (*Propping himself up on his elbow.*) The desert is really getting crazy. Used to be safe. I'm gonna start spending my vacations in Minnesota from now on.

CANDY: Hey! I thought you were asleep.

RON (THE BIKER): Time was when you could feel free *and* safe out here. Now—well, you have to choose, I guess.

SHELLEY: You're an eavesdropper, aren't you? That's rude.

RON (THE BIKER): Sorry. There didn't seem to be anyplace to go at the moment.

CANDY: (*As they cover themselves up.*) You're an eyedropper, too. (*They jump down from the rock and dress.*)

RON (THE BIKER): You guys are okay, you know that? I liked hearing you. Like music that makes you feel good. You know, not supermarket stuff.

(*Ron starts to shed his outer layer of biker clothes. Underneath the leather he has on a midwestern-looking pair of shorts, somewhat baggy, and a corny t-shirt.*)

CANDY: Say. What are you?

RON (THE BIKER): Huh? You mean my sign?

CANDY: No. Are you a biker or what?

RON (THE BIKER): Sure.

CANDY: A Hell's Angel? Born to be wild?

RON (THE BIKER): Uh, well, no. (*Beat.*) Hi. My name's Ron.

CANDY: This guy *is* a fake.

RON (THE BIKER): Look, I've got a nice little Honda—fixed her up myself. Drove her all the way out from Michigan.

SHELLEY: I'll bet.

RON (THE BIKER): Ypsilanti.

CANDY: Nothing is exciting anymore. There is no romance left in life.

RON (THE BIKER): Gee. That makes me feel sad.

SHELLEY: It's hard to be a woman.

RON (THE BIKER): Is it?

CANDY: Oh yeah.

RON (THE BIKER): Gee, I would've thought—well, gee. Well. Wow. (*Beat.*) Hard to be a biker, too. Hard to be a man. Life's too crazy. I get lost.

SHELLEY: Our map has orange juice on it.

RON (THE BIKER): Yeah. I know what you mean.

CANDY: We had such great plans.

RON (THE BIKER): Yeah. I know.

SHELLEY: I just meant the map got wet. (*Shelley climbs up on the rock.*) I just wondered how far we'd have to go to walk to the Interstate. Come up here. Come on. Both of you. Get up here. Look. (*Candy and Ron reluctantly climb up on the rock.*)

CANDY: Shelley, stop playing around.

SHELLEY: Now sit and be quiet. I was getting somewhere before.

RON (THE BIKER): Oh. Whoa. You mean she is doing a spell or something?

SHELLEY: Sssshhh.

RON (THE BIKER): I better, uh—

SHELLEY: Quiet! I have to return to a former feeling. A really good feeling.

CANDY: Does this mean we'll all three have sex?

RON (THE BIKER): Uh, gee, guys, I, uh . . . I don't think I'm ready for this. Look. I'm sorry I was listening to your secret stuff, but—

SHELLEY: Relax. I'm just getting filled up. Candy—you, too. Ron. Try it. Come on. We've got a lot of stuff ahead of us. We need to take something away with us from here.

RON (THE BIKER): It is a secret rite. It is, isn't it?

SHELLEY: Sure. If you insist. (*There is a long, still, full moment, as the three of them all bask in the wildly colored glow of the desert sunset.*) Reality. Who'd believe it?

CANDY: Ooooohhhh. (*Beat.*) Ron, you got anymore of that Kool-aid?

RON (THE BIKER): Huh. Sure. (*Transfixed by the desert colors, Ron hands Candy the goatskin. She drinks. Ron and Shelley stare into the distance. Candy begins to take another drink—stops.*)

CANDY: Shelley! Shelley!

SHELLEY: What? What?

CANDY: The car might like some Kool-aid!

SHELLEY: Sure. Cars are human, too, you know.

CANDY: Grape Kool-aid—

RON (THE BIKER): Black cherry.

CANDY: Black cherry Kool-aid into the radiator, and then we could drive Ron to his bike and we could siphon some of our gas right into his tank and—oh—

SHELLEY: I don't know, the radiator's bigger than that.

CANDY: We've got a flat Pepsi with a bug in it. Two-liter disposable bottle. We can use that too.

SHELLEY: Pepsi is really bad for you, you shouldn't drink it.

CANDY: The car!

SHELLEY: Okay! (*Candy and Shelley climb down from the rock and gather up all their stuff.*) Come on, Ron dear. You help, too. This is the old pioneer spirit, you know, the settlers all pitching in together to raise the corn, to save the wheat crop. You've seen the movies.

CANDY: Yeah, America, America.

RON (THE BIKER): Yeah. Yeah, okay. Just a moment. I'm almost getting the feeling.

SHELLEY: (*To Candy.*) He's getting the feeling.

CANDY: It's a nice bonus.

SHELLEY: Anytime you're ready, Ronaldo.

CANDY: Whatever happens.

SHELLEY: Ron! Not too much now—you'll want to get more later! (*To Candy.*) Interesting man. Hmmmm.

CANDY: Shelley.

SHELLEY: Take it easy. We have all just drunk from the fountain of life. I suggest we get on with it.

CANDY: Whatever happens.

SHELLEY: Ron! (*Candy and Shelley go off to the car, leaving Ron on the rock.*)

CANDY: (*Offstage.*) Hi, happy Mr. Radiator Cap. There you go. Don't like grape?

SHELLEY: (*Offstage.*) Oh sure he does. It's black cherry anyway. And some cola. Num num.

RON (THE BIKER): I feel like I'm growing bigger. Taller. Fuller.

SHELLEY: Ron! Come on, Ron. We're saving you, too.

RON (THE BIKER): I am. I'm sure of it. (*Offstage—the car starts.*)

CANDY AND SHELLEY: (*Offstage.*) HURRAY!

RON (THE BIKER): Nice.

(*Ron exits to the car. Sound of the car pulling out, heading down the highway, as the brilliant sky fades to the first purple of night.*)

SHELLEY: (*Offstage.*) Candy. Candy. Keep your eyes on the road. Keep driving. You know, I don't think I even made it with Roger—I'm sure I fell asleep. Watch it! You almost ran over a coyote! Ron, stop fidgeting, I can't see the map. I've gotta go to the bathroom. Do you think the Pacific's really cold? Let's get a coke. (*Sounds and lights fade.*)

END

Authors' Biographies

Kathleen Collins received a 1983 National Endowment for the Arts Playwriting grant for *The Brothers* which was also nominated for an Audelco Award ("Best Play 1982" category) and was a finalist in the 1982 Susan Blackburn International Prize for Playwriting. *The Brothers* was produced off-Broadway at the American Place Theatre and in Pittsburgh at the Kuntu Repertory Theatre. Her *In the Midnight Hour* was produced off-Broadway at the Richard Allen Center for Culture and Art and at the Kuntu Repertory Theatre. Ms. Collins has also directed two films: an hour dramatic movie, *The Cruz Brothers and Miss Malloy,* and a feature film, *Losing Ground,* based on her original screenplay. She won the Prize for First Feature at Portugal's International Film Festival, and has received a National Endowment for the Arts Media grant and an American Film Institute grant. Her films have appeared at numerous festivals in Berlin, London and Paris, and been sold to German, Swiss, British and Australian television. She is about to direct her second feature, *A Summer Diary,* based on her original screenplay. Ms. Collins teaches Film History and Production at City College in New York and has just recently completed a novel, *Woman Waiting at a Window.*

Lavonne Mueller's first play, *Warriors from a Long Childhood,* was produced by The Women's Project and another, *Killings on the Last Line,* produced on the main stage of The American Place Theatre. *Crimes and Crimes* appeared Off-Broadway. A children's play, *Oyster Crackers, Undershirts and Mauve Lemonade* was published by Baker's Plays. She has won playwriting grants from the Guggenheim and Rockefeller Foundations and the National Endowment for the Arts.

Carol K. Mack is a graduate of Mount Holyoke College where she majored in theatre and studied playwriting with Denis Johnston. In the early '60s she wrote book and lyrics for five musicals for children and studied acting with Uta Hagen. While her three children were young she worked as film reader, wrote educational film strips and fiction. In the early '70s she became a member of The New Dramatists where three of her plays were produced including *Esther,* later shown at The White Barn Theatre Foundation and Off Broadway; *A Safe Place* premiered at The Berkshire Theatre Festival in association with The Kennedy Center; and last season E.S.T. produced *Postcards* in their One Act Marathon and she received two commissions from The Actors Theatre of Louisville. *Postcards, Gazebo* and *A Safe Place* have each received awards. In other media, a novel and short fiction have recently been published and she is currently working on a screenplay.

Terry Galloway divided her formative years between Berlin and Fort Hood, Texas. She received her BA in American Studies from the University of Texas at Austin, and later taught as a research associate at Shakespeare at Winedale, an experimental English program at that university. In 1976 she helped found Esther's Follies, a political cabaret still popular in the Southwest, for which she wrote, performed and directed. That same year she worked with the East German playwright Heiner Muller on the American production of his play *Mauser.* She has written one book of poetry, articles for *Texas Monthly* and *Third Coast* magazines, and an award winning PBS television series for handicapped children. She has performed in New York at the Limbo Lounge, the W.O.W. Cafe, the Pyramid Club, and American Place Theatre. In 1983 she won the New York Villager's Theatre Award for Outstanding Solo Performance.

Paula Cizmar was a newspaper reporter, radio news writer, and magazine feature writer before she became a playwright. Her work has appeared in *Mother Jones,* the *Detroit Free Press, San Francisco Chronicle, Books & Arts* and other publications. She began writing plays after studying acting in San Francisco, and early impetus for her theatre writing came from studying physical theatre with Bob Ernst of the Blake Street Hawkeyes in Berkeley, California. One of her plays, *The Death of a Miner,* was co-produced by the Women's Project and Portland Stage Company in 1982. The play has gone on to other productions around the country and the Los Angeles production won four Drama-Logue Awards. Other plays include: *Madonna of the Powder Room,* produced at Portland Stage; *Cupcakes,* produced at Actors Theatre of Louisville's Stages Festival; *Apocryphal Stories, Exceptional Friends; Escape from the 44th Floor;* and *The Girl Room,* produced in Berkeley. In addition, Ms. Cizmar (with her husband Douglas Gower) has written two screenplays: *Tough Girls* and *M.U.T.H.R.* With John Griesemer and Douglas Gower, she was a writer for *The Voyage of the Mimi,* a 13-part science/adventure series for children, aired on PBS.

Julia Miles is a graduate of Northwestern University and began her career as an actress. In the early 1960s she co-founded Theatre Current in Brooklyn Heights, where production of Arnold Weinstein's *Red Eye of Love*, directed by John Wulp, was moved to Off-Broadway. She then co-produced a season of new plays Off-Broadway and in 1964 joined The American Place Theatre on its first production, Robert Lowell's *The Old Glory*. Ms. Miles is currently Project Director of The Women's Project and Associate Director of The American Place Theatre. She is also president of "Four Women Productions" and was Executive Producer of Steve Tesich's film, *Four Friends,* directed by Arthur Penn. She is founder and Chair of The League of Professional Theatre Women / New York and is on the Board of The Bridge and Performing Artists for Nuclear Disarmament. Ms. Miles is married and has three daughters.

PAJ PLAYSCRIPT SERIES

OTHER TITLES IN THE SERIES: